A Highpoint Church Women's Bible Study

MISS PERFECT
DISCOVERING GOD'S PURPOSE WITHOUT THE PRESSURE

KARIN CONLEE
with Chris Kuhlman

I want to express the greatest amount of gratitude and love for the women of Highpoint Church. It is an incredible joy to serve the Lord with you. A team of people were critical to the completion and quality of this project. First, I want to thank Chris Kuhlman for her constant dedication as a friend and partner in this project. Your heart for holiness is an inspiration. Thank you to the editors who worked tirelessly to make this project great including, Rachel Cuccias, Amber Fournier, Cris Moore, Martha Nicolas, Elissa Roberts, Robyn Smith, Emily Wilson, Kim Woody, Kim Trefz and executive editor my husband, Chris Conlee. Thank you for investing your best for God's glory in this project.

–Karin Conlee

Copyright © 2012 by Karin Conlee & Highpoint Church
Cover design and layout by Speak Creative; www.speakcreative.com
Photography by Ava Grace Photography; www.avagracephotography.com
Executive producer, Andy Savage

Request for information should be addressed to: Highpoint Church, PO Box 341425, Memphis, TN 38184; phone (901) 762-0071.

All scripture quotations, unless otherwise noted, are taken from The Holy Bible, English Standard Version®. ESV®. Copyright© 2001 by Crossway Bibles, a publishing ministry of Good News Publishers. Used by permission. All rights reserved.

Emphases in scripture quotations have been added by the authors.

Printed in the United States of America.
www.missperfectbook.com
www.highpointmemphis.com

INTRODUCTION

While the process of naming this study was a laborious one, I have since realized that the title *Miss Perfect* ironically represents the battle of the first two decades of my life. For my first 20 years, I was a sponge absorbing all the cultural messages and standards for success. From grades, to looks, to sports, to professional aspirations, to relationships, perfection was the elusive goal. Neither my successes nor my failures brought any lasting satisfaction, just the need to try to reach the next goal.

As I now approach completing my fourth decade, I am so grateful for what the Lord has taught me about Himself and myself since I became a Christian my freshman year at Wake Forest University. Through God's strategic placement of godly men and women in my life, especially my husband, I have been exposed to a significantly more meaningful life as I seek to live a life of purpose.

From its inception, this project has had one focus: to help women be set free from the world's expectations by exposing the emptiness of the world and the fullness of life under God's direction. No matter your stage of life, from college student to retiree, I pray that you will boldly choose to evaluate your life in light of God's Word and choose to live a life with an eternal perspective. It will look different for each of us, but be gloriously satisfying for all of us.

I have asked a co-laborer in Christ, Chris Kuhlman, to join us on this adventure. She has walked her faithful journey a season ahead of me and offers great insights of her own. Our desire is for you to stop long enough to consider what really matters. Examine the truths of Scripture with us and begin adjusting your life to do what has value–nothing more and nothing less. So many of us work so hard and yet never seem to be at peace. We missed perfection a long time ago, so what if we lay aside that empty pursuit of worldly affirmation, and exchange it for a truly satisfying life?

You can use this study in either a small group format or as a guide for one-on-one mentoring relationships. Each of the 9 weeks of homework contains 5 days of material requiring approximately 30 minutes each day to complete. For those using either the small group or mentoring format, you can also access 10 corresponding teaching sessions and listening guides at missperfectbook.com. While we strongly desire you to be turning the pages of your own Bible, we have tried to incorporate as much Scripture into the printed material as space would allow so you can spend more time applying God's truth. It is not just reading God's Word that transforms. It is the applying of God's Word to our lives that will make the difference. I beg you–please take the time to answer the application questions. Do not short-circuit your growth by skimming over questions.

May we leave the pursuit of perfection behind and find a life rich with purpose!

In Him,
Karin Conlee

CONTENTS

WEEK SIX
Prayer without Pretense BY CHRIS KUHLMAN 136

WEEK SEVEN
Purity without Pressure BY KARIN CONLEE 162

WEEK EIGHT
Contentment without Conditions BY CHRIS KUHLMAN 186

WEEK NINE
Mission with Meaning BY KARIN CONLEE 210

IDENTITY WITHOUT INSECURITY

A woman discovers her identity by turning to God and turning from substitutes.

MISTAKEN IDENTITY PART 1

KARIN CONLEE

Are you ready? Today is day one of a ten-week journey. Chris and I (Karin) will be your guides, your encouragers, and your challengers through our time together. I hope you are like us and you are sick of trying to be Miss Perfect. Are you ready to stop running toward a finish line that is always moving? Do you want a life where you are spending your time on the things that matter? This life will never be perfect and neither will we, but there is an amazing opportunity to leave our self-imposed pressure behind.

As women in the 21st century, there is a weird dichotomy of selfishness and selflessness in our culture. Our world screams to make everything about us. Aren't we told to do whatever feels right or makes us happy? At the very same time, however, most women have this enormous web of people we care for either practically or emotionally. Who is it for you? Your friends? Your mom? Your husband? Your children? Your co-workers? Don't you feel like there are always so many people going through your mind that need something from you? If you are like me, it makes it hard to make time for yourself. Or, if I find it, I feel guilty that I am not helping one of the many people that I love.

Well, guess what? For this week and, to some extent, for this semester, we are asking you to make it about you! Why? Because God wants YOU to BE SET FREE from the lies of perfection. It is time to stop pleasing everyone and start pleasing God. Allow God to show you His purpose for your life as you remove the pressures that the world loves to pile on.

We are going to spend this semester looking at nine different aspects of our lives that will help us grasp that... A WOMAN DISCOVERS GOD'S PURPOSE BY EMBRACING THE HUMILITY, IDENTITY, AND PERSPECTIVE OF CHRIST SO THAT SHE CAN BE KNOWN BY LOVE.

As we dive into our first subject, I want you to take a step back and think about your identity. We usually hear the word tossed around by LifeLock discussing identity theft. I want you to contemplate the following question, "Where do you find your worth?" Consider how we can find our true identity:

A woman discovers her identity by turning to God and turning from substitutes.

As women desiring to follow the Lord, we likely know the typical answer of where we should find our identity, right? Of course, like almost every child answers in a Sunday school class, we respond, "Jesus." That answer may work on Sunday mornings, but all of us need to slow down and even stop to contemplate where we really find our value. Where do I gain my sense of identity? How do I truthfully evaluate that question?

We need to be honest with ourselves and identify where we are tempted to find or create an identity. If we do this, we will be one step closer to getting to the place where we are no longer battling with our insecurities.

Where do women typically look to find their sense of identity?

After a relatively smooth path through school, I had drawn in my mind the picture of the life I wanted. I was imagining expensive suits, high profile meetings, corporate jets, and speaking engagements. As I inched a little closer to pursuing that dream, God gave me a sneak peek into corporate life in the form of an internship and eventual entry level job at Maybelline's national headquarters. I remember one of my first days on the job in the department of Business Acquisitions when I met the Director of Mascara. Here was a man in his early thirties, well-dressed, an up-and-comer, who had studied hard and earned his M.B.A. to be Mr. Mascara. Seriously? How ridiculous! I began to second-guess whether this world I had longed to be a part of would bring any lasting satisfaction.

Have you ever had an aspiration that later seemed disappointing or disillusioning as you got closer?

If so, how did you respond to the disappointment?

Depending upon their stage of life, there are four common areas in which women mistakenly try to find their identity. Today we will tackle the first two:

1. HER POSITION

God has given women amazing minds that can accomplish much good in this world. Since the 1960's, our culture has urged women to reach for the greatest level of success that they can achieve. In 2006, the *New York Times* front page read, "Women are Leaving Men in the Dust." This article gives statistics that there are thirty percent more women in college than men. These women are also thirty-three percent more likely to graduate than their male counterparts.[1] The question is not whether women have the ability to succeed. "All indications are that women will gain a clear majority in most professional fields as the 21st century progresses."[2]

The question we must now ask is the same question that many men face: What am I without my position, my paycheck, my power, and my sense of control? When a layoff comes, does that mean I have somehow lost my value? When I have to consider relocating for the benefit of my spouse, can I really start over after all I have achieved?

Have you had a time where a position or job gave you an added sense of importance or purpose? How did it impact your behavior?

As a female, God's design of women to bring life into this world can cause stagnation, delays, or even the end to a career if a couple chooses to add children to their family. As my husband, Chris, and I began to plan for the arrival of our first child, I finally had to act on my new paradigm as a believer. My lifelong dream had not been motherhood. I became a Christian in college and only as I grew in my relationship with Christ did I begin to see value in serving others. I had spent so many years geared towards a career that I knew that I would not do three jobs well. Being a wife, mother, and employee was going to require some juggling. Given my experiences, I feared that the expectations of the workforce would receive my best energy and attitude. We decided that I would resign from my position and come home to care for our child when he arrived.

Whether right or wrong, the decision brought me face-to-face with the reality of where I truly found my sense of value. It also reinforced that achieving Miss Perfect is an illusion. Ironically, as I left the opportunity for raises, travel, and the affirmation that I enjoyed, I quickly realized that the organization I worked for went on just fine without me. Did my previous efforts really matter? Yes, but I was just an interchangeable part after all! I think I needed the position (and its validation) more than it needed me!

2. HIS WIFE

For as many women who long for a powerful career, thankfully, there are still many women who aspire to be a wife.

What does Genesis 2:18 show you about God's purpose in creating women?

According to Genesis 2:21-24, how did God physically create Eve?

If God designed woman from the body of a man to be his helper, it makes sense that there is a God-given desire for a woman to find a husband. If this desire is God-given, how can it be dangerous to find one's identity in her husband?

Of all the erroneous places to find our identity, this is likely the most acceptable if you have grown up in church. After all, we take our husband's last name and we become one flesh.

However, the danger lies in looking to another human being to define us and meet all of our needs. When finding a man becomes a stronger desire than finding God's man for me, we must evaluate if this title of "wife" (or should we say "Mrs. Perfect") is where we are placing our value.

Have you ever known someone who desired to be married so badly that she may have short-circuited God's plan in exchange for her own?

What caution do you wish you could have given her?

We must look at our entire created purpose, not just our roles, to determine if we are allowing ourselves to find our value in a way that underestimates God's best or if we are trusting His plan and His timing.

Does the young widow cease to have value if a husband is truly God's place for her to find her identity? What about the woman who has never been married?

What does Paul's teaching in 1 Corinthians 7:32-35, 39-40 reveal about the opportunities for focus outside of marriage?

From God's perspective, do you have any less value or identity if you are not married?

As women, we must remember that God has a plan for each of our lives. If you are unmarried, then treasure the ability to have undivided devotion to the Lord. He is your husband now. He will forever be the only one who loves you perfectly, so treasure the time! Allow yourself to remove the pressure of finding a husband, and focus on His purpose for you. If you are married, then embrace the role God has for you and know that our identity comes from One greater than even the most loving spouse.

What was the most meaningful statement or Scripture you read today?

What does God want you to do in response to today's study?

MISTAKEN IDENTITY PART 2

KARIN CONLEE

Yesterday, we contemplated two places that we, as women, might mistakenly try to find our identity.

List the two areas we discussed:

1.
2.

Today, we will move on to consider two other common possibilities where we find our identity. As we move through different stages of life, the reality exists that we can try to find our identity in different areas at different times. I strongly encourage you to evaluate where you find your validation. If it is anywhere other than in the Lord, your priorities will be in this area, and it will cause you to compromise your designed purpose. Consider if these last two common areas are of danger to you....

3. MOTHERHOOD

I have observed that God uses different stages of life as seasons of purifying. For some, the entire education process was sandpaper. For others, school was a breeze, but the dating scene brought much anguish and reflection. Some women seem to naturally be at ease as they transition into motherhood while others quickly fall to their knees in complete awareness of their need for the Lord to give them wisdom about this new world. Regardless of the season, most of us don't escape trying to become Miss Perfect. It is amazing how God can give women so many similarities but also make us so unique in our journey. Interestingly, our identity battle usually is rooted in our greatest area of strength.

We tend to attach our identity to what we think we are best at.

Do you think this is true in your life? Explain why women fall into this temptation.

For the first few years of a child's life, the tender bundle is in need of our full attention. If the Lord brings more than one child, this stage of being available to meet an infant's continuous needs can last for years. It is easy to understand that, with the sacrifices required to love our children well, we would wrap our identity around being "Mark's mom," or the best mom in your child's class, or the most creative mom, or even just the best mom to your family.

Why could finding your primary value in being a mother be problematic?

Noted parenting expert John Rosemond makes an interesting case that through the later half of the 20th century, women no longer saw their child's behavior as a reflection of the child. Mothers began to see their child's behavior as a reflection of themselves. His assertion is that this shift in a woman finding her identity in her children has crippled her from being able to correct her children. We take everything so personally that we are quick to justify or rationalize their behavior or even look for a diagnosis because we attach a feeling of personal failure to a child's childish ways.[3]

If you are a mother who can relate to this, describe a time where you took your child's failure as a personal failure.

Finding our identity in motherhood is also extremely tempting when our marriage is not meeting our expectations. Instead of working on our marriage, we can choose to focus all of our energy on our children. We ignore the Holy Spirit's encouragement to grow in all relationships and just focus on the one that brings us comfort or value.

For those who are married, have you ever found yourself investing more in your children than your marriage?

Whether you are married or not, describe some dangers of continuing in this pattern.

While the children may enjoy the extra attention, there are hazards for every member of your family when these patterns occur. Your children are learning an unhealthy model of home life. They need to see you model how a wife should treat her husband. By giving the children first place, they are not learning their proper position in the family and are missing an opportunity to find security in knowing that their parents are healthy. A significant part of being a great mom is being a faithful wife. Additionally, if you minimize working on your marriage, when your children leave home you are left with the reality of a double void. Your home is now empty of children and your relationship with your spouse is a shadow of what it was.

Obviously, relationships are complicated and can take time to heal if they have been damaged. Finding your identity in the Lord will help you work on your marriage and love your children while being at peace with who you are.

When you are freed from depending upon others to validate your worth, you can enter into the process of reconciliation with security.

It is now possible to humbly examine your involvement without feeling threatened if you need to ask for or extend forgiveness.

I cannot leave the subject of motherhood without also addressing the women struggling with infertility. The desire to be a mother and the inability to conceive a child is a painful combination that I only experienced for a year. Many women experience this unmet desire for a lifetime. While I cannot ease the longing, I beg you to guard yourself from becoming singularly focused on this specific role you desire to have. In the same way, it is dangerous for mothers to lose themselves in their children, you also face the danger of longing to put your identity where it should not be.

You need not go far in Scripture (see Genesis 21:1-2, Genesis 30:22, Judges 13:3-4, Luke 1:36-37) to find barren women whom God chose to eventually bless with children. We know that God is able, and we cry out to Him for this blessing. However, He is no less God and you are no less valuable if He delays or denies your request.

4. BEAUTY

Of all the places we can find our identity outside of God's design, this is the most curious and perhaps the most dangerous. The vast majority of us grow up acutely aware of the shortcomings in our external appearance. You do not even have to make it all the way to middle school before your peers have identified all of your blemishes. As I was chaperoning a field trip recently, I overheard four 11-year-old girls asking each other, "What is my least attractive feature?"

All of us can remember someone we wanted to look like or dress like. Often that girl or that woman became our role model of Miss Perfect... regardless of her actions or character. As the world affirms the beauty of some, there can be a temptation to make the world's affirmation our goal.

How do women take external beauty to an extreme?

What does God say about beauty in Proverbs 31:30?

What beauty is precious to God according to 1 Peter 3:3-4?

Of the 4 areas, where are you most tempted to find your value?

Is there another area not discussed where you might be attempting to find your identity? If so, what is it?

One way to evaluate possible areas is to examine what you talk about, what you spend your time doing, and where you spend your money. We can also ask the question, "Where do I sense I am putting myself under a lot of pressure?"

If you have identified any area you are depending upon to fulfill you and validate who you are outside of the Lord, what is one active step you can take to correct your pattern?

An idol, by definition, is anything we give more time or importance to than God.

It is anything outside of God that we look to in order to meet our needs. Much of this is a matter of the heart. You must evaluate if you conduct yourself in these areas because you love the Lord and are serving Him through your position, relationships, etc., or if you are motivated by a desire to feel important through these avenues. If it is the latter, then you are worshipping an idol.

Read Exodus 20:2-4 below. Underline the first two commandments.

² I am the Lord your God who brought you out of the land of Egypt, out of the house of slavery. ³ You shall have no other gods before me. ⁴ You shall not make for yourself a carved image, or any likeness of anything that is in the heaven above, or that is in the earth beneath, or that is in the water under the earth.

The first idol recorded that the children of Israel made was a golden calf. Read Exodus 32:1-10 and 19-24. What reasons did Aaron give for the making of the calf?

The children of God were impatient! They decided to find something easier to fulfill them rather than to obey and wait upon the Lord.

Have you chosen an easier idol to find peace and satisfaction in rather than obeying what God has told you to do and waiting upon Him? If so, what is your idol?

Read Exodus 32:30-35. Does God take idolatry lightly? What is His response to Moses' interceding?

The areas we have been discussing these last two days may not classify as gods of gold, but if we find our identity in anything less than God, we are building our own 21st century idol. There is significant temptation to find your value as a woman in a position, in beauty, or in a relationship. After all, if we are so busy serving our husbands, children, style of living, social life, or job, who has time to sit at the Lord's feet and get to know Him? Can you see how you might hinder the development of your love relationship with God by looking elsewhere for your identity? Do you now see how trying to become Miss Perfect in any one of these areas can cause you to completely miss God's purpose for you?

Something within our soul longs to know we are valuable. That longing is by design. In reality, we ARE designed to find our value in a relationship: *our relationship with God.* It is only in our culture that confusion lurks. By finding our value and security as a child of God, we actually give our loved ones a more beautiful woman to love and cherish. We will bring security and contentment to these precious relationships to strengthen them, rather than unknowingly depend upon others to satisfy a need that only God can fill. I urge you to find your identity in the only One who is perfect and then allow those you love to experience the same freedom from the world's pressure by leading them to His throne!

What was the most meaningful statement or Scripture you read today?

What does God want you to do in response to today's study?

PREVIOUS IDENTITY

KARIN CONLEE

We have spent the first part of the week looking at the places that women commonly try to find their sense of worth. From our job to our looks to our relationships, we can subtly or not so subtly be pulled into the world's value system. You may think, "Does it really matter where I find my identity? I get along just fine without analyzing myself." The catch is that there is an enemy that desperately wants any believer to be powerless. The enemy cannot take our salvation once we are saved, so the next best thing he can do is try to make us ineffective.

Perhaps you are distracted by a position or a relationship to such a degree that you really only give God whatever is left at the end of the week. Maybe while you are trying to find perfection in all of these areas, you are missing the One who is perfect? If this is true, Satan scores. Another way Satan can score is to keep us focused on our past failures so we feel unusable.

Have you ever felt like something from your past haunted you?

What types of things do women commonly feel guilty about from their past?

The primary nature of (the) battle is (for Satan) to destroy our concept of God, distort the relationship we have with Him, or discredit the truth of who we really are as children of God. Satan's lies are aimed at causing each of us to think, "I'm stupid, I'm no good, I'm ugly, God doesn't love me, I can't be forgiven, and Christianity doesn't work for me."[4] Nothing could be further from the truth! If you are a woman who has entered into a personal relationship with Christ, then you have all the power you need to have victory.

Read 2 Corinthians 5:17-21:

> [17] Therefore, if anyone is in Christ, the new creation has come: The old has gone, the new is here! [18] All this is from God, who reconciled us to himself through Christ and gave us the ministry of reconciliation: [19] that God was reconciling the world to himself in Christ, not counting people's sins against them. And he has committed to us the message of reconciliation. [20] We are therefore Christ's ambassadors, as though God were making his appeal through us. We implore you on Christ's behalf: Be reconciled to God. [21] God made him who had no sin to be sin for us, so that in him we might become the righteousness of God. (NIV)

What three things are true "if anyone is in Christ?" (v17)

Are you in Christ?

To be in Christ means that there was a specific time where you saw your sinfulness, realized your need to be forgiven of your sins, and asked Jesus to forgive you and to become your Lord and Savior. If you have made this decision, then the old things have passed away!

Church attendance, growing up under parents who are Christians (even a pastor), or memorizing Scripture does not mean you are in Christ. All of those good things can be done with the right intentions, but the only way to be in Christ is to surrender all of your attempts, admit your attempts are not good enough and neither are you, then ask Him to become your Lord. We must give up chasing what it means to be Miss Perfect! If you cannot remember a specific time when you surrendered your life to the Lord, I encourage you to stop RIGHT now. In your own words, pray and ask God to forgive you of your sins. Name specific sins that come to your mind. Then ask God to save you. You can conclude by thanking the Lord. You can be encouraged to read Romans 10:9-10 for the confidence that God has just saved you. Then, tell someone you know who is a Christian and ask them to help you as you begin this journey as a new follower of Christ.

Read 2 Corinthians 5:17-21 again. Instead of staying ashamed of our sin, what privilege do we have now that we are reconciled to Christ?

The words *reconcile* and *reconciliation* are the pictures of an exchange or to bring into favor. In the New Testament, reconciliation is the restoration of the favor of God to sinners who repent and put their trust in the death and resurrection of Christ.[5] Get this: because God allowed Christ to be the exchange for our sin, now we get the privilege of helping others see that the favor of God can be restored in their lives, too. What an amazing exchange!

If you are a child of God and are still battling with sins of your past, then you are not trusting in the power of God's forgiveness.

Do not let the enemy cause you to doubt what God has already done.

His forgiveness is enough. He truly is powerful enough! The enemy wants us to believe we are still indebted and unworthy. Let the word of God tell you what is true.

Read Psalm 103:1-12. How many iniquities (sins) does the Lord remove? (v3)

Who does David, the author of this song, say these truths apply to? (v11)

How far has God removed our transgressions? (v12)

Have you ever heard someone say, "I know God forgives me, but I can't forgive myself"? The enemy has allowed us to believe that it is our role to forgive ourselves and since we can't, then we are paralyzed again. If you have to forgive yourself, then you are judging yourself. If you are playing judge over yourself, then you are no longer being yourself. You are playing the God role. Instead of assuming the role of judge to forgive yourself, you must humble yourself and move back to just being the one who needs mercy.[6]

There are sins of the past that the enemy will continue to drag up to keep us from living a life that is on mission for the Lord. There is another place where we can find ourselves off course: through the destruction of habitual sins. You might say, "It would be easy to find forgiveness for something in my past, but what about the sin that has entangled me for years that I still can't seem to beat?"

You are not alone in dealing with habitual sin. At Highpoint, we hear that "you only change when it costs you too much not to change." If you see that your habitual sin is destroying the life God intends you to victoriously live, then there is amazing hope. The first step is admitting your struggle. There is no healing in hiding. Whatever your struggle, you are neither the first nor the last to have this specific battle. From eating disorders to adultery, the enemy wants you to believe that there is no way out. You must admit your need for help so you can get the support and tools you need to be set free.

God sees a woman created in His image. He wants you to live triumphantly. Victory begins when we stop believing the lies the enemy tells us. Christian author John Eldredge describes this process as breaking agreements. What are the lies that you believe about yourself? These lies might have come from guilt associated with past failures, or perhaps it came in the form of critical words from someone you cared about.

> If we evaluate where we struggle, we can often find an area that we have decided to agree with the enemy about our identity.

For me, I had to break the agreement that I was not a good mother. Somewhere along the way, I had decided that I was not meant to be a mom. When a common struggle came in parenting I immediately, without realizing it, would agree with the enemy. "You are right, I am a bad mom. I can't do this." It was only through realizing I believed a lie that I was able to consciously break that agreement with the enemy. Now, when the occasional doubt in me arises, I literally rebuke Satan and let him know that his lies are ineffective on me.

For some of you, this is a new idea that may even seem a little odd. Our culture tries to make Satan seem like a fictitious cartoon character, but as John 10:10 says, Satan comes to steal, kill, and destroy. He is real, but he is also a liar (see John 8:44). I can make him powerless if I choose to believe what is true about my identity instead of his lies. The next time you realize you are believing a lie, audibly tell the enemy that you will believe the One who gives life and no longer believe his lies.

What types of agreements do you need to break to be able to free yourself from a false identity?

We will expand on this idea of recognizing, renouncing, and replacing the lies of the enemy next week. I encourage you to spend this week being alert to lies you are believing about yourself. You do not have to be entangled in your past or current sins any longer! Allow God's Word to have victory in you! Decisions can be made in a moment, but the enemy will likely cause you to doubt whether you can truly break the agreement. It is essential to have a support system of godly people who are encouraging you as you establish new God-given agreements about who you are. If healthy Christians are not a part of your daily life, seeking out these relationships is key to long-term victory.

Finish today by reading and re-reading the truth about how God views you. Look up the following verses in Ephesians, or better yet, take time to journal through the entire second chapter of Ephesians.

Ephesians 2:1-7

What did the Lord make you? (v5)

Where did He seat us? (v6)

Why? (v7)

Ephesians 2:12-13

Where were we brought?

Ephesians 2:19-22

What were we? (v19)

What are we now? (v19)

What is God building within you? (v22)

What was the most meaningful statement or Scripture you read today?

What does God want you to do in response to today's study?

Day Four

STOLEN IDENTITY
KARIN CONLEE

As we enter into a new day of study, let me encourage you to do two things before we dive in and explore another facet of our identity. First, would you turn back to yesterday's lesson and be reminded of what the Lord showed you? Is there an agreement that you need to make sure you break with the enemy? Second, stop and pray. Ask the Lord to both remind you of truths He has shown you and prepare your heart as we honestly evaluate the influences in our lives.

What did the Lord show you? What lies are you not going to tolerate from the enemy the next time he tries?

I encourage you to begin your Bible study with prayer every day. My words and Chris's words are just that- words. But if your heart is sensitive to the Lord, He may have a life changing truth for you to receive. One word from Him can be more powerful than a lifetime of words from any human being.

Now as we shift to consider another angle of our identity, consider this question: Would you want your children to get their values from the television, movies, or even from a well-meaning group of older children? No! Instead, most parents try to protect their children from the influences of culture! We attempt to shape our children's understanding of the world through meaningful conversations, God's Word, and by being a good role model.

Strangely, the very sources we try to protect our children from become our subtle teachers of womanhood. How did you decide what it truly meant to be a woman? How did you determine your priorities and goals?

Many of us unintentionally absorbed the world's definition of success and then acted upon it.

We would hardly let a stranger go pick out a pair of jeans for us to wear, but we will accept a stranger's message of what we should value. The world has stolen the God-designed identity of many women and replaced it by continually projecting an image of what culture desires women to be.

How has the world's view of what a woman should be shaped you?

There are so many aspects of life that we are intentional about! We like our specific brand of coffee or a certain store where we prefer to shop. We will take time to coordinate an outfit or find just the right shade of hair color. Yet, we have not stepped back and looked at the big picture of our lives to ask the larger questions and, more importantly, determine our answers. As if we were a young student in school who forgot to study, we look over the shoulders of the students next to us and assume their answers look good enough.

As a Christian, we look to the Bible to guide us in many areas, but seldom do we ask, "What was God's purpose when He created women? How does His design influence me?" If God created the universe as Genesis says He did and you believe it, then you are called to embrace a breathtaking dignity and fixed meaning to your life and to your womanhood.

> You are purposeful, designed, intentional, and God has put you here because He is out to achieve something in the gender He has wrapped you in.[7]

Read Genesis 1:26-31. What actions does God give to Adam and Eve to fulfill? (v28)

Adam and Eve are called to fulfill two fundamental purposes: to bring life into the world and to provide leadership over the earth. This is not simply a call to have babies! What a small view of God's desires! We must look only to the many cults that choose to procreate in mass to pass on a false religion to know that there is more to God's intended purpose than just a headcount. He wants us to produce followers of God! Even the couple who has been unable to conceive still has incredible value in God's kingdom of multiplying! It is a precious gift to have your own biological child, but it should not be the limit of our multiplying!

Genesis 2 expands on what was described in Genesis chapter 1. Read Genesis 2:18-25. What reason did God give for the creation of woman? (v18)

When we take the truths of Genesis 1:28 in light of Genesis 2:18, we begin to have the context of God's instructions. We are to help Adam rule the earth and provide him companionship. Think of the parallel of helping your child with his or her homework. You are to help provide some encouragement and clarity where needed, NOT take the book and do it for them! God designed us to assist our husband, not take the book and do it for him! The culture would have us believe that men originally overpowered us and coerced us into a role of lesser strength. As women, we have a powerful role of influence and have the ability to cause our husbands to thrive or wither. If you have issues with helping your husband, your issue is with God. No worries, we will get back to this subject later.

What actions does God tell man and woman to fulfill in verse 24?

Do these verses in Genesis just apply to Adam and Eve? Explain your answer.

God gave these instructions before Adam and Eve sinned in the garden. God's plan for a woman and man were not the consequences of sin. His perfect design is for a woman to be a helper to a man and for them to come together as one, have children, and rule over the earth. Genesis is not about what is unique to you as a woman but rather what is common and enduring for all women. Genesis presents three core callings for women to build their lives around: Be Fruitful and Multiply, Subdue and Rule, and Leave and Cleave.[8]

How does the culture's definition of a woman's purpose compare to God's definition?

How do YOUR views of womanhood compare to God's plan for women?

As Robert Lewis coined the terms in his book *The New Eve*, we must decide whether we are going to live from the inside-out or from the outside-in. *We must decide if the outside world will shape our convictions or if our convictions will determine how we interact with the world.* The choice is ours! As women, we are given the freedom to choose what our femininity looks like.

> But outside-in living exacts a heavy toll on women. It reshapes and molds life to fit values and attitudes that are not native to the true femininity God has placed within every woman's heart. To go against this divine grain is an invitation to heart ache. Our roots in Genesis shout this warning. Women who forsake their core and choose forbidden fruit of this world find that in time it leaves them lonely or angry or childless or with angry children or with an angry husband or with no husband or empty or with everything but true happiness. Outside-in living looks delicious on the front end, but it has a deadly back side. Just ask Eve.[9]

We were not created as women to be weak. We were given the responsibility to be a helper to our husbands as they rule. Women hold a unique power to make life better, and in the beginning God named this as a core calling for all women.[10] God has designed a path that will allow us to use our unique gifts in a way that brings great glory to Him and great satisfaction to our feminine souls.

Go along with me for a minute, especially if you are familiar with the life of Jesus. If Jesus had chosen to listen to the world, how might He have used His gifts differently?

Perhaps the sinless nature of Jesus and His sacrifice unto death seems too great a stretch for us to relate to. Read John 12:41-43 below. Circle what kept some from following Christ.

[41] Isaiah said these things because he saw his glory and spoke of him. [42] Nevertheless, many even of the authorities believed in him (Jesus), but for fear of the Pharisees they did not confess it, so that they would not be put out of the synagogue; [43] for they loved the glory that comes from man more than the glory that comes from God.

Were these leaders choosing to live from the Outside-In or from the Inside-Out?

While we may not have the threat of Pharisees putting us out of the temples, in what ways does your desire for approval from people hinder you from seeking the approval of God?

We are given the freedom to choose how we live our lives as women. We must take hold of the decisions before us and determine if we will follow God's design or the world's. We must decide if our convictions will determine how we interact with the world or if we will allow the world's ever changing values to determine our next move. Are you going to continue to subject yourself to the pressure of the world or choose God's purpose? Consider your choice wisely.

What was the most meaningful statement or Scripture you read today?

What does God want you to do in response to today's study?

TRUE IDENTITY
KARIN CONLEE

———————

Up to this point in our study of our identity, we have focused on the ways we can try to find our identity in the wrong places. Sometimes, we are tempted to find our identity through power or through human relationships we care deeply about. At other times, we may hear the whisper of the enemy telling us that if people really knew our identity and our past we would face unbearable pain or embarrassment. As women of faith, we can even be at war within ourselves, adding our own pressure and insecurities as we try to satisfy both God and the world. So, is there somewhere we can find our identity that will not disappoint or delude us?

YES! I am so excited to reassure you. Yes! Yes! Yes! As I mentioned earlier, I also bought into the world's value system of a woman's identity. It was no longer the world's way. It had become my value system. As I left the work force after having our son, I was trying to make the emotional transition of losing esteem while gaining a beautiful, and by this time, long-sought-after baby. I felt guilty about my mixed emotions until Clyde Cranford, a godly man who discipled my husband, spoke great clarity into my mental gymnastics. He told me one night over dinner, "Whatever you do, Karin, do not change your identity from being the Associate Director of Admissions to being Mark's mom or Chris's wife. You are not promised those identities forever, either. You must find your entire identity in Christ. It is the only identity that will never change and never disappoint."

The question must be answered: What does it mean to find your identity in Christ?

As I was writing this section, I was using the wording "We must place our identity in Christ." Then it struck me; this is part of the problem!

> We act as if we can pack up our identity and place it at option A or B. No!
> Our true identity can't be transported.

Looking below at Ephesians 1:3-5.

> [3] Blessed be the God and Father of our Lord Jesus Christ, who has blessed us in Christ with every spiritual blessing in the heavenly places, [4] even as he chose us in him before the foundation of the world, that we should be holy and blameless before him. In love [5] he predestined us for adoption as sons through Jesus Christ, according to the purpose of his will.

When was our identity determined? (v4)

Who was the one doing the choosing? (v4 and 5)

What are the results of us being chosen and adopted?

Paul was writing to the believers in Ephesus, and if you are a believer in Jesus Christ, it applies to you. Whether you understood it or not, when you humbled yourself and acknowledged your sinfulness and asked for God to save you, you found the identity that was created for you before the foundation of the earth! Now we must embrace that identity and allow ourselves to stop trying to create an alternative identity. We will never be able to improve on being the child of the most High God!

After this week of study, where are you on this journey of embracing your identity in Christ? For the analytical among us, where are you on a scale of 1 (struggling!) to 10 (completely at peace that my identity and value come from Christ and Christ alone)? Why?

If you are still wrestling, what is one step you must take to overcome old patterns and live according to God's purpose?

Now the reality is we don't always feel like the daughter of a king, do we? Think of it this way: when you were a little girl, did you ever want to run away? Sometimes we think our plans are better, and we decide we don't want to be a part of our family anymore. However, even if we packed a bag and walked down the street, we never stopped being our father's daughter.

In a sinful, fallen world, many of us are accustomed to the pain of broken relationships. Sometimes, it has been through this pain that we have put up walls and determined we will make our own identity so we can never be hurt again. How can we trust that our identity in Christ is secure?

Read Romans 8:35-39. List all the things that CANNOT separate us from the love of Christ.

As a child of God, it is not oversimplifying it to come to a place where we can say, "I love God and He loves me, therefore I am okay."[11]

> When our identity is no longer attached to our performance or our past or our interactions with others, we now become women at peace with who we are.

We can let go of the self-imposed and world-imposed pressure. We can stop striving for the unattainable perfection. We can discover God's purpose. We can now make choices based on God's desires and how we are wired instead of trying to keep up a facade or to impress those we want to admire us. The Lord has already fulfilled that void and now we can be free to love and serve without needing something in return.

Look at the following scenarios. Describe how the woman's response would be different if she found her identity in Christ rather than the area in jeopardy.

A woman in her mid 40's finds out her husband has lost his job. They will have to downsize to a smaller house and significantly decrease their discretionary spending to make ends meet.

After ten years of marriage, a woman discovers that her husband has had an affair and has decided to leave her for this new relationship. She faces life now as a single mom.

A mother finds out that her teenage son has been stealing to support a drug addiction.

Three of your longtime friends have begun planning activities together without you. Your feelings are hurt and you feel betrayed.

All of these scenarios play themselves out in our fallen world. If your identity is in your position, then perhaps in scenario one you begin to blame your spouse or try to fix the problem so you can keep up with the Joneses… or at least the image you have created. When your identity is in Christ, the situation is still difficult, but you are able to trust in what God wants to teach you and you can be content without all the worldly luxuries you once had. You likely begin to treasure relationships more, and you know that who you are is not determined by the size of your home or the labels in your clothes! Discuss the scenarios in your small group time.

Read Psalm 91. What security can you have if you put your identity in Christ?

What specifically does David say the Lord protects you from?

The Lord does not promise there will not be tribulation in our lives. He actually promises we will encounter trials (James 1:2-4), but what does Psalm 91:15-16 promise?

As we wrap up our study of our identity, be encouraged by the words in Isaiah 54:10,

For the mountains may be removed and the hills may shake, but My lovingkindness will not be removed from you, and My covenant of peace will not be shaken,' says the LORD who has compassion on you. (NASB)

When your identity is in Christ, you can be at peace even when the world around you shakes! Take courage, women! We were given an identity! We do not have to find one or create one. We only have to embrace the one our perfect, loving Heavenly Father designed for us. He knows us and wants us to discover joy and satisfaction as we carry out the purposes He created us to accomplish.

What was the most meaningful statement or Scripture you read today?

What does God want you to do in response to today's study?

NOTES FOR THE WEEK

HOLINESS WITHOUT HANG-UPS

A woman discovers her holiness by responding to the fear and awe of God with a life that is set apart.

Day One
UNDERSTANDING GOD'S IDENTITY

Day Two
REPLACING YOUR FEAR OF THE ENEMY

Day Three
REPLACING YOUR FEAR OF THE "WHAT-IFS"

Day Four
GAINING A BIGGER VIEW

Day Five
TAKING THE PLUNGE

UNDERSTANDING GOD'S IDENTITY
CHRIS KUHLMAN

I (Chris) am so glad to be joining you on this journey of *Discovering God's Purpose Without the Pressure*. Like Karin, and most women, I spent many years of my walk with Christ trying to be Miss Perfect. For countless reasons, I kept "missing" the perfect part. I could never quite reach perfection and regularly fell short of my own expectations. I could never figure out how to be the "perfect friend," "perfect wife," or "perfect mom." MOST of us can identify with the desire to be perfect, but ALL of us can identify with falling short of that perfection. The truth is, God is more interested in our progress than He is in us being perfect. But only Christ can free us from the performance trap, because only Christ loves us based upon *His* goodness instead of our goodness. He only wants progress, but it isn't possible apart from understanding who God is.

Last week, we learned that our identity must be found in Christ. As important as it is to understand OUR identity, it is even more critical to grasp God's identity. If we have an inaccurate view of God, then we will continually be disappointed, confused, and frustrated when God does not act the way we imagine He should. Several years ago, I made a shift in my thinking. I realized that I needed to "know God" to truly be able to experience Him. Instead of just reacting to life, I desired to respond to life's circumstances based on my relationship with Him. There is a huge difference between reacting and responding!

Do you ever find yourself just reacting to whatever comes your way? If so, give an example.

Not long ago I felt that Satan was attacking my family. I spent the following days and months crying out to God to make it better. But I realized that my tears were coming out of my efforts to try to get to God while God was teaching me that I need to submit to Him, however He decided to work. Getting to know God in His holiness has allowed me to really begin to trust Him with every part of my life. It has allowed this very fearful person to exchange the fears of my insecurities for a "fear" of an awesome and loving God who I can trust with every single part of my life. We can know a lot about God and still not know WHO He is. And until we know WHO God is, we won't trust Him with the deepest, closest, and most vulnerable areas of our lives.

If we are to contemplate God's identity and understand who He is, holiness is the place to start. If you have spent a lot of time in church, you likely have heard that God is holy or even the hymn "Holy, Holy, Holy," but what does *holiness* really mean?

What do you think of when you hear the word "holy"?

For some, it conjures up pictures of grandeur... maybe a royal throne. For others, holiness brings a feeling of harshness or legalism. Sometimes we get all hung up in our stereotypes when a person espousing to be "holy" tells us how to act. Holiness means to be set apart and totally different, unique. God's Word never says that God is love, love, love; it does say that He is holy, holy, holy. It is God's holiness that shapes every other attribute He has. Here is what is so amazing: there is no one else or nothing else that is holy apart from God. As His children, Christians are seen as holy, but only because of Him. None of us are holy in our own strength.

The fact that God alone is holy should drive us to respond to Him differently than anyone else. When we truly grasp how amazingly separate God is from all of us, it should bring us to a place of having a healthy fear of God. Now in our culture, the word *fear* is used mainly in a negative way. But when God tells us to "fear Him" it is for our good.

In our study this week, we will spend the first few days trying to grasp how powerful and mighty God is. In this sense, our fear is literally defined as being afraid or terrified. We should have a wholesome dread of displeasing Him.[1] Later this week, we will look at fear from the perspective of how we also will stand in awe of Him. In reality, these two definitions of fear are both used in Scripture and are sometimes hard to separate. Many times it is a combination of both meanings of fear at the same time. There are times you experience fear because He is a holy and just God, but you also experience awe because He still pursues you and extends forgiveness to you. Put another way: God is intimately intimidating. This is a big subject and we will just touch the tip of the iceberg, but let it deepen your view of our great and awesome God.

> A woman discovers her holiness by responding to the fear and awe of God
> with a life that is set apart.

This week, we aren't going to run away from the word *fear*. I think it's safe to say that we've all felt some type of fear in our lives. Fear can be crippling, but it can also serve a positive purpose. We teach our toddlers to fear a hot stove because it will burn them. It is for their safety and their comfort. In the same way, God's Word tells us over 400 times to "fear God." We will not dodge it because it makes us feel uncomfortable or because it is confrontational. Allow it to confront you. Let's use it to find out WHO God is and why we are to fear Him. Like the hot stove to a toddler- fear can be for our good, our safety, and our comfort.

Let me set up the scene for our main passage today from the book of Exodus. From the time Jacob brought his family to Egypt during the famine until the exodus, the Israelites had lived in Egypt 430 years. When the time came for God to deliver the children of Israel from their bondage, He took not only Pharaoh but His own people through ten plagues to reveal to them all WHO He is. For 430 years, the Israelites had lived among a people who believed Pharaoh was a god. God wanted to show His people that He alone is God, and He alone is to be feared.

Read Exodus 3:14-15. By what name are we to remember God?

In Exodus chapters 7-11, we see God revealing Himself not only to Pharaoh and the Egyptians but also to His own people. God uses the first three plagues to proclaim, "I AM THE LORD." But Pharaoh tries to compromise with God (Ex. 8:28). He sees that the Israelites' God is great but does not see Him as GOD ALONE. We often try to compromise with God to get Him to ease the pain of our own trials, but many times God wants to reveal WHO He is to us through those very trials. He knows that compromising with us would stifle our ability to see Him for WHO He is. It's our choice: we can harden our hearts because God won't remove the obstacle or hardship, or we can allow God to change our hearts through the discomfort. Each plague God placed on Egypt was a message to His people that their God was fighting FOR them, and they did not have to worry or be afraid.

Have you ever tried to compromise with God? If so, describe the circumstances.

Give one reason why God does not compromise or negotiate.

Is there any circumstance in your life NOW where you could be tempted to harden your heart toward God because you have not received the answer you desire? If so, describe.

In the rest of these passages about the plagues, God is building on the truth that He has set them apart from the Egyptians. Look at Exodus 9:4.

> But the Lord will make a distinction between the livestock of Israel and the livestock of Egypt, so that nothing of all that belongs to the people of Israel shall die.

What do you think God was trying to teach the Israelites?

God protected His children from the plagues. He wanted the Israelites and the surrounding nations to experience His great power to ensure that they knew HE ALONE IS GOD. He was radically different than the false gods.

Then we have the great exodus. As the Israelites watched God at work on their behalf, not only did the their faith increase, but their awe and trust in Him increased. God's kindness and majestic power inspired them to obey. It can inspire us to do the same.

Remember the movie *What About Bob?* Bob suffered from excessive phobias. He wouldn't leave his apartment. He couldn't make friends. His fears caused him to stay closed up to the outside world. Bob's transformation came when he took his psychiatrist's advice and read the book *Baby Steps.* Bob relied solely on his psychiatrist for help, and when Dr. Leo leaves for a family vacation, Bob is unable to cope. So he reluctantly sets out to follow him on his vacation, causing him to take his first "baby steps." But it didn't feel like a baby step to him in the beginning; he just had faith and followed what his psychiatrist told him. Likewise, the Israelites were learning day-by-day, simply taking "baby steps." Trusting one day at a time. Some days, they were taking a step because they were literally afraid of His power. Other times, they were in awe of Him as He proved Himself a faithful protector of His people. And in the same way, we will learn by taking our own baby steps. We must allow our fears to help us develop a complete trust in our God.

So does it benefit me to fear God? Absolutely! "To the woman who fears God He will show the way she should live" (Psalm 25:12,14). "She will lack nothing" (Psalm 34:9). "He gives safety when she is attacked by the enemy" (Psalm 60:4). And "She will gain insight"(Psalm 111:9-10).

What specific blessings do we see offered to the one who fears God in the following verses?

Psalm 103:13

Psalm 130:4

Proverbs 3:7-8

Do you need direction in your life? Do you need God's safe, protective hand to cover you? Do you need His forgiveness, His healing, and His refreshment?

Yes! Of course we do. Everyday we are in need of the blessings that God offers to the woman who would "Fear Him." And we will only fear Him and revere Him if we KNOW HIM. He does not say *I was* or *I will be,* but I AM. He is here now in this moment to be everything you need. He is for you, and He desires for you to KNOW HIM. Take hold of His holiness, even if it requires you to approach with both terror and awe. You will never regret pressing in to become connected to our intimately intimidating God.

What was the most meaningful statement or Scripture you read today?

What does God want you to do in response to today's study?

REPLACING YOUR FEAR OF THE ENEMY

CHRIS KUHLMAN

When I was 11 years old, I would walk to a park a couple of blocks from my home. One of my favorite things to do there was climb the tall pine trees. One day, I was feeling extra adventurous and I made it all the way to the very top of one of the trees. After making it to the top and getting a full view of my favorite park, I was pretty proud of my climbing accomplishment. But at that very moment there was a strong wind that caused the tree to begin swaying, and I began to sway with it. I can't remember how, but apparently that breeze caused me to fall straight to the ground, hitting pine tree limbs all the way down.

I don't know if I lost consciousness before I fell and that was what caused the fall, or if I simply don't remember the fall because I lost consciousness after I hit the ground. But what I do remember is being flat on my back, opening my eyes to the startled faces of curious onlookers. Ever since that accident, I have had an intense fear of heights. But not too long ago, I was thinking about that accident, and I realized that I am not actually afraid of the height, (after all, I'm not afraid to fly in an airplane), I am just afraid of the falling. That fall caused a great fear in me, and I am now conditioned to fear whenever I'm in a place where falling is possible.

Yesterday, we saw that before the Israelites could take one step with God, they had to believe that He was able to deliver them. God, in His perfect way, opened up heaven and allowed Himself to become known by the Israelites. The Egyptians were the enemy, and these children of Abraham were conditioned to fear them. But God wanted them to have a greater awe of *His* power than of anything the Egyptians could do. He wanted them to see that He is holy. As women of God who desire to grow and take those baby steps in our faith, we must have a greater fear of God than we have of the enemy. The awe and reverence we have for the Lord should far outweigh any fear we have of what the enemy can do in our lives, but we can easily fall prey to our own conditioned fears just like the Israelites.

In what areas of your life have you become conditioned to assume the worst and become full of fear?

If we were to truly grasp how powerful and holy our God is, we would be unstoppable. The enemy and our flesh would be defeated, if we would only live out what we say we believe about God. Unfortunately, instead of standing in reverent awe of our God and allowing His power to protect us, we frequently give greater weight to earthly fears. There are two significant hang-ups we are going to examine over the next two days: the fear of the enemy and the fear of the unknown. Let's look at how the fear of the enemy keeps us from partaking in God's holiness.

God's presence was always with the Israelites in a pillar of fire by night and in a pillar of cloud by day. His presence guided them on their journey toward the Promised Land. As long as their eyes were on God and they believed Him to be their fortress, they were secure, strong, and unconquerable. It even says in Exodus 14:8 that the Israelites were "marching out boldly." But then one day they heard their enemy coming and they took their eyes off the pillar of cloud and they "looked up, and there were the Egyptians..." They were terrified! They instinctively began to fear! That overwhelming feeling of reverence and awe they had put in God and His power was transferred to being terrified of their enemy. I can imagine they remembered the torturous years of laboring under Egyptian rule, luring their minds back to what had caused them to cry out to God in the first place.

We may not have a physical enemy attacking us, but we have the same choice when we come face to face with the enemy's activity.

> We can keep grounded in who God is or we can cave into the lie that we should be afraid of the enemy's power.

Has someone close to you ever said something so hurtful that it just sucked the wind out of you? In that moment, we have a decision to make. We can quickly succumb to all the horrible thoughts that the enemy wants to plant in our minds OR we can identify the fear that the comment aroused in us, determine what is legitimate and what is not, and then replace the fear with faith. We must decide if we are going to allow fear (often disguised as hurt) to control us, or if we will remember God's unmatchable power and trust Him to take care of us.

Can you recollect a time where you realized that you were in the midst of deciding if you were going to stand strong against fear or fall to it? If so, describe what you were thinking.

Choosing to remember who God is sounds so easy when you are not in the heat of the battle. As an observer, you can see the enemy play his hand like a stack of cards. But in the moment, it is hard to be so methodical and rational, isn't it? We looked at this concept briefly in our week on Identity. We must remember that the enemy is a liar. He is good at it, too. Sometimes we latch on to our own negative thoughts. Other times, we take something someone says to us and allow the enemy to have a field day in our heart and mind. When it comes to criticism, sometimes it is justified and sometimes it is not. So what are we to do to keep from giving into the fear that the enemy is trying to paralyze us with?

I am a very literal person. It helps me to have concrete steps to follow. So let's make this very practical. Let's say that something has happened to trigger you to have an internal battle.

For sake of an example, imagine that you were criticized at work or by your husband. If you are left with thoughts like "I'll never be good enough" then apply these steps:

Step 1 - Recognize the lie
"I am consciously or subconsciously believing that I'll never be good enough."

Step 2 - Renounce the lie
If you have ever wondered what spiritual warfare is, this is it! The enemy never fights nice. This battle requires you to stand against the lie by confidently saying out loud or determining in your spirit, "I am not going to believe that lie again." You've just defended yourself from the lie; now it is time to move to step three and play offense.

Step 3 - Replace the lie
Don't make this too complicated. In the clearest and most direct way, replace the lie with truth. Once you identify the lie, the truth becomes obvious. The most powerful way to do this is to imitate what Jesus did in Matthew 4 when He said "it is written..." and quote the Scriptures that best refutes your specific lie. For example, "'God has not given (me) a spirit of fear, but of power and love and discipline' (2 Tim 1:7). [7] I am choosing right now to replace fear with confidence."

If there was any truth within the criticism, you can now address the issue from a context of security and peace. You may need to approach your boss and see what steps you can take to regain his or her confidence. Perhaps you were misunderstood and you need to clarify some things. Some criticisms are unfounded and now that you are believing what is true about you, you can let the criticism go. Regardless of the action you need to take, you are no longer trapped in fear and you can trust the Lord to lead you to respond out of faith instead of fear.

We give the enemy too much credit and we fear him more than we fear the power of our God. Fredrick W. Cropp said, "There is much in the world to make us afraid. There is much more in our faith to make us unafraid."[2] How true! Yet, we are frequently guilty of keeping our focus on the enemy's power and overlooking the One who has true authority and dominion over all. The Israelites were guilty of this same pattern. It was only a short time before the Israelites began fearing the Egyptians attack that they saw God do amazing and wondrous miracles. Yet at the first sign of their Egyptian enemy, they were ready to go back to bondage. But God had determined to bring them deliverance, and just as He wanted to deliver them, He wants to bring deliverance to us as well.

Exodus 14:13-14 says,

> [13] And Moses said to the people, "Fear not, stand firm, and see the salvation of the Lord, which he will work for you today... [14] The Lord will fight for you, and you have only to be silent.

What did Moses tell them they needed to do?

Did you catch the instruction to be silent? Sometimes, circumstances force us to take action, but more often than not we choose to take action instead of trusting God to fight for us. When we are in a place where fear is descending on us like a thick, opaque fog, we must discipline our minds to "Fear not, Stand firm, and see the salvation of the LORD." We only have to be silent. Yes, of course, being silent is one of the hardest things to do when we are afraid. But our silence is an indication of our trust in the One who fights for us. We can be silent when we'd rather run and scream. And we can KNOW that He is working on our behalf.

What is an example of a situation where you need to be silent and trust the Lord to fight for you?

We know that God did come through that day with a victory for His children and it produced in them a mighty awe of the Lord, and they "believed Him" (Exodus 14:31). This is such an important truth that we must grab tightly. As we stand in awe of the Lord, we can simultaneously put our trust in Him. He can be trusted completely, and that trust will melt away any fear we have of the enemy while creating a reverence for the Lord. There is a cycle. Do you see it? When we are silent and let Him fight, we will see His magnificence and power. As we see His power and Sovereignty, we will trust Him with more and more until we trust Him with all that we are. He is holy. He is waiting for us to step out of the way to see it.

Let's finish this journey with the Israelites and see where God led them when the enemy pursued. In Exodus 14:2, they were commanded to camp between Migdol and the sea. It was the most vulnerable place to be when a hot blooded pursuit was imminent. God put them in a position where they had no other choice but to depend completely on Him. They had to trust God more than they feared their enemy. God was going to fight this battle for them; they simply needed to listen and obey. The Israelites did what God instructed, and their lives were spared in a miraculous event we know as the "parting of the Red Sea."

Can you relate to the children of Israel being in that most vulnerable place? Do you feel like you are at a "dead end" where victory seems out of reach? You may be in this place because of your own unwise decisions, or you may be in a predicament through no fault of your own. Maybe someone else made a few unwise decisions and you are reaping the consequences. It could be a prodigal child you desperately want to walk with God. Your "dead end" may be related to your work, school, or home. Whatever it is, right now you feel squeezed in a tight place with nowhere to run. Take heart! When we have nowhere to turn, feel out of control, and all looks hopeless, that is precisely where God does His best work!

You will yield to that which you fear most. Do you fear the enemy and what he can do? Remember Romans 8:31."What shall we say to these things? If God is for us, who can be against us?"

According to this verse, what can we KNOW when we are trapped by our fears?

What should our response be to this truth?

Let us enter into each day realizing that God is for us!

Moses instructed the Israelites not to fear the enemy. But how could they NOT fear? The enemy was right there! They could see the threat! They felt the ground shake beneath them from the thunderous beating of the horses hooves! God didn't promise it would be easy, but He did promise He would fight for them. We must do what the Israelites had to do--remember WHO God is and what He promises. Remember what He did during the plagues. Remember the Red Sea. Remember His promises. Remember what He has done in your life. God wants us to wait for Him. Stand firmly and do not waver from what you know about Him. When you find yourself in a frightening, dead end situation, it's likely God is about to do His best work in you. Respond according to WHO you know God to be!

What was the most meaningful statement or Scripture you read today?

What does God want you to do in response to today's study?

REPLACING YOUR FEAR OF THE "WHAT-IFS"
CHRIS KUHLMAN

Yesterday we explored how we can be tragically misled to fear the enemy more than God. Whether we knew it or not, we have all given the enemy more authority than he ever deserves. We are learning to recognize his lies so he can remain powerless over us. When we choose to put our eyes on the One who is worthy to be feared, we are in a position to experience the fullness of life as God intended. Today we will turn our attention to one other fear that distracts us from seeing God's holiness: the fear of the unknown.

Fearing the unknown can be debilitating. As a mother, I have a strong tendency to fear unknowns in my life. My son Taylor lives out of town. He can go a couple of weeks without feeling the need to call "just to talk." There are times I let my imagination take hold of my thoughts, and I begin to allow the "what-ifs" to gain some ground. I don't want to voice the questions that start circulating in my mind as though to speak them out loud would make them come true. What if something bad happens to him and I won't know soon enough? What if he makes a bad choice that leads to consequences I can't prevent? What if he can't pay his bills? What if he forgets God in his life? If I do not stop myself when my imagination gets the best of me and remember that God knows the future and that He is bigger than any "what-if," I become immobilized by fear. I have to take action quickly! I have to intercept my thoughts, and make a determined decision to entrust them to God.

Do you struggle with the "what-ifs"? If so, what is the unknown that causes you the most fear?

We all have a tendency to fear the unknown. But when we learn WHO God is, that He is trustworthy and cares for us intensely, it awakens an emotional response in us that will lead us to complete trust and surrender. When I begin to fear the "what-ifs," I remember that God only allows circumstances to come into my life and into Taylor's life that have the potential to draw us closer to Him. I remember that He loves me, and He loves Taylor, and that He is always present with us. He never forgets about me, and He is the One who has placed in me this motherly affection for my son. He will take care of my baby. I need not worry about the "what-ifs." He can handle everything in my life, and NOTHING surprises Him. Taylor is in good hands. Based on this knowledge of God, I know that I can trust Him with Taylor.

What are two things you know are true about God that can combat your fear of the unknown?

I love to read deep, engaging novels. I thoroughly enjoy getting wrapped up in the storyline and the characters, and becoming fully engaged in the plot. However, after reading the first few chapters, I absolutely have to know if it ends well or not. I so desperately want to be prepared for what may happen, that I usually turn to the last few pages to check the ending. I know, I know....this ruins the whole book! But I really love a happy ending! Anyway, after peeking into the final destination of the characters, only then can I comfortably continue reading.

Unfortunately, we cannot do this with our own lives. When we read the stories in the Bible we forget that the people in the "story" did not know if they would have a happy ending. They either trusted God, or they gave into their desire to control their circumstances. We all have this innate desire to be in control. We want it, and we never want to lose it.

We allow control to give us a false sense of security.

When we feel we are out of control, we tend to rely on our own perceived strengths to put us back in the driver's seat. But we must fully rely on His promises and His character, and only then will we see firsthand how we can trust Him with every part of our lives. When we begin to trust Him, we will see that there is no greater place to be than in His control.

On a scale of 1-10, how would your closest friend rate how much you struggle with control? (1=She is not controlling, 10= She attempts to control anything she can)

In the early days of my walk with Christ, I compartmentalized the areas of my life. There were some areas I was comfortable entrusting to God, but there were other areas I wanted to keep to myself. I thought I could handle them well enough on my own, but if I'm honest, it was usually because I wanted to control the outcome. Most of the time, those areas of my life did not turn out well and I had to endure the pain of my decisions. How foolish I was to think I could handle these areas of my life according to my own understanding. I have learned that when I submit to God in every area of my life, I can be assured that He has my good in store.

Proverbs 3:5-6 says,

[5] Trust in the Lord with all your heart, and do not lean on your own understanding.
[6] In all your ways acknowledge him and he will make straight your paths.

The word translated *vvtt* in this verse means "to lie helpless, face down." It is a picture of a servant waiting in readiness to obey his master's command, or a soldier yielding himself to the conquering general. We are told to view ourselves as utterly helpless, and without God totally hopeless. Complete trust is so against our earthly nature that we instead yield ourselves to self-reliance, believing that we can handle whatever might come. Our self-reliance must go before we can replace it with complete trust in the Lord. Do not be fooled; self-reliance will keep us from experiencing God's holiness.

How do you think self-reliance impacts your relationship with God?

J.I. Packer's book, *Knowing God*, says, "Not until we have become humble and teachable, standing in awe of God's holiness and sovereignty, acknowledging our own littleness, distrusting our own thoughts and willing to have our minds turned upside down, can divine wisdom become ours."[3] "We can be sure that the God who made this marvelously complex world order, and who compassed the great redemption from Egypt, and who later compassed the even greater redemption from sin and Satan, knows what He is doing, and '[does] all things well,' even if for the moment He hides His hand. We can trust Him and rejoice in Him, even when we cannot discern His path."[4]

Circle the word trust and rejoice in that last sentence. In what specific areas do you struggle letting go of control? Why?

We will never eliminate our fears by simply telling ourselves not to be afraid.

Our only hope for relieving the fear in our lives is to make a determined decision to take our eyes off of the fear and instead place our focus on the One who can conquer every fear that ails us. When you are focusing on your fear, all you see is that fear. But when you are constantly directing your mind and your heart toward God, your focus will change. You will see His power in your life and begin to entrust the worries of your life to Him.

Sadly, most people barely get to the place of entrusting God with their worries. Yet beyond worries, there is an entirely deeper dimension to God's power that we can experience, if we let Him. Not only can He be entrusted with our worries, but He can be entrusted with our lives. He is sovereign. This means that He is the One truly in control of all that occurs in our lives. When we can live in a place of acknowledging this, we are truly able to grasp God's holiness. He really is set apart and different. Do you realize that He is the only One in control? Any control but God's is pure deception. If we want to discover God's purpose for our lives without the pressure, we can start by replacing our confidence in ourselves with a confidence in the One who truly is in control.

Earlier we asked where you struggle letting go of control. How does this new perspective on control impact your struggle?

It's time for a fresh look at the God who promises us that He is *for us*. We CAN trust Him. We are foolish not to trust Him. Trust should occur when someone has both character and competence. Ironically, we trust ourselves even though we know when it is all said and done we do not have the ability to guarantee our future. We are incompetent and our character on our best day leaves much to be desired. In contrast, God's character is perfect and He defines competency. We can trust Him and in trusting Him we CAN rejoice.

What was the most meaningful statement or Scripture you read today?

What does God want you to do in response to today's study?

GAINING A BIGGER VIEW

CHRIS KUHLMAN

We have spent the early portion of this week looking at the places where we get hung-up or distracted from grasping who God really is. Louie Giglio of Passion Ministries has said, "I don't know how big your God is, but He is as big as you want Him to be."[5] There is so much truth to this statement and it explains why so much of the modern church remains powerless and fearful. If we keep our view of God small, we can miss His holiness and spend our time fearing the evil in this world and all the unknowns. When we choose to have an accurate view of our mighty God, and a reverence for His power and authority, we will develop a trust in Him that encourages us to lean into His strength.

Do you act like you have a big God or a little God? Explain your answer.

Do you genuinely desire a bigger view of God?

Why or why not?

As we continue discussing God's holiness, I want us to shift perspectives. We have talked about the fact that God is intimately intimidating. We should be both scared and awed. From a human perspective, I think about that enormous football player that is described as a teddy bear by people who know him. You sure would not want to meet him in a dark alley, but everyone who is close to him says he is such a tender guy. But we are not discussing a football player! We are discussing the creator and ruler of the universe.

Why would He want us to fear Him? What is His motive?

After all, He owns everything. He does not need us. He is not a human on a power trip. He is not insecure. He does not have the Napolean complex. If we are to grasp that God is totally unique and understand His heart towards us, we must grasp His perspective.

Read 1 Peter 1:10, 13-16 below.

[10] Concerning this salvation, the prophets who prophesied about the grace that was to be yours searched and inquired carefully.... [13] Therefore, preparing your minds for action, and being sober-minded, set your hope fully on the grace that will be brought to you at the revelation of Jesus Christ. [14] As obedient children, do not be conformed to the passions of your former ignorance, [15] but as he who called you is holy, you also be holy in all your conduct, [16] since it is written, "You shall be holy, for I am holy."

God's bottom line is found in verse 16, "You shall be holy, for I am holy." Peter is actually quoting what God told the Israelites in Leviticus. On the other side of the resurrection, God now uses Peter to bring greater revelation to His urging. Peter shows these believers the heartbeat of God.

Left unchallenged, most of us probably bring an inaccurate view of God or of holiness to this passage. First, we might mistakenly imagine God's perspective as punitive or strict when He says "be holy," but if we look closely that can't be. Peter is telling believers that they can have hope because they have the salvation that was spoken of by the prophets (v10). Our second danger is to have a negative view of holiness.

If we have a negative view of holiness, we have an inaccurate view of holiness.

Holiness is an invitation to be like Him. When God says, "Be holy," He is saying be "set apart" like Me, be "unique" like Me, and be "radically different" like Me.

Have you ever viewed holiness as an invitation?

We are already positionally viewed as holy through salvation, but now God is calling us to be holy in our daily behavior. He isn't telling us to become something that we can't become; He is simply telling us to become who we are as His children, "be holy for I am holy." He saw the effects of sin on His first two precious children. He knows that pursuing holiness is the only pursuit that helps us.

Holiness protects us from unholiness. In this respect, holiness is an appeal to love. He wants us to be holy because there is nothing greater than being like Him. Everything else is a substitute and is ultimately less than His best.

How could looking at sin from God's perspective help us run towards His holiness rather than away from it?

In Exodus 20, after God gives the Ten Commandments to Moses, He sends a powerful storm, one with loud thunder and bright lightning. In Scripture, a storm is often a representation of the awesome presence and power of God.[6] In the midst of the darkness and the clouds, the thunder and lightning, the earthquake or the fire, the storm declared to all those watching the greatness of the One true God. This storm produced in the Israelites a holy fear. He overwhelmed them with His magnificent display of power in order to reveal how GREAT He is.

Why do you think God reminded them of His power at this time?

Have you ever been overwhelmed by the greatness of God's power? If so, describe why you think God allowed you to have this experience.

These mighty demonstrations of God's power were designed to prepare His children's hearts for obedience. The Israelites were called to be a holy people, set apart from the nations around them. God was going to deliver them to a land all their own, overflowing with His goodness, but only through obedience to Him could they truly enjoy the blessings He had waiting.

After the people saw the storm, they "trembled with fear." But in Exodus 20:20, Moses said to the people, "Do not fear, for God has come to test you, that the fear of him may be before you, that you may not sin."

Underline that phrase, "that you may not sin."

The test for the Israelites was whether they would choose to fear God and refuse to sin. This was the beginning of a nation set apart to God, a nation that had been living in Egypt for so long they looked like Egypt, talked like Egypt, and thought like Egypt! God had to do a work mighty enough that it would scare the Egypt out of them!

When the storm came, the Israelites were in awe of God, but it was not long before they started second guessing what God was doing. When we are tempted to question God's actions, we must be careful how we respond. God is big enough to handle our questions. Unfortunately, many times instead of trusting God with our question, we allow the lies of the enemy to creep in our minds and cause us to doubt WHO God is.

A few months ago, Tim and I found out that a house we have always daydreamed about was in foreclosure, so we quickly decided to put our house on the market. This new house would give us more room, but wouldn't cost us any more financially. I began to give God all the reasons why this new house would work out so well for us, and I tried my best to persuade Him into working out all the details to our benefit. *Of course* I would use it for ministry, and it would allow us to do so much more for Him! Well, to our disappointment, our house didn't sell. I went through a process of questioning God about His actions. It just didn't make sense (at the time). I could have allowed it to make me doubt His best for me, because I certainly knew that this house was best for me! Ha! But no matter what I did, I could not get away from my concrete belief that He always knows best. I knew that His ways are so far above my thinking, reasoning, and planning. It didn't take long for me to get my head back on straight, because I know WHO He is. And I am resting and rejoicing in that! So I had to make a decision in that moment of disappointment. Who was I going to trust? Did I know best, or did He?

Each time a situation arises in my life where I have the opportunity to let go of the control and give to Him what I want to hang on to so badly, I lose a little bit more of the fear that entangles me. I am reminded over and over that He designs circumstances in my life to teach me to TRUST Him.

> **In some situations, it's pretty easy to trust that "God knows best." Then there are situations where it is much harder to trust Him. When was the last time you wanted something so badly but God acted differently than you planned and you were left questioning the outcome? Describe how it felt and what you chose to do.**

There are so many situations that appear dreadfully wrong from our perspective. We can be left choosing to doubt God or we can remember His character and trust that even though we want an explanation that His heart is for us. I love the way the American Standard Version translates Deuteronomy 5:29. Allow yourself to feel the emotion that is embedded in these words, spoken from the very mouth of our loving God.

> Oh that there were such a heart in them, that they would fear me, and keep all my commandments always, that it might go well with them, and with their children forever.

God desires for it to go well for us! His heart is completely for us! I want to put 100 exclamation points on the end of that verse because it stirs up such emotion in me! Do you hear God's heart in the words He chose for that verse? Can you feel how much He cares for you?

The language of the original Hebrew is emphatic: "Who will give that there may be such a heart in them?" Ok- I can hardly keep my seat here! My eyes well up when I see God revealed in such a personal way. We know the answer to such a profound question. God would give His greatest and most precious gift to us, His Son, in order that, as Jeremiah 32:40 (NIV) says, "I will make an everlasting covenant with them: I will never stop doing good to them, and I will inspire them to fear me, so that they will never turn away from me."

What does God say He will never stop doing?

Why does He want us to stand in awe of Him?

The sense of fear and awe of the Lord is placed in our hearts only by the grace of God. With that grace we see our sin, which brings us to a place of humility and dependence on Him alone. When we combine reverent fear and dependence, a deep love will result. There is security knowing that He keeps us and will not ever leave us. Listen to how Jonathan Edwards puts it in his book, *Lover of God*.

[She] does not merely rationally believe that God is glorious, but [she] has a sense of the gloriousness in [her] heart. There is not only a rational belief that God is holy, and that holiness is a good thing, but there is a sense of the loveliness of God's holiness. There is not only a speculatively judging that God is gracious, but a sense of how amiable God is upon that account, or a sense of the beauty of this divine attribute.[7]

> God is holy. His holiness should make Him unapproachable,
> and yet He actually longs for us to come to Him.

He wants a loving, thriving, growing relationship with you. Throughout the Bible we see His desire for that relationship, and how He went to great lengths to make a way for us to have that relationship! The God of the universe, full of glory, came to us, and lived among us. He stayed with the children of Israel, close by. And He stays with us. He is in us. Let's be purposeful and prayerful to give God the glory for WHO He is!

What was the most meaningful statement or Scripture you read today?

What does God want you to do in response to today's study?

TAKING THE PLUNGE

CHRIS KUHLMAN

Are you getting a more accurate picture of God and His heart toward you? We started the week from the premise that we needed to have an accurate view of God's identity. His holiness is what sets Him apart from all others. Are you seeing that God uses His strength and power to protect us and love us? Everything God does is designed to draw us into a deeper love relationship with Him. I am so emotionally stirred when I think about His everlasting love for me. For many years in my Christian life, I held His love at arms length. Not on purpose--I just didn't fully understand what it meant to be loved wholly and eternally by God. And I think I'll always be somewhere in the process of learning why God would love me and how it is that He chooses to show me.

For so much of my life, I stood at the shoreline of the ocean of His love and stuck my foot in, just to let the foamy water roll over my ankles. But it wasn't until I decided to jump in and let the waves crash over my whole body that my relationship with God changed. I began getting up in the morning and reading His Word. I was eager to just spend time in His presence, and I want the same for you. Spending time with the Lord in His Word and prayer is so personal.

Each one of us has to take the plunge for ourselves.

Take my advice—it's worth it! Come to the water and dive in!

I realize as some of you read this, you might be perplexed or even frustrated. Maybe your relationship with God does not drum up such strong positive emotions. Each of us are on a journey. If we are ever going to make progress, we must be honest with where we are on the journey.

So, how would you describe where you are on your journey of truly being in awe of God and His heart for you?

If you don't sense the intimacy with God that you desire, you are not alone. In Genesis 32, Jacob wrestled with the angel of God. It says that he wouldn't let go of the angel until he received a blessing. He was at a place in his life where He wanted God's blessing more than anything else. He wanted to know that the Lord knew him, was with him, and would take care of his family. Nothing else would satisfy.

Can you identify with Jacob? If so, how?

Are you satisfied to stay where you are, or are you at a place where you truly want more from your relationship with God?

Our desire is that through this study, you will truly discover the fullness of the life God created for you. That discovery is possible if you are truly hungry for more than just life as usual.

Wherever you are, let Jacob's journey challenge and encourage you. Genesis 32:24 begins, "So Jacob was left alone..." All of his family went on ahead of him. He had no one. God orchestrated some alone-time for Jacob so that He could get his full attention. Now in our culture, especially as women, alone time is a rare commodity! Sometimes we lack alone time because we have too many responsibilities. Other times, we avoid solitude because we don't want to be alone with our thoughts.

How about you? When was the last time you had some time alone to ask God to show you more of Himself?

We have to get to a place where it is okay to be alone with God, because when we're alone we cannot be distracted by others, and we can do the hard work of facing ourselves. If this intimidates you or feels awkward, start with a journal and begin writing a letter to God sharing what holds you back. Perhaps, you begin writing out prayers of what you desire from your relationship with Him. Remember, our God desires a meaningful relationship with us. In that place of solitude, we are able to recognize that God shows us great love by coming to us despite our sinfulness, and we bow in reverence before Him. Our hearts become pliable, and God shows up ready to work.

Twenty years earlier, Jacob met the Lord. He was alone at Bethel, and in his dream he saw a stairway reaching to heaven. There above it stood the Lord, and He said, "I am the Lord"(Genesis 28:12-13). Here is Jacob, 20 years later, having exhausted all of his own efforts, and once again, praying for deliverance. Does this sound familiar? Do you tend to do the same thing? I know I do. I'll go and go until I can't figure out what to do next, then I finally go to God.

Read Genesis 32:24-32.

Genesis 32:24 says, "...and a man wrestled with him till daybreak." The word wrestled means to strive, to agonize, to be diligent in the use of means. This same word is used in Luke 13:24.

> Make every effort to enter through the narrow door, because many, I tell you, will try to enter and will not be able to. (NIV)

Underline the words "make every effort." Do you make every effort to look to God, to pray for spiritual light, knowledge, and grace to press through difficulties in your life? Just as it was for Jacob, it is for us: the only way to victory is through active surrender.

What do you need to surrender in your life?

Before we can be intimate in our relationship with the Lord, we must confess to Him on what we are depending. Did you notice that the Lord asked Jacob his name in verse 27? He knew that Jacob was depending on himself. In asking Jacob this question, God's meaning was clear. "Are you going to continue living up to your name?" Jacob's name meant deceiver, and he indeed had a reputation for being a schemer and a deceiver. Deception is what got him into this predicament in the first place. He was afraid of his brother Esau, whom he had deceived and fled from 20 years earlier. Jacob feared that Esau would attack him and his family, so he was pleading with God to protect him from the unknowns of this whole situation he had caused. *He was at the end of himself.* His schemes would no longer work, and his only option was to meet with God face-to-face. But this was right where God wanted Him.

It's right where God wants us - at the end of ourselves.

After three years of studying music in college, I made the difficult decision to transfer to a new school. My brother was going to be a college freshman at John Brown University, so I decided to join him. I was burned out in my major, and I wanted to make a complete change and start over. John Brown didn't have a bunch of rules like my previous college did, so I got lax in my church attendance, which led to me to get lazy about my time with the Lord. I slowly became complacent in life. I was restless, and my appetite for God's Word was waning. I had let the life drain out of me. But God never left me. He kept pursuing me. One night He spoke clearly to me, asking if this was the way I wanted to continue to live my life. And so the wrestling match began. I was at the end of myself. My flesh was weak, but my spirit was willing. I had to let go of my agenda to make way for what I really wanted. I wanted Jesus living in and through me. I wanted abundance. I wanted to grab on to Jesus and say, "Whatever it looks like, I want the life You have purposed for me, because walking side by side with You is better than me trying to do it my way." This defining moment in my life has led me to the place I am today, in a growing, thriving relationship with Jesus Christ.

Genesis 32:25 says, "When the man (Angel of God) saw that he did not prevail against Jacob..." This does not mean he could not, but that he would not–He is encouraging Jacob's faith. This divine person knew the promises made to Jacob, and Jacob's faith was so strong at this time that he was clinging to the angel with everything he had in him. It was not in his own strength he wrestled, nor by his own strength he prevailed. It was a strength that came from God alone.

What does it reveal about the heart of God that He will even give us the strength to wrestle so we can draw closer to Him?

God changed Jacob's name. His name changed from "deceiver" to a name meaning "God's fighter" or "he struggles with God." "Your name will be Israel- a prince of God." The new name, Israel, is indicative of a new nature which had come to Jacob as he clung to his oppressor. When depending on his own strength, Jacob was no match for God, but by depending on God, he could prevail. After this encounter, Jacob could no longer doubt who he was. He had the blessing of a new name. When we struggle, but then get to a place where we realize we can do nothing without Him, we will begin to desire Him with a love that yearns for intimacy.

Genesis 32:31 says, "The sun rose above him as he passed Peniel." If you've ever met with God face-to-face, determined to wrestle your way through, but then finding sweet surrender and a renewed claim on His promises, you have felt that sun rise. Jacob limped away with a permanent reminder of his need for dependency on God. As he leaned on his staff, he was reminded to lean heavily on Him who is able–Our eternal, sovereign, holy God.

Jacob was far from perfect, but God loved him anyway. Because of the promises He made to Jacob, He never left him. He knew how to lovingly bring Jacob to the place of surrender. Does Jacob remind you a little bit of yourself? He does for me. I try so hard to make everything turn out well. But eventually I'm always reminded that only through dependence on God will things turn out for the best. Thank goodness God has that same fervent love for us that He did for Jacob.

God is holy. Whether you believe it or not...

> He alone knows what is best for you. He alone wants what is best for you.
> He alone can give you what is best for you.

If there is any part of you that is not completely convinced of this, I beg you to care enough to ask the Lord to show you His holiness in such a way that you too will feel the sun rise on your relationship with the Lord as Jacob did. Take some time now and specifically tell the Lord where you have struggled in your own strength. Then ask Him to give you the strength to cling to Him until you can see His holiness in such a way that you are never the same again.

What was the most meaningful statement or Scripture you read today?

What does God want you to do in response to today's study?

NOTES FOR THE WEEK

ATTITUDE WITHOUT ATTITUDE

A woman develops her attitude by choosing to see relationships and circumstances from Christ's perspective.

Day One
ATTITUDE OF LOVE

Day Two
ATTITUDE OF MERCY

Day Three
ATTITUDE WITHOUT JUDGMENT

Day Four
A POST-PLANK ATTITUDE

Day Five
ATTITUDE OF ANTICIPATION

Day One

ATTITUDE OF LOVE

KARIN CONLEE

Today we begin a week-long journey on the topic of attitude. Now I must say, men can certainly have their own issues with attitude, but from the youngest of ages females get the reputation for having the bad 'TUDE. We can get so busy trying to become Miss Perfect that we get a pretty sour disposition while attempting to appear to have it all together.

I have a miserable memory, but my earliest recollection of girl attitude is crystal clear. It happened at Montclair Elementary School. I moved to Florida in the first grade and became best buddies with a girl named Lisa. We did everything together until the beginning of the third grade when a new girl, Cherelle, showed up.

After a few weeks, I could see the writing on the wall. Cherelle wanted to take our original two-some and make it a three-some. I labored over a note to Cherelle. I told her that I realized "she was DETERMINED to ruin my friendship with Lisa." With my stomach in knots, I gave her the note after school. The next morning, I found the reply on my desk. Cherelle wrote, "How dare you call me DETER MINDED!"

While I laughed then at her misunderstanding and I laugh now at our immaturity; grown women can be almost as quick to jump to conclusions and cop an attitude. Even as women, at one time or another, have we not all had the thought that women can be so hard to deal with?

At some point, all of us have been the victim of some person's bad attitude, but if we are going to spend an entire week examining our own attitude, we should define it. In a secular context attitude is defined as follows:

> manner, disposition, feeling, position, etc., with regard to a person or thing; tendency or orientation, especially of the mind[1]

Circle the last four words of the definition. I will spare you the lineage of the word attitude, but suffice it to say that the overlap between the secular definition and the biblical definition is found in the four words you just circled. The Greek word for attitude frequently translates as mind. We are told in Philippians 2:5 to "have this mind among yourselves, which is yours in Christ Jesus." We are called to have Christ's mind or attitude.

Before we dive headlong into our discussion on our attitude, I want to make an observation now that we will revisit later this week: there is a huge distinction between perspective and attitude. Our attitude is how we feel about something. Our perspective is how we look at something.

Let me illustrate the difference. A few weeks ago, I was really frustrated with my son. He perpetually stalls when it gets close to bed time. Finally, it got quiet in the house, so I assumed he had gone to bed. About an hour later, as I walked to my bedroom, I noticed his light was still on. I was furious. My mind was rattling off all the things I was planning on saying about his direct defiance when I got to his door. Just as I climbed the last stair and arrived at his room, I decided to look through the crack in the door first. Mark was lying on his bed reading his Bible. The perspective through the sliver of open space between the door and the wall radically changed my attitude! Instead of being furious, I became grateful. What more could a mother of a 13-year-old hope for? He knew he needed the Lord to keep from repeating a tough day. One enormous key to both discovering God's purpose for our lives AND having a good attitude is to gain God's perspective.

> **A woman develops her attitude by choosing to see relationships and circumstances from Christ's perspective.**

One of the reasons we linger and are not truly motivated to change our attitude is because we allow other people to be our standard instead of the Lord. We can all point to several people we know that have worse attitudes than ours, right? Typically, we are content as long as we can justify that it is not our attitude causing our problems. At the same time, in our honest moments, we know that we struggle to have victory in this area. Rarely is our goal to have an attitude that is good enough to bless others. We should not take this struggle lightly. Do not believe the subtle lie that "this is just the way I am" or "no one really has a good attitude." If we are going to live as God intended, we need to begin to raise the bar and acknowledge that our attitude really does impact our lives and everyone around us.

What is one example of where your attitude made a problem worse?

What is one example of where your attitude made a problem better?

What would be different in your life if you conquered your battle with your poor attitude?

Let's tackle the Scripture with an open heart this week and ask God to give us the grace to have sustained victory in this area!

We will pick up in Luke's retelling of Jesus' sermon on the Mount. In the preceding verses, Jesus has addressed those in the audience who would be blessed and those who should be fearful. Now He addresses everyone. Put on your seat belt and read Luke 6:27-31.

List the four instructions that Jesus gives us in verses 27 and 28.

I hope you were adequately prepared to jump in with both feet. If you are like me, you may have days where it is hard to love, do good, bless, and pray for those whom you love, let alone your enemies. Typically, we want to be the receiver of these actions more than the giver. Here is the deal…if we can learn how to change our attitudes and how to conduct ourselves when we are dealing with our enemies, I am confident we can have victory in more pleasant situations.

If you wrote your answer to the last question in the order they are presented in the text, then the first thing you listed is "love your enemies." So often we are told WHAT to do, but we are not provided with the next step that explains HOW. We cannot use that excuse this time! How we love our enemies are the other 3 items you wrote down. In your answer above, go back and circle the three practical ways you can love your enemies.

Thinking of a particular person that you are currently struggling with or have previously, did you find yourself doing good to them, blessing them, and praying for them?

What do you think would be different about YOU, if you applied Jesus' instructions to your situation?

Let's get really specific. These situations can be intensely personal. If you are like me, I need something tangible to do or some step-by-step instructions when my buttons are being pushed. What does it look like to "do good" to an enemy? It means that you do something nice for them even when your feelings are not leading the way.

You need to act first and trust your feelings to catch up.

Many times in life, we have to obey our way into our feelings instead of allowing our feelings to lead us into disobedience. If we wait on our feelings, we will never "do good" to our enemies.

I am trusting we all have one person who at least gets on our nerves, even if we are too sophisticated to call them an enemy. (I don't care how spiritual you are; some people are difficult to love.) What is one nice thing you could do for your "enemy"?

The other two action points of blessing and praying are connected to our tongue. James 3:9-10 reminds us of the power of the tongue.

> [9] With it we bless our Lord and Father, and with it we curse people who are made in the likeness of God. [10] From the same mouth come blessing and cursing. My brothers, these things ought not to be so.

When we have a bad attitude, we need to be on guard. If we don't plan to use our tongue for good, we will usually allow it to cause harm. When Luke tells us to bless those who curse us, one major way that occurs is in how we speak about our enemy. Truth be told, this is where we can get in serious trouble. We often can be so swept away by our desire to defend ourselves that we rush to speak as negatively as possible about the one who has offended us.

With discretion, describe a time when you spoke negatively about someone else instead of obeying this passage.

If you had trouble remembering a time you spoke negatively about someone, I am sure you can more easily remember when someone said something hurtful to you or about you. The tongue is a powerful tool. It can inflict incredible pain and leave enormous scars. As women seeking to learn to live as God purposed, we must speak differently about our enemies than the rest of the world does. When you are speaking with your enemy, you can bless them by sticking to the problem at hand and not making the conflict about the person. You can bless your enemy when you are outside of their presence by doing what you may have been taught as a child: If you can't think of anything nice to say, don't say anything at all!

The last way that we can love our enemy is to pray for them. While this may feel forced at first, God will begin to soften our heart towards them. If we want to discover God's purpose for our lives, we will take a giant step forward when we treat difficult people with the same compassion He did.

At one point, someone I knew accidentally sent an email to my husband and I that was about us. It was not intended for us to read. It had some false information in it and revealed that several other people we knew had been circulating these emails. It would have been so easy to point out all of their flaws and the lies that they were contributing to, but that would have been just what the enemy wanted. We cannot be pawns in his game to keep Christians at odds with one another. We must trust that God knows what is best. To keep myself from becoming bitter or jaded, I began praying for the person who sent the email. It took some time, but eventually I could see the hurt fade and my heart begin to see beyond the one email to the bigger picture.

> Even if you cannot fix every situation, you can be at peace that
> you have handled adversity with character.

Who do you need to start praying for?

Before we wrap up for today, let's try to put our new attitudes into practice. Imagine with me that you have just learned that an acquaintance of yours said some critical things about you to someone you really respect and admire. You are embarrassed and stunned that this person would be so cruel. You feel betrayed.

Having studied Luke 6:27-28, how should you put these verses into practice? Be specific and ready to discuss this in your small group.

We have just touched the tip of the iceberg today. We will pick up in this passage tomorrow and continue allowing God's truth to impact our lives. As we conclude, I challenge you to go ahead and begin applying what you are learning. Delayed obedience is disobedience. I challenge you to do good to an enemy before tomorrow, begin praying for them today. You'll never regret knowing that you have pleased your Heavenly Father and taken a step in improving your attitude.

What was the most meaningful statement or Scripture you read today?

What does God want you to do in response to today's study?

ATTITUDE OF MERCY
KARIN CONLEE

Yesterday we kicked off our week on attitude with a kick in the gut... or maybe since we are all girls.... a bad day of cramps! I admit that there is probably a softer entry into attitude. As we discussed loving our enemies, I imagine it stirred up emotions. Just thinking about keeping a good attitude in the midst of conflict can be exhausting. My prayer is that if we address attitude in the context of the hard "stuff," then the truths we are learning will truly stick.

Do you remember from yesterday how practically can we show our enemies love? List them below. Peek if you are drawing a blank! (Luke 6:27-28)

1.

2.

3.

Today we will pick up right where we left off. Just when we thought we had considered all the dynamics of dealing with difficult situations, we see that God has more to show us. He gives us clear directions on how we can handle adversity with a God honoring attitude. Read Luke 6:29-31 below.

[29] To one who strikes you on the cheek, offer the other also, and from one who takes away your cloak do not withhold your tunic either. [30] Give to everyone who begs from you, and from one who takes away your goods do not demand them back. [31] And as you wish that others would do to you, do so to them.

Now for clarity in verse 29, Jesus is not talking about being passive in the face of a physical assault. He means we should not defend ourselves when we are insulted. Culturally, the slap on the cheek was more an attack on honor than a physical assault. Jesus isn't prohibiting *defense*, but *retaliation*.[2] The thought of not retaliating is so foreign to us. Usually, we see this as a sign of weakness. In reality, it takes much more strength to hold our tongue than to get down in the mud and start returning insults with insults. As Ravi Zacharias says, "Only two things happen when we throw mud: You get dirty and you lose a lot of ground."[3]

Can you think of a time when your honor or character was attacked? If so, describe in a few words.

How would God have coached you to respond in that circumstance?

Early in our marriage, my husband and I were put in a challenging place. We developed concerns over some ministry dynamics and, yet, were not in a position to be able to cause change. We decided to remove ourselves from the situation, but did not have the freedom to explain ourselves. Several friends began to distance themselves from us as if we were enemies.

During that challenging season, a woman by the name of Lillian Lubbert told me, "You must lay your reputation at the foot of the cross." I have lived by this truth from that day forward. Instead of allowing myself to get tied in knots and overflow with frustration,

I can focus on the fact that God is in charge of protecting my reputation.

Taking that perspective frees me and keeps me out of so much trouble. When I feel like I am in a no-win situation, I have a choice to develop a bad attitude (and sin) or I can rest in God's ultimate protection. It took five years, but one day out of the blue we received a call asking for forgiveness as God brought truth to light. I am certain that if I had chosen to cop an attitude that I would have spent those five years conflicted and not in peace.

Where do you currently need to lay your reputation at the foot of the cross?

Looking back again at the passage from Luke 6:29-30, you can see that in just the last two verses we have some pretty difficult circumstances. Think about your normal response when you are insulted or when someone takes something that belongs to you. Jesus is instructing us to completely baffle those that may be trying to cause us pain. When we truly love our enemies, they will not even know how to respond. Isn't it interesting that the famous Golden Rule in verse 31 is in the context of loving our enemies? We are called to treat everyone the way we want to be treated...even our enemies.

Before we continue our study by looking at the next few verses in Luke 6, we must come to grips with one fact: human beings are terrible self-evaluators. Last night, my daughter announced that she was cutting back on desserts. She has an incredible sweet tooth, so we all chuckled at her declaration (I have repeatedly given her the diabetes speech til I am blue in the face!). Then we started talking about what she had already consumed that day. The girl had just opted not to finish the last cookie, but she had already consumed six since lunch! She may have had good intentions, but she was deceiving herself if she thought that saying no to a seventh cookie was showing restraint! As we continue in Luke, God calls us out to make sure we are not deceiving ourselves.

Notice what verses follow up God's instructions on loving our enemies.

Read Luke 6:32-34 below.

> [32] If you love those who love you, what benefit is that to you? For even sinners love those who love them. [33] And if you do good to those who do good to you, what benefit is that to you? For even sinners do the same. [34] And if you lend to those from whom you expect to receive, what credit is that to you? Even sinners lend to sinners, to get back the same amount.

It is as if God was reading our mail. Can't you just see it! God used Luke to call our bluff. We called ourselves obeying. We thought we were obeying because we were being "nice" or because we were comparing ourselves to others. We were acting all sweet, doing good, loving, and lending to people... just not the ones that we dislike.

Did God bring specific conviction to mind? If so, write it below. No one is looking!

Who does God compare the reader to in these verses?

Currently, do you treat your enemies differently than those who don't proclaim to follow Christ treat their enemies? If so, how?

Continue reading Luke 6:35-36 (below).

> [35] But love your enemies, and do good, and lend, expecting nothing in return, and your reward will be great, and you will be sons of the Most High, for he is kind to the ungrateful and the evil. [36] Be merciful, even as your Father is merciful.

If the verses did not blow you away, go back and read them again. Maybe you were multi-tasking? Focus first on verse 35 (I will wait for you, I promise). These instructions are mostly a reiteration of what Jesus told the disciples a few verses earlier, but then Luke answers the question WHY.

Why should you "love your enemies, and do good, and lend, expecting nothing in return"?

We all relate to the concept of trying to be Miss Perfect, yet we all know it is impossible. We will never get it all right. But if there was ever a passage where we could follow the One who is Perfect, this is it! When we truly embrace God's way, our reward is great. When we embrace His way, we are no longer among the sinners and tax collectors, we are now His child. We no longer act like sinners, we act like Christ. Not only is our reward great, but when we live this out we are under the protection of the Most High. We certainly can't muster up enough goodness in us to carry this out alone, but through His strength we will love our enemies and by our actions declare to the whole world that we are His.

Now go back to Luke 6:35-36 and circle who Jesus is kind to.

What thoughts come to your mind when you see who Jesus is kind to?

The passage does not say that the Lord is tolerant of the evil and ungrateful. It does not even say that He is restraining Himself from the evil and ungrateful. It is not the picture of avoidance or stiff-arming. The Lord is kind to them. The Lord moves towards the evil and ungrateful. Most of us have people in our lives that we could categorize as takers. They are the "joysuckers" of life. You know, the person that you decline when their number pops up on your phone. The person you avoid. What would it look like if you actually moved toward them? We also can think of someone we have deemed evil. As long is there is no emotional or physical danger, we should extend kindness through the grace our King supplies to us.

Who is one person you need to move towards?

For some of you, this may be the same person you listed yesterday. For others, you have multiple people the Lord is bringing to your mind. Either way, take the first step towards them. Think how different our approach would be on a daily basis if we lived out these instructions. Our very own Savior was kind to the ungrateful and evil. As a matter of fact, He did not only show mercy to "those kind of people," He showed that mercy to us. We were among the ungrateful and evil that Christ went to the cross to spare.

Mercy is when God withholds punishment that you deserve. Describe how God has shown you mercy.

I hate to beat a dead horse, but for our attitude to honor the Lord, we must embrace two core truths. We must embrace God's holiness and our identity in Him. Sound familiar? Why would you want to live as the rest of the world when He offers us a greater reward? God does not just promise us a life in heaven if we follow Him, He offers us a life of abundance now. We can have freedom here on earth and lead others to a life of freedom and peace.

Why continue in the pressure cooker of life chasing unattainable perfection when you can have a life full of loving well? You know in your soul that God has called you to something so much greater. I challenge you to never get over the mercy that God extended to you so that you can have the perspective of Christ and demonstrate mercy to others.

What was the most meaningful statement or Scripture you read today?

What does God want you to do in response to today's study?

Day Three

ATTITUDE WITHOUT JUDGMENT

KARIN CONLEE

We have reached hump day in our week on attitude. I am hoping you are truly taking steps each day to obey God's word. No one else can do it for you and no else will reap the blessings more than you, if you bring yourself into alignment with God's word.

Yesterday, we saw two types of people that Jesus was kind to. Who were they? (See Luke 6:35)

1.

2.

Today, we will continue on in our study of Luke 6 as we see how God desires us to look at the world. When we can see the world through His eyes, we will have an attitude that is pleasing to Him. I am sure you have heard the expression, "Perspective is everything." It is so true.

In 2011, our family had the opportunity to travel to Arizona for a family reunion. Since my children had never been out west, we wanted to make sure that they got to see the Grand Canyon. After the family reunion, we drove about two hours out of our way to make the trek. It was the worst two hours of the entire week. We were all exhausted and barely had any breakfast in our hurry to get on the road. We thought we could save a little money and just combine breakfast and lunch into one meal. As lunch time approached, we couldn't decide on a place to eat and before we knew it we'd missed all our options. Suddenly, we had two hungry children, no food, and four bad attitudes.

As we continued the miserable drive, we saw a few mountains and hills. Mark kept insisting he had seen enough and suggested we shorten our detour and instead head directly to our final destination for the night. Compared to Memphis and other places we had traveled, the view along the way was impressive enough to him. Having seen the Grand Canyon before, my husband and I knew what was ahead. When we finally arrived at the canyon's edge and were able to look out at the incredible living mural of God's creation, Mark realized the drive was worth it. He was blown away! The "impressive enough" mountains and hills paled in comparison to the sight of the Grand Canyon. Moments later, Annika said, "I would hate to be the second grandest canyon." It is all in your perspective!

Read Luke 6:37-42.

Did you notice how Jesus gives instructions first and then paints an almost comical picture to show us His perspective on our attitude? We'll address the instructions today and Jesus' parable tomorrow.

Following my example, write down the contrasting pairs of actions from Luke 6:37-38a.

[37] Judge not, and you will not be judged; condemn not, and you will not be condemned; forgive, and you will be forgiven; [38] give, and it will be given to you. Good measure, pressed down, shaken together, running over, will be put into your lap. For with the measure you use it will be measured back to you.

DO NOT..**SO YOU**

1. Judge.. won't be judged

2.

DO...**SO YOU**

3.

4.

There is a spiritual economy. We cannot expect to have a bad attitude, treat people poorly, and never be negatively impacted by our actions. Cause and effect does occur. The Bible calls it reaping and sowing. If we can choose to have an attitude of mercy as Christ called us to in the earlier verses, we will be protecting ourselves from much anguish.

After all, if you could do something to prevent yourself from being judged and condemned, wouldn't you? If you knew there was a way to cause people to be forgiving and giving to you, does that not sound like something you would prefer to act upon? We do have some say in the matter! Sometimes we forget that the Bible is not just a good idea or a bunch of suggestions, but His directions for living your life.

> Deciding to obey God's direction brings blessings, whereas deciding to ignore God's direction brings consequences.

Most of us understand what it means to be forgiving and giving, but there tends to be a lack of clarity when it comes to being judgmental and condemning. Those who choose not to follow Christ frequently throw this idea of "judge not" back at Christians to justify that any way of thinking is acceptable and believers are wrong to judge. Perhaps you can even think of a time when you were conflicted about whether you should or should not judge in a particular situation. I see this issue arising as my children are now old enough to have their own social lives. Is it "judging" to make an assessment of my child's friend or their parents and prevent my child from participating in an activity? If you are new on a college campus, is it being judgmental to decide not to hang out with a particular person or group because you observe behavior that concerns you?

If you can think of a time where you questioned whether you were right or wrong to judge someone, describe it below.

We only need to look a few verses further in Luke 6:43-45 to realize that we ARE called to make assessments. Jesus is not calling us to universal acceptance of all behavior or teachings. So what is the difference between Jesus' reference to examining fruit and the sin of judging? To put it succinctly: "The Christian is not called to unconditional approval but he is called to unconditional *love*."[4] Assessing or evaluating is for the purpose of making a wise choice about our own course of action or providing developmental feedback, not critical feedback. Assessing is for the purpose of praying and loving. If our assessment of a situation goes past the details and causes us to be less than loving, merciful, and compassionate to the person, then we are judging. If we are using the opinion or information to make ourselves look better, then we are judging.

> We really can love people who do things we do not approve of.
> The Lord does it with us everyday.

Where have you crossed the line and started judging someone?

Again, we must examine fruit. Matthew 10:16 says,

> Behold, I am sending you out as sheep in the midst of wolves, so be wise as serpents and innocent as doves.

Jesus actually gives this warning to the disciples as they go out into the world to proclaim the Good News. I think we can apply the warning to our lives, too. When you determine there is a situation that is unhealthy for you or your child, then make wise choices. Just be sure to make the assessment in a way that you are gentle like a dove to the people involved.

So what is condemning? *Strong's Concordance* defines it most clearly as "to pronounce guilty." This is a lighthearted example, but one day I was driving home with a beautiful fresh flower arrangement in my car. I kept thinking that the drivers around me must be livid, but if I went any faster or took turns any sharper, I was going to have water all over my car and my once-a-decade bouquet would be toast! I thought, how often do I get behind someone who is seemingly trying to make me late or annoy me when I truly have no idea what is going on in that car?

On a more serious note, we must realize that "we can judge the *fruit* of others, but we can rarely judge their motives with accuracy."[5] How many times have we jumped ahead of ourselves when we met someone? Within a few moments, we put someone in a category and determine by their look or profession how we will view them. One beautiful aspect of ministry is that my husband and I have the privilege of hearing the life stories of many people. Behind every precious face, we each have scars from living in a fallen world. If not handled with tender care and provided time for healing, our scars cause most of us to put up unhealthy defense mechanisms to guard from pains we have already experienced and cannot bear to endure again. When we determine someone is guilty, we have stepped into God's place as judge and have condemned him or her.

Describe a time where you condemned someone only to learn later that you were wrong?

Of the four attitudes: judgmental, condemning, unforgiving, and stingy, which negative attitude do you struggle with the most?

Why do you think this is your most challenging of the four attitudes?

What consequence will you experience, if you continue to allow this pattern in your attitude?

What consequences will others you care about experience, if you do not change your attitude?

As the mother of a 13 and 12-year-old, I can already see how my struggles have not only caused my children to repeat some of my negative attitudes, but my negative attitude has also wounded them at times. We need to get this attitude thing right! This is far more important than any of us realize.

There is also one other math principle introduced here in the last sentence of verse 38. Jesus says that the measure we use is how it will be measured to us. This makes me both smile and cringe. I have one generous child and, let's say, one working on his or her generosity. As any good mom on a budget or a diet, there will be times that I will get them a treat and I won't get one for myself. Yolo's and Yogurt Mountain are frequently requested stops. My desire is that they will share with me. One child freely hands over the entire bowl of frozen yogurt and allows me the pleasure of partaking. You have to get a little yogurt, some toppings, and a touch of whip cream to make it an exceptional bite. My other child will measure out a small bite (of yogurt only!) on the end of the spoon, hold the spoon while I try to take a bite, and literally pull it out of my mouth before I can get the little dollop off the end of the utensil. I don't know about you, but I sure need big bites of forgiveness and generosity. Let's not be found guilty of withholding these "big bites" from others.

Which child would you be in the previous illustration?

Ladies, some of us have carried on generational sins of judgment, condemnation, and unforgiveness. Some of us have started new patterns of unhealthiness on our own. We must honestly assess how we view the world and our attitudes towards the people we encounter.

Do you generally believe the best about people? Or, do you find it easier to quickly judge and condemn?

Who would think that two little verses could stir up so much need for renovation in our own hearts? Our world models the philosophy that we can take the pressure off ourselves to achieve perfection by pointing out the faults of others. It takes a lot less work to show others their shortcomings than to address our own, but the victory of establishing healthy attitudes must push us beyond our current failed methods. God's way is the only path that can guarantee the joy we are seeking. The best opportunity we have to truly find fulfillment is to be one who wisely loves in such a way that it is returned to us. Will you take a step forward with me?

What was the most meaningful statement or Scripture you read today?

What does God want you to do in response to today's study?

A POST-PLANK ATTITUDE

KARIN CONLEE

Did all the talk of being judgmental and condemning get you discouraged yesterday? Sometimes it can be so hard to look in the mirror. Take comfort; I am right there with you. I find great peace knowing that I am not alone on this journey. I hope that encourages you, too. If you feel like you have so much attitude work to do, instead of being discouraged you must realize that the Lord cares enough about you to open your eyes to see there is a more fulfilling life available.

When my husband was being discipled by a gentleman named Clyde, I remember Clyde repeatedly telling us, "The closer you get to the Lord the more you see His holiness. The more you see His holiness, the more you are aware of your sin." Just as we have said all week, perspective is everything. Grasp the truth that conviction is actually a sign of spiritual health. He shows us our sin because He deeply desires for us to deal with it so we can live in victory and freedom. You should be more concerned if you don't sense you have any attitude problems, than if you do!

As we return to Luke 6, we see Jesus paint an absurd picture to illustrate the valuable truths we studied yesterday. Shortly after telling them not to judge and condemn, but rather to give and forgive, Jesus gives us a vivid image that helps visual learners out there like me.

Reread Luke 6:37-42 to make sure we get the context of this parable.

Draw a picture to represent the 2 people described in verses 41 and 42.

Among your stick figures or masterpieces, hopefully, what is noticeable is the big piece of wood in the eye of one and the barely visible speck in the second person.

What does Jesus call the first person in verse 42?

A hypocrite is an actor or a pretender. When we are so quick to point out someone else's flaws, we are pretending to be someone we are not. We are not the judges (remember yesterday, right?) and we do not have our act together, but we give the appearance we do when we point out the flaws of others.

What is significant about the difference between the log (or plank, depending upon your translation) and the speck?

I have read this passage many times. On the surface, I always walk away with the truth that I must deal with my own junk first. This is an appropriate application of this parable, but I want to point out two other aspects that are equally important to consider in the context of our attitude.

First, there is a problem that prevents the hypocrite from removing the log. The hypocrite does not even see the log that is in his own eye. On some levels, he is not even aware he is a hypocrite. So, what are we to do with that? How do you correct a problem that you do not even know you have? I can hear it now, "For crying out loud, Karin! I have enough problems I am aware of and now you are telling me I need to consider that there might be another area of my life that I need to address that I am currently oblivious to?" My response is (very gently...), "Yes."

Think of it this way. In our heart of hearts, we all desire to live a purposeful, God-glorifying life. We want our life to matter and yet we also are weary of trying to do it our way and failing. Our entire world and our flesh fight against us living a life of purpose. So, what if we trust our Heavenly Father, anchor our identity in Christ, give up the whole Miss Perfect mirage, and then ask God to gently reveal our log?

I love the image of the log, but we might also relate well to the more modern idea of blind spots. I remember my dad teaching me to drive. Whether it was changing lanes on the highway or just backing up in a parking lot, you had to turn your head to make sure you could see what was not obvious in a scan of the car mirrors. We call them blind spots because we can't see them even though we have three mirrors in their correct positions. It does not matter how expensive or cheap your car is; everyone has to deal with blind spots. The same is true in our walk with the Lord.

> No matter how long we have been a Christian, we all have blind spots that left unchecked can put us in danger.

What are some ways that God might choose to show you your log or blind spots?

Sometimes, He does it through your Priority Time. Other times, He may reveal it to you in circumstances or through other believers. We might receive the correction when God keeps it just between Him and us, but when He uses someone else, our pride can make it stickier. In our flesh, we might get defensive when another person points out our blind spot. We might even want to quickly show them their blind spots, too. It is ironic and sad how this cycle can go round and round, if we remain in our flesh. The Lord, however, did not design Christians to live in isolation. If we are living in community with other believers, we must make ourselves vulnerable to allow someone to speak truth into our lives.

> Refusing to listen is refusing to remove your blind spot.

How would God want you to view someone He is using to reveal an area in your life that needs to be addressed?

The second aspect that we cannot ignore is WHY we must deal with our issue FIRST. In the end of verse 42, what does Jesus say will happen to the hypocrite when he takes the log out of his own eye?

I would urge you to consider that it is not just the absence of the log that brings clarity. Clarity occurs through the process of the removal.

Let me illustrate this idea another way. Have you ever asked someone without children for advice on parenting? Not if you are smart! Usually, you ask someone for advice that already has a child of his or her own. The counsel a person without children offers may or may not be similar, but what usually is remarkably different is the approach. It is so easy to have all the answers if you have never been tested. If you are a parent, however, your approach SHOULD be one of empathy and compassion instead of one of authority and pride.

The example of parenting advice is not even "a log." Move the same concept to a situation where you are struggling with a particular sin. Do you want to ask someone who has never acknowledged his or her sin to hold you accountable, or would you rather ask that of someone who understands that they are completely dependent upon the Lord? If you have walked through having to confess a particular sin, you see the world differently. When we have accepted and addressed our own blind spots, we can offer compassion to others without compromising the truth.

I love how Matthew Henry puts it:

> To help to pull the (speck) out of our brother's eye is a good work, but then we must qualify ourselves for it by beginning with ourselves; and our reforming our own lives may, by the influence of example, contribute to others reforming theirs.[6]

Wow! In the pain of acknowledging and repenting of our own sin, God gives us the clarity and humility that qualifies us to help others deal with their own speck.

Did you catch the phrase "by the influence of example"? Have you ever been moved to confession or repentance after watching someone else respond to the Lord's conviction?

Almost every week at Highpoint Church, we have *Going Public* stories. These short video testimonies are played prior to each person's baptism (Check them out at highpointmemphis. com/goingpublic if you need a shot of encouragement!). In the video, the person shared how God showed the sin in her life and her need for a Savior. Each story is different. Each log is different, but we frequently see the honest confession of one new believer generate confession in another person in the service (and online!).

Who is one person in your circle of influence that might be moved by seeing your humility before the Lord?

As we prepare to conclude for today, let's role play for just a moment. If you had a blind spot that a friend became aware of, how would you want them to approach you? Be specific.

We are all on this journey called life. As you read your list above, keep it in mind the next time God wants you to be His gentle instrument in restoring a sister to Christ. We have not experienced our last log or our last speck. The more humbly we come before the Lord, the less we will have to endure the pain of log removal. None of us want to have surgery. None of us want to be in the position to assist the Master Surgeon, but how different our perspective is towards others who are struggling when we ourselves are sensitive and responsive to God's conviction! Isn't your attitude completely different when you acknowledge that you don't have your whole act together either? Jesus gives us the parable in the context of telling us not to judge and condemn. You can be a hypocrite, or you can be humble. You can act like Miss Perfect, or you can humble yourself and treasure the perfection of Christ washing away your sin. Let's follow God's plan and allow God to work on our log first!

What was the most meaningful statement or Scripture you read today?

What does God want you to do in response to today's study?

ATTITUDE OF ANTICIPATION
KARIN CONLEE

We have covered a lot of ground this week. For our good, I hope that the Lord has made each of us aware of any shortcomings in our attitude and is helping us take strides to improve it. Our attitude towards our enemies cannot remain unchanged, but there is one more piece to the attitude puzzle we must also address. Our attitude struggles revolve around more than just difficult people. The great news is that this ONE piece can actually help us take an enormous leap forward in having an attitude that honors the Lord.

In order for us to simplify this attitude journey and have sustained victory, I need you to reach back in your mind (or workbook) to some statements I introduced on Day 1. Do you remember when I told you about the time I rushed up the stairs mad only to find Mark reading his Bible? Fill in the blanks below to remind us the difference between attitude and perspective.

_____ - how we feel about something

_____ - how we look at something

Our perspective determines our attitude. Put another way: how we feel about something is determined by how we look at something.

As I approached this final day on attitude, I began to contemplate: Is having a good attitude supposed to be this difficult? Did God intend for us to spend so much energy keeping our feelings and emotions in check? Is a half-full view of life really available to everyone who walks around half empty? Then it occurred to me that having a good attitude as a believer is not the impossible task we make it out to be.

> **The vast majority of the time a good attitude actually boils down to just one thing: seeing life from God's perspective!**

We can all nod in agreement with my statement, but knowing we *should* have God's perspective in our everyday lives and knowing *how to* have His perspective are two very different things. In our culture, even those who love the Lord with great conviction can miss God's perspective. Read our passage for today and let me illustrate my point.

Read Luke 12:22-34.

If you have been in church much, you have likely heard a sermon on this passage before. It is one I frequent when I recognize that I am struggling with worry. I'm the type of person who can tough it out for a long time, but when I hit my breaking point, the dam breaks, and I start flooding. At least that's what my husband calls it. Once I start flooding, I see everything negatively and my perspective is completely distorted. Have you ever been there?

What would you say is your major takeaway from reading Luke 12:22-34?

Why do you think Jesus spoke these truths to the disciples?

For most of us, our first read of this passage brings relief. We think, "Oh, good. God cares about me and promises to take care of my needs." Or maybe your takeaway is, "I need to be less materialistic." The problem is that both of these views come from a man-centered approach. Without getting too churchy, being man-centered is another way of saying that we view life as if it revolves around us. We are man-centered when we think God is here to help us accomplish our goals. In reality, we were created to glorify Him and so we should have a God-centered perspective. Our attitudes stink much of the time because we have not exchanged our perspective for a God-centered perspective.

Does God promise to provide our basic needs in this passage? Yes! BUT, He is telling us this so we can take our mind off worldly distractions and be concerned about more important things. He tells us this so we can keep focused on our real mission. We can start having God's perspective when we stop thinking, "How am I being affected by this situation?" and start asking, "How can I use this situation to point someone to my King?" If you make this shift in your perspective, it will radically change your attitude!

What Jesus wanted the disciples to remember as a result of this particular conversation is found in Luke 12:31. Reread Luke 12:31 below and circle what we should be doing with our time instead of worrying.

Instead, seek his kingdom, and these things will be added to you.

If we seek His kingdom, God promises to provide these basic needs. Our basic needs are a side note in God's eyes. He has a mission and vision for each of us.

He knows if we are seeking His kingdom, then we will have His perspective.

When we have His perspective we will become passionate about His priorities. Our attitude battles become attitude victories when we are viewing our lives through His eyes. God goes one step further after affirming we will not be in need and reminds us of His amazing heart towards us. Read verse 32 below.

Fear not, little flock, for it is your Father's good pleasure to give you the kingdom.

Write the first 2 words of verse 32 (see above) in the blanks:

_____ _____

In verse 32, why should we NOT have fear?

Jesus knows we need to eat and be clothed, but the enemy is perfectly happy if he can periodically just get us so wrapped up in things that we lose the perspective that God has given us life to be a part of an amazing mission. I honestly don't think the enemy cares if we are distracted by basic needs, extravagant wants, or even relational struggles. All three keep us from seeking the Lord's kingdom. All three keep us self-centered. All three keep us from accomplishing God's priorities.

This particular passage speaks to our basic needs like food, clothing, and shelter, but every Miss-Perfect-wanna-be worries about many other things, right? I am sure I won't get them all, but check off the ones below that you have worried over at some point:

_____children's health, safety, behavior _____inability to have children
_____spiritual condition of family and friends _____future spouse
_____aging parents _____children's future
_____prodigal children _____marriage

Now go back and read Luke 12:25-26 again. This truth applies to all of our hand wringing, not just food and clothes. So cross-out anything listed above that will NOT be helped by being anxious.

I hope you see that if our worry will not even add an hour to our life, it certainly can't help with any other problems. Again, I do not say these things lightly, but if we can keep our eyes fixed on the fact that we have a God who loves us and cares more about our family, friends, and future even more than we do, then we can stop allowing our attitude to be hijacked by our anxiety. Our anxiety is useless!

So how do we overcome stress, worry, and anxiety so it does not overtake our attitude? We must replace our perspective with God's perspective. When we have God's perspective, it will influence how we feel. We need to take in a few more verses to comprehend ALL of God's perspective. He cares about all the specifics of our lives, but He also sees a bigger picture.

Read Luke 12:35-40.

Jesus says we are to be like men who are waiting on their master to come home from a wedding feast. By the time we get to verse 40, Jesus is no longer making an analogy. He is speaking in literal terms to the disciples.

What is the command given in verse 40? BE_____!

Why do they need to be ready? (v40)

I hope you see this! God has called us to have His perspective. He has told the disciples: Don't be anxious! Fear Not! Be ready!

We are called to be ALWAYS READY and NEVER AFRAID.

Jesus knows that the enemy is going to try everything he can to keep us worried, fearful, and anxious. If we are waiting on circumstances to be right for us to have a good attitude, we never will! Jesus is warning us that this is one of the enemy's tactics. It is as if He is saying, "Don't fall for it. DON'T GET ANXIOUS about your basic needs, I have them covered." If we did not get it in verse 25, Jesus tells us in verse 32, "Fear not... it is my dad's pleasure to give you the kingdom." Not only should we not fear having enough today, but don't forget God can't wait to give you His kingdom, too. As a matter of fact, we really can take our eyes off all the possessions of the world because there is something so much greater AND everlasting that we should focus on.

How do we keep ourselves from being anxious and fearful? Focus on being ready! Focus on the future!

Fear generates some of the strongest emotions we can experience. What would happen to our attitudes if we began to replace our fears over a circumstance with the questions:

What might God be trying to accomplish in me or through me with this trial? (Go ahead...give it a shot and answer!)

How does looking at this trial in light of the Lord's return help you to turn away from your fear?

Jesus is not going to remove the enemy's influence, but we are both warned of his tactics and equipped to overcome his lies, if we choose to adopt God's agenda. We can be like Eve and think God is holding back, or we can trust He will meet our needs now and He joyfully anticipates giving us His kingdom.

The key to keeping our attitude in check is to keep our perspective on God's greater promise. We are called to be ready for the Son of Man to return. All of our issues and struggles fade into the periphery when we put our eyes toward a future full of hope and relief from this world's troubles. When we take on God's perspective, we will embrace an attitude of anticipation. We will see things in such a way that we are ALWAYS READY and NEVER AFRAID.

What was the most meaningful statement or Scripture you read today?

What does God want you to do in response to today's study?

NOTES FOR THE WEEK

DISCIPLINES WITHOUT DISAPPOINTMENT

A woman discovers her true heart for God by developing
the disciplines of the relationship.

Day One
CHANGING OUR VIEW

Day Two
OUR LOVE LETTER

Day Three
THE DISCIPLINE DETAILS

Day Four
OWNING THE TRUTH

Day Five
IT IS WRITTEN

CHANGING OUR VIEW

CHRIS KUHLMAN

As I sit down to write this week on spiritual disciplines, I have wrestled with what to say and how to say it. If you have been around church for long, the term "spiritual disciplines" can stir up all sorts of emotions both positive and negative. I am very aware that the disciplines we will talk about, and even others that we don't, can become "rules" that we use for judgment and self-righteousness if we are not careful. There are those of us who are rule followers, and as long as we follow the rules we feel good. Then, there are those of us who hate rules. To these people, rules stir up rebellion, and they are a burden, an unwelcome enemy. I can relate to both of these ideas.

Are you more of a rule follower or a rebel?

Regardless of which camp you lean towards, spiritual disciplines, such as being in God's Word, prayer, Scripture memory, and meditation, are our lifeline to growth in our relationship with the Lord. While they are an amazing gift to us, many Christians don't see disciplines as a gift. Instead, they bring us frustration or fear of disappointment. If we are battling to be Miss Perfect, disciplines can feel like another place we don't quite measure up. You might be thinking, "I've tried this before and I never stick with it," or "I have never seen any great benefit from all this spiritual discipline stuff."

Do you resonate with either of these 2 concerns? If so, which one and why?

This week we are going to ask God to help us to see the subject of spiritual disciplines from His viewpoint. The more we can understand God's perspective on them, the more we will clear up some common misperceptions and be drawn to develop these disciplines.

The first misperception I want to eliminate might be best removed by changing our terminology. As we have already indicated, spiritual disciplines are incorporated into our lives not as habits to perform, but based on a relationship. What we will learn how to develop this week are not skills to later be proven on a spiritual achievement test. This week is actually about developing a strong relationship with the Lord. So, let's ditch the terminology of spiritual disciplines and begin referring to them as relational disciplines.

A woman discovers her true heart for God by developing the disciplines of the relationship.

If you miss this concept that disciplines are for the purpose of increasing your love for the Lord, you will likely look at disciplines the same way that the Pharisees looked at the Law. The Pharisees tried to use the Law to prove their religious superiority.

They missed the entire point of the Law:

> The Law was to help them see God as holy.
> The Law was meant to separate them from other nations.
> The Law was meant to show them that they were not good enough to keep all the laws.
> The Law was meant to be a tutor to lead them to Christ.

As we explore the disciplines of being in God's Word, meditating on it, and memorizing it (we'll save prayer until Week 6), let's not make the same mistake as the Pharisees of thinking relational disciplines somehow make us better than others!

Relational disciplines should give us a higher view of God, not of ourselves!

Consider a few of the reasons we need to make relational disciplines a part of our lives:

> Relational disciplines help us attach our heart to the Lord...instead of the world.
> Relational disciplines keep our mind focused on what is true....instead of lies.
> Relational disciplines help us to focus on eternal value...instead of temporary value.
> Relational disciplines protect us from sin.

In Days 2 through 5, we will define and explain three primary relational disciplines. Many times we are told what to do ("study your Bible" or "meditate on Scripture"), but we are rarely shown how to do it. The remainder of the week we will get very practical, but before we get practical, we have to get honest. Truth be told, sometimes we might be resisting relational disciplines because we are comfortable with where we are. We may use busyness as a convenient excuse, but if we step back, busyness may not be the complete reason. We think that if we let God get any closer to us it means we will have to give up something we would rather hang on to.

Are you afraid you will have to give something up to grow closer to the Lord? If so, what is it that you feel like may be threatened?

If you still look at your relationship with God as something that keeps you from what you want to do, then this week can really help you. Sometimes, we have an encounter with God and recognize our need for Him. We genuinely trust Him as our Savior, but then don't learn how to develop our relationship with the Lord. We get stuck. This usually happens either because we don't have someone there to show us how to take our first steps as a new Christian, or we think we can handle it on our own and just keep on our old path. We won't sense much change if we don't begin any relational disciplines. If we are not careful, we can continue this path for years and then just resign ourselves to the fact that this must be all there is to the Christian life. Do not be deceived! It would be like meeting a guy, deciding to date, and never seeing him again. He might be an amazing guy, but you would never know. In this case, I promise you this relationship is even better than the man of your dreams. Don't miss out!

The result of salvation is that God begins to change us to be more like Him. In church lingo, we call this sanctification. Sanctification is the process of being made more like Christ. Don't be afraid of that word. It simply means that God loves us so much that He does not want to leave us just the way we are. He knows that if we are left to ourselves, we will make choices that will harm us. The most obvious way to begin to get to know God and follow His ways is through His Word. The Bible is available to us to lead us in the sanctification process, if we will choose to engage.

Have you ever had to assemble a complicated toy? Imagine as you open up the box that there are several bags of different parts. You can either read the owner's manual and have a predetermined, positive outcome, or you can try to guess how to assemble the toy and see what happens. Usually when we guess, we leave out parts or put them in the wrong place. Both errors seriously compromise the safety of the toy. It is no big deal if it is a small doll house that your daughter may use for her little dolls. What if it is a swing set that you are trusting to be well-assembled as it holds the weight of your precious children swinging high in the air? There is too much on the line in our lives to hope for the best. God's Word and these disciplines are how you can make yourself accessible to His owner's manual.

If you know anything about the life of Paul, you'll remember that he had a pretty impressive resume before he was radically saved. He could have decided to just try to make some adjustments in his own strength, but he didn't. He put his entire life before Christ in the rearview mirror and jumped in with both feet.

Read Philippians 3:10-11 from the Amplified Text and see what I mean.

> For my determined purpose is that I may know Him, that I may progressively become more deeply and intimately acquainted with Him, perceiving and recognizing and understanding the wonders of His person more strongly and more clearly, and that I may in that same way come to know the power outflowing from His resurrection [which it exerts over believers], and that I may so share His sufferings as to be continually transformed [in spirit into His likeness even] to his death, in the hope that if possible I may attain to the spiritual and moral resurrection that lifts me out from among the dead even while in the body.

When Paul became a Christian, his new life was not about what he was giving up. Instead, it was about all that he was gaining! Paul did what God desires for every believer to do... to fall deeply in love with Him and take great joy in following Him. So, what was Paul's secret? What was it that prevented Paul from just going through the spiritual motions?

Read a few verses earlier in Philippians 3:7-8 below and see if you can find the key to Paul's victory:

> ⁷ But whatever things were gain to me, those things I have counted as loss for the sake of Christ. ⁸ More than that, I count all things to be loss in view of the surpassing value of knowing Christ Jesus my Lord, for whom I have suffered the loss of all things, and count them but rubbish so that I may gain Christ. (NASB)

Why does Paul count all things as loss (v8)?

There is a four letter word in verse 8 that is the difference between Paul and the Pharisees. This four letter word can also be the key to your spiritual growth. Paul had an accurate VIEW of Christ. We can teach you the practical steps to relational disciplines all day long, but they will eventually fall on deaf ears if you do not have an accurate view of what you can gain by spending time developing your relationship with God. Go back to Philippians 3:10-11 and circle what Paul wanted to grasp about Christ.

Paul had a desire to learn all the riches of Christ. Paul had a view of what he was gaining that was so strong that it moved him to pursue the Lord. If you view relational disciplines as laborious or boring or dutiful, you'll likely never get much out of them. If you have a view of what is available to you, your desire will be your pathway to disciplines. Your desire must precede your discipline!

What if you decided to ignore the lies that the enemy whispers about God and His Word and instead jump in to discover the view for yourself?

For some women, you have developed consistent disciplines in your relationship with the Lord. You may be in the Word daily, consistent in prayer, meditation, and Scripture memorization. Do not think that you are exempt from this topic! Desire must be the motivator for each of us everyday or we will become like the Pharisees and just focus on the discipline. Our pride can creep in without us even realizing it. Whether you are an old pro at relational disciplines or a rookie, continue to ask the Lord to give you His view!

Paul used the imagery of a race and athletes often in his letters, and we will look at them several times during the study. An athlete must be disciplined. Discipline means reaching for the best. Relational disciplines boil down to spending time reaching for the richest relationship with God that is available to us.

Read how we are to run in Hebrews 12:1-2.

How are we to run? (v1)

Where should be keep our eyes? (v2)

God wants us to put our trust in Him and not ourselves. As we yield to Him, our hearts will be stirred to know Him and obey Him. The believer devotes herself to "running the race," keeping her eyes on the goal of knowing her Lord and not letting anything distract her. How does she do this? Paul tells us how in Philippians 3:13-14. Look up these verses and fill in the blanks below.

...One thing I do:

_____what lies behind

_____to what lies ahead

_____toward the goal.

WEEK FOUR

The Christian running the race looks to the future. She keeps her view on Christ and all of eternity. Two things stick out in my mind about my training from my days of high school track. 1) Do not look back to see how far ahead or how close the next runner is. It will slow you down. 2) When jumping hurdles, look to each hurdle, one at a time.

Instead of looking to the past, Hebrews 12 tells us to look to Jesus. "To forget" does not mean "to fail to remember." We don't forget what has happened to us in the past. We can't erase those memories, even though some of us wish we could! "To forget" in the Bible means to not allow it to have influence. Hebrews 10:17 says, "I will remember their sins and lawless deeds no more."

God is not saying He will conveniently forget. That is impossible with God. But He is saying, "I will not hold their sins against them. Their sins will no longer affect their standing with Me or influence My attitude toward them." If God has a view towards our future, surely we can too.

No matter how faithful or unfaithful you have been to develop relational disciplines in the past, I pray that you will have a fresh excitement as we proceed this week. Like any relationship we have, it takes work to develop deeper intimacy. The very Creator of the universe offers us a way to draw closer to Him. Let us keep our eyes on Him and His surpassing value and decide to run hard after Him. He waits with open arms to comfort and amaze us. We will never be disappointed.

What was the most meaningful statement or Scripture you read today?

What does God want you to do in response to today's study?

OUR LOVE LETTER
CHRIS KUHLMAN

Our lives are defined by our relationships. We fill our days with all kinds of activities based on the relationships that are in our lives. When you get up and get breakfast for your children, get them ready for the day, take them to school, etc., you do this because you have a love relationship with them and want what's best for them. If you have a friend who is struggling with a decision, you make time to meet with her even in the midst of your busiest week because you value the relationship. Sometimes, I reserve time for myself and that is based on the love relationship I have with myself. I care about myself over other relationships. If we care about our relationship with God, then we must invest meaningful time in this relationship, too.

The first discipline we are going to look at is spending time in God's Word. While God is beyond our comprehension and physical grasp, He left us an amazing letter so we can develop an intimate relationship with Him. His Word is the primary tool we have to learn His heart and purpose for us. Believing in Him is not all He wants from us. Belief in Him is not the same as personal knowledge from experience. We will not daily surrender our lives over to someone we don't know. We will defer to whom we do know - ourselves. We must get to know Him so we will trust His ways.

Read what the psalmist said about God's Word in Psalm 19:7-11 (NIV) and then fill in the blanks below.

> [7] The law of the LORD is perfect, reviving the soul. The statutes of the LORD are trustworthy, making wise the simple. [8] The precepts of the LORD are right, giving joy to the heart. The commands of the LORD are radiant, giving light to the eyes. [9] The fear of the LORD is pure, enduring forever. The ordinances of the LORD are sure and altogether righteous. [10] They are more precious than gold, than much pure gold; they are sweeter than honey, than honey from the comb. [11] By them is your servant warned; in keeping them there is great reward.

The law of the Lord is_____.

...making_____**the**_____.

...giving_____**to the**_____.

...giving_____**to the**_____.

From these verses we see that when we need direction and answers to the things we don't know, we go to God's Word. When we lack joy, when we find ourselves in a defeated state, when we are emotionally drained, when we feel raw grief, we go to God's Word where we find the joy we desire and the comfort we need. Psalm 119:130 says, "The unfolding of your words gives light; it imparts understanding to the simple." David is overcome with what God has provided. God's words hold a high priority in his life. They can only hold this place if it is based in an intimate relationship.

When Tim and I were dating, during the summer breaks from college we wrote letters to one another. This was before cell phones and Facebook! I remember the excitement of coming home from work, eager to see if I had a letter waiting for me. If I wanted to know what Tim was feeling for me, I had to read those letters. Just having them on my nightstand wouldn't produce much in me. But when I picked up the letters and read them, the words I read were Tim speaking to me. We have a love letter from God. This is how we know who God is, what is in His heart, how we come to Him, how we live. In it He introduces me to my need and to His Son, the answer to my need. We seem to be looking everywhere else for answers to our life questions when God has already given them to us. He actively speaks to us in His Word.

We must read the Word of God to know the God of the Word. It gives life.

Read Hebrews 4:12 in the Amplified Version.

> For the Word that God speaks is alive and full of power [making it active, operative, energizing, and effective]; it is sharper than any two-edged sword, penetrating to the dividing line of the breath of life (soul) and [the immortal] spirit, and of joints and marrow [of the deepest parts of our nature], exposing and sifting and analyzing and judging the very thoughts and purposes of the heart.

How does the author of Hebrews describe the Word of God?

What does this verse say the Word of God actively does? (hint: look for the verbs)

The Word of God is powerful! It can expose, sift, analyze, and judge our thoughts and purposes. Before that freaks you out and scares you off, don't forget God already knows every thought you have anyway! We can sit down with God's Word in our lap to hear His heart and to allow

Him to show us a better way. He will make His Word true in me because of His Almighty power in my heart to accomplish every blessing of which it speaks.

Since the Bible is God-breathed and unique to any other piece of literature, we want to approach it differently than a book, blog, or newspaper. You may have heard a new believer say, "I am reading my Bible, but I am not getting much out of it." Others have read the Bible for years, but it still remains more of a historic lesson than a life changing process. Let's address that now so we can experience the full benefit of spending time with the Lord through His Word.

There are a few basic skills that will transform your time in the Word from an academic exercise to the meaningful encounter that we have been describing. These skills will help the Word come alive to you. The first skill is what we call Focused Thinking. The second skill is Personal Application.

At Highpoint, we call our time in the Word and prayer a Priority Time. A Priority Time is a daily, unhurried time to get to know God through the Bible and prayer. Some people call it a quiet time or a devotional time. The terms can be used interchangeably, but we prefer Priority Time because (1) God should not be quiet during your time in His Word, and (2) we must make Him our priority that directs all other priorities.

> **The first skill of Focused Thinking is the discipline of asking questions for the purpose of discovering and obeying truth.**

Instead of just reading quickly through a few verses, we want to be intentional to slow down and ask questions that will cause us to think and apply. The first six questions you will remember from seventh grade English class (The seventh question is what we were all thinking in class anyway!). They are who, what, when, why, where, how, and so what. You won't ask every question for every passage, but if you take time to ask these questions, then you can grasp what God is trying to communicate. Let's give it a try:

Read Psalm 139:1-12. Now let's try some FOCUSED THINKING. Ask the journalistic questions of the verses you just read... for example:

1. Who does David say has searched him?

2. Who is David writing about?

3. What does David say God does?

4. Where does David say that God is?

If I were having my Priority Time, I would have seen that David is writing this psalm to God about God and himself. David describes that God knows him and searches out his path. God lays His hand on David and hems him in. David says that God's spirit is everywhere. He cannot get away from it and it guides him.

All of this information is very interesting. It is neat to see how much David recognizes God's love for him, but if we just take information from the passage then we have cheated ourselves. We must follow *Focused Thinking* with *Personal Application*. Failing to spend time applying God's Word to us in a personal way is the number one reason people feel frustrated that they are not getting anything out of their time in the Word. It is easy to learn a few historical Bible facts, close the Bible, and forget what you learned by lunch.

> We must take the truth of God's Word and ask how it applies to our own lives right now.

We must ask questions to discover how God wants us to apply His truth to our lives. Transformation will only occur if we have information PLUS application. Far too many people close their Bible after they read a passage and never ask the Lord, "What does this mean for me?"

Here are some great questions that can help you make personal application:

> What did it mean to the original hearers?
> What is the underlying timeless truth?
> How should knowing this truth change me?
> What should I stop doing?
> What should I start doing?

Let's try some PERSONAL APPLICATION. Answer these questions for our passage in Psalm 139:1-12.

1. What did it mean to the original hearers?

2. What is the underlying timeless truth?

3. How should knowing this truth change me? What should I start/stop doing?

This passage is one of great encouragement. To the original hearers, they would have been reminded that God is everywhere and God intimately cares about each of them. This is a timeless truth that applies to us, too. The truth remains the same: God knows each of us intimately and is always there for us. When it comes to "how should knowing this truth change me?" you might also ask yourself, "Why does this truth matter?" Some passages will reveal areas of sin that you need to repent of while other passages will remind you of God's amazing character.

In this passage, you might be led to confess that you are not living a life trusting that God knows you intimately and is there for you. You might be convicted that you are trying to live your life in your strength instead of His strength. You might treasure being reminded that even in a tough situation your Heavenly Father is right there with you. You may need to stop depending upon your own strength in a specific situation you are facing. You may need to stop being afraid and start trusting God in a specific way.

Make your application specific.

Generic application is not application. All of us know we need to trust God more, but if you move to specific application, you will confess that you need to trust God regarding finances, or a health issue, or a relationship struggle. You will see God's activity and answers to prayer much clearer if you are applying, confessing, and praying specifically. Let me reiterate - be specific! You will be tempted to believe the misperception that God is distant if you don't get specific.

Do not make your time in God's Word too complicated. If you simply choose to slow down, ask what the text says, and then ask the Lord to show you how you are to respond, you will be on your way. Don't get hung up if you don't understand something in the passage. There is usually plenty of truth we do understand. Focus on obeying what you do understand!

This is God's love letter to you! Until you hear God's message in the stories of real people that lived with hang-ups and issues like your own, you will not trust that His power can enter your story. He is a personal God and wants you to know Him in that way. Open up your Bible daily to see His love for you and His interest in all the details of where you are.

What was the most meaningful statement or Scripture you read today?

What does God want you to do in response to today's study?

For more information and expanded instructions on Priority Time, visit chrisconlee.net.

THE DISCIPLINE DETAILS
CHRIS KUHLMAN

Yesterday we looked at how to spend time in God's Word in such a way that we truly allow it to transform our lives. Unless you grew up with a mom or dad that modeled this discipline, you may have been left with the simple instructions to "read your Bible." Because most of us went to school, we just assume that reading the Bible must be just like reading a history textbook, right? I hope you grasped this before, but the Bible is a love letter and our guide, not a boring outdated book.

When we can move from an academic model that focuses on facts to a more relational approach, two amazing dynamics emerge. First, we now approach God's Word out of relationship, not obligation. We want to learn about our Heavenly Father. Every Priority Time you have should give you a greater understanding of who He is. Some passages will remind you of His grace and mercy. Other passages will remind you of His holiness and wrath. Whatever attribute you discover, you are gaining a more accurate picture of who your Father is. The second dynamic is we see how the unchanging, timeless truth of the passage applies to our own life today. When we begin to see God's Word as personal and relevant, our hearts become teachable and tender towards Him so we begin to obey His Word.

Usually when believers get a handle on these skills of Focused Thinking and Personal Application, it opens up lots of practical questions. Often people want to know where in the Bible they should start their time in the Word. Quite frankly, there are also some practical things that you can do that will help you make the most of your time. We are going to spend today addressing some of those questions and then introducing a great little tool that will be an asset to all the relational disciplines we discuss this week.

AN UNHURRIED TIME

When we defined a Priority Time yesterday, we said that it was a daily, unhurried time to get to know God through the Bible and prayer. I am not sure about you, but I don't know many women who are unhurried about anything! So how do you really have an unhurried time?

1. Pick the length of time you are going to spend in your Priority Time (20 minutes is recommended if you are just starting).
2. Back up your morning routine by that amount of time.
3. When you have your Priority Time, set a timer for that length of time. This will allow you to be focused and unhurried during your Priority Time and not distracted checking the clock every three minutes afraid that you are going to go too long and be late to your next commitment.

Now I can already imagine the grumbles. "In the MORNING, really?" "I am not an early riser" or "I already get up at 5:00 AM." I'll spare you a lot of reasons why this is the best approach and have you turn to Mark 1:35.

When did Jesus get up?

What did the sky look like?

Where did He go?

What did He do there?

> If the Son of God needed to get alone with God before His day started, I think it is safe to say that we have an even greater need.

Our mornings are the most predictable part of our day. No matter your stage of life, it is almost always easier to have consistency early in the morning before the pace of the day increases. Not to mention, if you wait to spend time with the Lord in the evening, you'll likely spend most of your time asking for forgiveness for what you already did that day instead of attaching your heart to the Lord and asking Him to guide you.

Women don't have simple lives, especially if you are still trying to please both God and man. (I hope you have decided to give up that losing battle by now!) If we are going to really discover our purpose without the pressure, then we have to get our hearts connected to God each day and stop trying to act like we are Miss Perfect and can do it without Him. If you are not convinced it is worth it to get up in the morning or that your life circumstances are the exception, look back and read Mark 1:32-34.

So what did Jesus do the night before He was getting up early?

Yeah. You got it. Jesus was up all night healing people and casting out demons. Stop making excuses and just commit to giving the Lord the first part of your day.

SO MANY BOOKS TO CHOOSE FROM

Once you have decided on when, you will want to decide where to start. Every book in the Bible has value, but for those who are newer to this discipline, start in one of the Gospels.

Whether Matthew, Mark, Luke, or John, start in the first verse of the first chapter. How long you have committed to your daily Priority Time will determine how many verses you read. It is better to read fewer verses and really apply God's Word than to read too much. Dr. Adrian Rogers has said that "for every minute you read, you should think."[1] If it takes you three months to get through Matthew, who cares? Each day just pick up where you left off the day before. When you complete a book, you might then rotate to an Old Testament book next.

LOCATION, LOCATION, LOCATION

As much as the location of your Priority Time may seem like a minor detail, it actually is a very critical one. Go back and read Mark 1:35 again.

Where was Jesus found?

Why do you think Jesus went to a secluded place?

I don't know about you, but I am easily distracted. If you decide to have your Priority Time in the middle of your kitchen when your roommates, husband, or children are up and getting ready for the day, you will inevitably get distracted. If you go to Starbucks, you may see someone you know and then you definitely will not allow yourself to be vulnerable before the Lord. I have never seen someone kneel to pray in Panera, have you? Do you get the picture? You need to find a secluded place. Maybe that is in your closet with the door locked or, if you are lucky, in a sunroom. Keep away from somewhere that tempts you to get to work (not near your laptop) or in your bed (can we say, "snooze?").

FORGET ME NOTS

The most common thing we do is to skip relational disciplines and convince ourselves that we can manage this world in our own strength. A tragedy. I hope the Holy Spirit has used this study to change your mind and to trust God to be your guide. The second most common thing we do is forget God's faithfulness. We will pray hard and God will answer our prayer. A week later, we cannot even remember what we prayed. We can ask Him to reveal to us our passions and purpose. God will speak powerfully to us. A month later, it is a vague memory. While there are MANY reasons to begin using a journal, our tendency to forget God's activity is the biggest one. So how does a journal fit into spending time in God's Word or other disciplines such as prayer, meditation, or Scripture memory? Here is how it can be used most effectively:

God's Word:
* Write down your questions and answers to your 7 questions (who, what, why...)
* Write down your application questions and answers
* Note significant insights that God gives you

Prayer:
- Write out your prayers, if you prefer
- If praying out loud, write down a summary of what you are praying for
- Go back and indicate when God answers each of your prayers

Others:
- Use your journal to keep track of the verses you are memorizing and use the list as a refresher as you add verses
- When you are waiting for God to answer a prayer, use the journal to remind you of how God has been faithful in the past
- Keep it as a record for the next generation of your family so they can look back and see God's faithfulness in your life

No one needs a bunch of rules. We have enough of those. We each need a sweet, safe place that becomes our most precious time of the day where we meet with the Lord.

This is the only appointment all day that will never disappoint.

What was the most meaningful statement or Scripture you read today?

What does God want you to do in response to today's study?

OWNING THE TRUTH
CHRIS KUHLMAN

My prayer for you over these last couple of days is that you have experienced more depth in your relationship with the Lord because of time spent in His Word. In Week 6, we will look at the discipline of prayer. The disciplines of spending time in God's Word and prayer go hand-in-hand. Right between the two is the discipline of meditation, which we will look at today. Let's be clear about what we mean when we say meditation.

> Meditation is taking time to focus on God - to focus on His character and His words so that we know better how to respond to Him and His will.

It is not eastern meditation where the goal is emptying our minds and checking out from the world. Even though some days we think that's exactly what we want to do! That can be a dangerous place for one to go.

What has been your previous understanding of meditation?

In the midst of our crazy, fast-paced culture, few of us have meditating on God's Word as a priority. Few of us really have ever been taught how to meditate on Scripture. Yet, this very discipline would strike at the heart of the temptation we face to stay busy with the wrong things. If we want to discover God's purpose and leave behind the worldly and self-imposed pressure of our day, keeping truth directly in front of us is a huge weapon.

God's Word has much to say about meditation. Read Psalm 119:97-99.

> [97] Oh how I love your law! It is my meditation all the day. [98] Your commandment makes me wiser than my enemies, for it is ever with me. [99] I have more understanding than all my teachers, for your testimonies are my meditation.

Who can we be wiser than if we know God's commands? (v98)

Who can we have more understanding than if we focus on God's word? (v99)

Meditation is loving the Lord and His Words by pondering them, reflecting on them, thinking about them all through the day and allowing the truths to penetrate our hearts. It is what Brother Lawrence meant when he talked about practicing the presence of God, "That our only business was to love and delight ourselves in God."[2] It is what Paul was talking about in his letter to the church of Colossae.

Read Colossians 3:2 and fill in the blanks.

_____ your _____ on _____

_____ and not on things that are on earth.

We don't abandon our daily responsibilities or ignore our work when we practice the discipline of meditation. Instead, our minds are so focused on Him that in doing our work and responsibilities, He shows us how to apply His Word. We begin to see everything through the eyes of the Word of God. If this is not where you are yet, do not worry! Remember that these disciplines need to be learned. This has become a sweet discipline in my life. It has been another building block to draw my focus up to the Heavenly Father and keep my thoughts and mind on Him. I know that as you practice meditation it *will* deepen your love for Him!

Before we look at the practical ways to meditate on Scripture, I want you to see how the practice of meditation plays a critical role in protecting us and allowing us to fulfill God's purpose for our lives. A first-hand example is provided to us through the life of Joshua. The passage we will look at today begins the entire book of Joshua. The backstory is nothing short of tragic.

Moses has been leading the children of Israel on their long, delayed, and detoured journey to the Promise Land. The disobedience of the people has caused God to allow an entire generation of Israelites to die in the wilderness without ever stepping foot in the Promise Land. Even Moses, their incredibly faithful leader who is referred to as "a friend of God" in Scripture, is forbidden to enter the long sought after land because of his disobedience. Moses, the leader of the children of Israel, has just died and now his apprentice is called upon by the Lord to lead.

Read Joshua 1:1-9.

Look carefully at verse 1. Who is speaking to Joshua in this passage?

What is God going to give to Joshua and his people? (v2-4)

What character qualities does God tell Joshua, not only once but twice, he must exhibit? (v6 & v7)

What must Joshua be careful to do? (v7)

What was at stake that Joshua needed to meditate on God's law? (v8)

When did God tell Joshua he should meditate on the law? (v8)

Do you get the picture? It is time for Joshua to put on his big boy pants and lead. The stakes are incredibly high. People have died and the remaining Israelites are weary at best. There is no room for repeating the sins of the past. God has a purpose for Joshua's life and in retrospect, this is a pretty critical part of his purpose. The only way that Joshua is not going to repeat the sins of his predecessor and find the strength and courage he needs is if he keeps God's Word in front of him at all times. Joshua was not a monk in a monastery. Joshua did not have all day to linger in his tent. Joshua had been given an assignment and was going to be on the move.

Do you know that God has a purpose for you, too? You can't succeed in your strength any more than Joshua could without the Word of God keeping you centered so you do not go to the left or the right. Meditating on Scripture is not for people with nothing to do. Meditating on Scripture is a discipline for anyone who wants to be able to carry out the purpose God has given him or her. You and I may not be conquering physical land, but we have our own battles that necessitate us to be equally prepared. I cannot escape the thought of how much this applies to generational sins. Just like Joshua could not afford to commit the same sins of the previous generation, neither can we! If we are going to be women who break the sins of our culture and our own family of origin, we need to follow the instructions God gave Joshua.

So what does this whole meditation thing look like? Let me first describe it by way of illustration. In a recent study, a group of kindergartners were asked how many ways they could think of to use a paper clip. You or I might come up with twenty or more, but more than 98% of the kindergartners came up with over 200 ways that a paper clip could be used.[3] What is my point? Adults are especially good at looking at the surface and not using our minds to think outside the obvious. We have trained ourselves to observe the surface and move on. Scripture is God-inspired, rich in its intricacies, and overflowing with application for our current lives.

> Meditating on Scripture means we are going to examine a verse in such a way that we see it come alive.

We are going to savor it and linger in a way that we do not linger with anything else our eyes read. We want to explore it from every angle and walk away owning the truth within it.

Let me show you what I mean. Find a watch, clock, or timer and set it for five minutes. Over the next five minutes I want you to look at the most familiar verse in Scripture, John 3:16, and meditate on it. In the "Notes for the Week" section, write down every thought and observation you have about the verse. Think about it from God's perspective, from the world's perspective, and from the Son's perspective.

John 3:16

> For God so loved the world, that he gave his only Son, that whoever believes in him should not perish but have eternal life.

At the conclusion of five minutes, write down your top 3 takeaways.

1.

2.

3.

Now let's turn to a less familiar verse, 1 John 3:16. Take another five minutes and write down every observation in the "Notes for the Week" section.

> By this we know love, that he laid down his life for us, and we ought to lay down our lives for the brothers.

What are your top three takeaways?

1.

2.

3.

Did you see anything new in these two passages by focusing your thinking and truly contemplating these truths? To prosper and be successful in God's perspective is to take those things we learn in His Word and to prove them in our lives. We can't prove them in our lives if we barely remember what we read. God "writes" His Word on our hearts so that we may be a living example in speech and in conduct and in love and faith and in purity (1 Timothy 4:12). How we live is important because it backs up what we say.

What area at home are you struggling with? A conflict with a parent? A sibling? Your husband? A child? Is there a specific temptation or sin (an issue with pride, submission, tongue, perfectionism, laziness, language, etc.) that continues to cause you to fall? Are you listening to the lies Satan is telling you? Does he tell you that you are unloved?

Using these questions to help you, what are a few areas that you need to begin to meditate on?

Use God's Word to combat these pitfalls. Choose a Bible verse or passage. You may do this by going to the concordance in the back of your Bible and looking up the key word. Or you may ask your Small Group Leader for a verse or passage. Or you may have a mentor or a friend you feel comfortable asking. God may speak to you as you are in your Priority Time, or in a worship service. Read the passage. Use the exercise above if you are just starting the discipline of meditation. Think about the truth as comprehensively as you can for the purpose of understanding and applying. Write a key verse from the passage or the Bible verse that pertains to what you are going through at the moment on a 3x5 card. Put it in a place where you will see it often.

Move beyond memorizing it to owning it, and speaking it. See yourself as an actress. These are your lines. You want them to become a part of you. You are not just quoting it, you are speaking it. Allow God's Word to saturate you. You will never be the same.

What was the most meaningful statement or Scripture you read today?

What does God want you to do in response to today's study?

IT IS WRITTEN

CHRIS KUHLMAN

We have made it to the last day of the week on relational disciplines! I hope that each day has provided you new understanding or a fresh perspective on each of the disciplines that give us access to a greater understanding, appreciation, and love for the Lord. Have you ditched the view of legalism surrounding disciplines yet? I hope you are motivated to take a step forward in your journey with the Lord by incorporating these disciplines into your daily life because you want to, not because you have to. If Miss Perfect is rearing her ugly head and trying to figure out how to add all these disciplines into her to-do list, just relax. Tell her to back off. At the conclusion of today's lesson we will see how they all fit together.

In the meantime, let's look at one last discipline—Scripture memorization. For a certain segment, this will be the easiest of the disciplines. A few lucky people can memorize with ease. For many others, like me, this is the one that truly requires work. If it takes me a little longer than others, that's okay. I will work at memorization because the benefits are significant. I recently heard John Piper, a very well respected pastor and author, talk about memorizing Scripture and felt a bit of relief as I listened. He said many times he will memorize a verse or passage and a few weeks later—it's gone! Left his mind! So at another time he will read it again and memorize it again! Wow! I thought if someone like John Piper has difficulty in this area then I don't have to feel bad if I don't remember every Scripture I have memorized! So, don't worry, you won't be Miss Perfect in this area either!

What is important is that you are consistently hiding God's Word in your heart.

> You never know how verses you are memorizing now will be an anchor to you later, especially when life gets tough.

I know Abraham thought often of the promise God spoke to him and it became a part of his life. In the same way, Romans 8:28 is a verse I go to often in my mind to remind myself that God is working all these things in my life for good, not so I will have an easy life, but it is for His purposes and His purposes will always bring glory to Himself.

Don't take my word for it! See how Psalm 119:9-11 speaks to the value of knowing the Word of God.

> [9] How can a young man keep his way pure? By guarding it according to your word.
> [10] With my whole heart I seek you; let me not wander from your commandments!
> [11] I have stored up your word in my heart, that I might not sin against you.

How does someone (yes, this applies to women too!) keep her way pure? (v9)

As we will see in a few weeks, all of us, regardless of age, are called to purity. God tells us right here through David how we can keep our way pure!

Why should one store the Word in her heart?

If David's words were not convincing enough, then hold on to your seat because the very Son of God used the Word of God to combat Satan in Matthew 4.

Right after Jesus was baptized, the Gospels tell us that the Spirit led Him into the wilderness where He was tempted by the devil. The devil came to Jesus three times. Christ was tempted that He might overcome the tempter. In the temptation we see that our enemy, Satan, is subtle and spiteful. But we also see that Christ showed us how to be victorious and not yield to the temptations of the devil.

Read Matthew 4:1-11.

Jesus had been fasting for 40 days and was hungry when the first temptation occurred. It seemed a logical request from Satan to turn the stones into bread. Satan loves to take advantage of our outward condition, to plant the seed that our Heavenly Father doesn't really care about us.

In what way have you specifically been tempted to doubt God's goodness to you?

Look how Jesus refuted Satan in Matthew 4:4. Fill in the missing word.

" It is_____..."

Jesus is fighting the temptation and the tempter with God's Word that He has in His heart.

Satan says, "Ok, I can use Scripture too." Only he takes it out of context. He tempts Him to question God's care of Him in safety and to put God to the test. When we try to take God's Word out of context to justify our wants and desires we are falling into a trap set by Satan himself.

How did Jesus begin His answer in verse 7?

It is important that we know God's Word and have it hidden in our hearts. We must know HIM who speaks the Word. This encounter is such a confirmation that these are relational disciplines. We will know His heart, not just recite words as we grow in our walk with Him.

Jesus knew God's heart well enough to know that Satan was taking God out of context and twisting His words. This has been a familiar trick of Satan since the Garden of Eden.

In the third exchange, Satan tempted Jesus to desire His own honor above the Father. Satan showed Him the world just like he tries to entice us with the desire to seek our own power or control. We make our desires more important than the will of God. Satan is saying, "I will provide for you better than God will." Jesus again resisted by quoting Scripture. If Jesus used Scripture to refute Satan, I think it would be safe to say that we should equip ourselves with the same ammunition that worked for Him.

I have a sweet young friend in college who struggled in her freshman year with a relationship she knew she should not be involved in. She knew the truth from God's Word. She came to the place where she said, "I know this is not God's best, but if this is as good as it gets, I'm okay with that." For a year she was convicted. She hardened her heart against the truth she knew and believed Satan's lie. But God, who is so rich in mercy, would not let her stay in that place. He began to work in her the truth of His Word that she had hidden in her heart. Once she began to listen to that still small voice, soften her heart, and stop believing the lie, she accepted God's truth for her. She was obedient to God even though it was difficult to end the relationship. With new found freedom she has a renewed love for the Lord. She told me recently she was "Falling in love with Jesus all over again!"

And again Jesus answers, (v10)

"Be gone, Satan!_____ _____ _____ _____...**"**

Satan comes at us with these same temptations. It is so important to see the example Jesus gave us.

> Our greatest defensive weapon against the enemy is the Sword of the Spirit, the Word of God, hidden in our hearts.

As we discipline ourselves to memorize God's Word, we tuck it away to be readily accessed when the enemy ambushes us with his subtle temptations, or when we are drawn away by our own lusts and worldly desires and tempted to turn from truth to the lies of the devil (James 1:13-15).

Often we think, "It's too difficult for me to memorize God's Word," but we memorize all the time. We memorize a grocery list, phone numbers, paint colors, songs, the list goes on and on. The things that we memorize easily are the ones that are repeated in our lives. This is where meditation works hand in hand with memorization. When we take a passage or even a verse and ponder it, think on it and let it linger in our minds, we are able to extract truth from it. Then it is worked into our minds and before we know it we have "learned" or memorized it and the Spirit can bring it to the forefront when we need it.

Think about yesterday's activity of identifying the temptation or sin that always seems to trip you up or something you are struggling with now. That Scripture you are meditating on—make a point to memorize it. Repeat it over in your mind and out loud.

Circumstances may change but God's Word remains true and powerful.

It is relevant to every circumstance. It is not our promises to the Lord that will bring victory but His promises to us! A familiar illustration seems to paint a picture of why we need to remember God's Word: Imagine yourself in a crisis and God rushes in and looks to see what of His Word you have hidden in your heart to use to help you. What would He find? Would John 3:16 be enough? We truly must be intentional to equip ourselves with the truth of God's Word so we are protected in any circumstance!

We have alluded to this throughout the week, but as we move on to our next chapter, let me make sure that there is clarity. These four disciplines are not linear. While each discipline can be separated for the sake of learning and understanding, the reality is that they will usually blend into a beautiful pattern as you engage with the Lord. Think of it this way: if you were to go out on a date and take a stroll through a park, you would never dedicate the first part of the date to talking, then stop talking and switch to only holding hands, only to stop holding hands and walk for the last part of your date. Of course not! You would weave in and out of all three throughout your time together.

Relational disciplines are the same way. In your Priority Time, you may start in the Word and God show you something that leads you to stop and pray. As you are praying, God may bring to mind a truth. You might journal the truth and then resume your time in God's Word. The next verse or two may speak directly to you and God will show you that verse for the purpose of leading you to what you should meditate on or memorize that week. Out of gratitude for Him showing you a truth that applies to exactly where you are, you will likely stop what you are doing to pray and thank Him. He is the "Grand Weaver," as Ravi Zacharias wisely called Him.[4] Your time getting to know Him can lead you to a love you never knew was possible.

What was the most meaningful statement or Scripture you read today?

What does God want you to do in response to today's study?

NOTES FOR THE WEEK

RELATIONSHIPS WITHOUT REGRET

A woman discovers her ability to love others by responding to God's love with love.

Day One
LOVING YOUR GOD

Day Two
HONORING YOUR PARENTS

Day Three
LEAVING YOUR HOME

Day Four
PASSING IT ON

Day Five
BEING AT PEACE

LOVING YOUR GOD

KARIN CONLEE

As we venture into the topic of relationships this week, each day we will highlight a different relationship that women typically have. In reality, an entire study could be written on each relationship. Aren't relationships the source of so much of the pressure we feel each day? Don't some of our biggest regrets in life come from relationships? So, where to begin?

The first relationship we will examine is our relationship with God. If you have made it this far in the study, I am trusting that while we may be at different places in our journey with God, we all acknowledge God's importance in our lives. Despite His importance, there may be a tendency to run quickly through this particular relationship and get on to the ones that scream for more of our attention. What woman does not grab for the magazine articles and books that help her sort out how to help her be a better wife, mom, or date? The stark reality is that if we don't get this relationship right, we threaten every earthly relationship we have. By not investing in our relationship with God, we will be left with a life full of relationships WITH regrets. The reality is that...

A woman discovers her ability to love others by responding to God's love with love.

Take comfort in knowing that we are not the first generation to struggle with prioritizing our relationships. Read Matthew 10:37 below and see what Jesus said on this topic.

> Whoever loves father or mother more than me is not worthy of me, and whoever loves son or daughter more than me is not worthy of me.

What do you think when you read this verse?

My guess is that your response is highly reflective of the health of your closest earthly relationships. Do you know who will struggle the most with this verse? Someone who has very strong, close family relationships will likely have the hardest time. If we are brutally honest, many women love their children or parents more than God.

Why would loving your family more than God be a problem?

In an honest assessment of your own heart, who is your first love?

In this verse, we are hearing loud and clear that God must be prioritized as our first relationship.

God is not asking us to love our family less; He desires that we love Him more.

He is asking us to love Him in such a way that our yes's are firmly in obedience to Him. If you love your family members more than God, you will choose to please them over pleasing God. Sometimes, we love our family in a way that is in alignment with how God would desire us to love them. Other times, our motives are not completely pure. But, we must always do what is best according to God, not according to what our family members desire or deserve. Think back to our study on Identity in Week 1. When we elevate people into first place, we have made them an idol and we have put both them and ourselves in a position to be hurt. Let's look at a familiar passage of a dad who had his priorities right.

Read Genesis 22:1-3 below.

> ¹ After these things God tested Abraham and said to him, "Abraham!" And he said, "Here I am." ² He said, "Take your son, your only son Isaac, whom you love, and go to the land of Moriah, and offer him there as a burnt offering on one of the mountains of which I shall tell you." ³ So Abraham rose early in the morning, saddled his donkey, and took two of his young men with him, and his son Isaac. And he cut the wood for the burnt offering and arose and went to the place of which God had told him.

How did God make Abraham live out Matthew 10:37?

Why was it critical for the Lord to know that Abraham loved God more than his own flesh? (Hint: see Genesis 17:1-5 for one answer)

Why is it critical that you love the Lord more than your own flesh?

We can breathe a sigh of relief that God did not require Abraham to follow through with sacrificing his son. Genesis 22:9-14 shows us that God provided a ram out of the bushes at the last moment to be sacrificed instead of Isaac. As the parent of a thirteen-year-old son, I can hardly fathom what faith this took of Abraham, but don't get lost in the "what ifs." For God to be able to use us, for our lives to be "bless-able," He wants to know that He is our God. We must prioritize our relationship with Him over all other relationships. This truth is not just for those super spiritual people! You may think, "I don't think God is going to start a nation through me, so I am content with how things are." Do not be fooled. Your obedience or disobedience impacts your children and grandchildren and great-grandchildren, not just you.

Read Genesis 22:15-18.

If Abraham had loved his son more than God, what is one thing that would have changed in history?

Let's look at one other example. In 1 Samuel, we learn of Hannah. She is married and dearly loved by her husband, Elkanah, but the Lord has closed Hannah's womb. In this culture, some men had multiple wives. This was the case with Elkanah. Unfortunately for Hannah, she has to share his love with one other woman. (I can't imagine!) Hannah has watched as her husband's other wife, Peninnah, has multiple children. Finally, after much anguish and prayer, Hannah finds that God has opened her womb. If there were ever a woman who would understandably be tempted to love her child more than God, it would be someone who finally conceived after years of desperation.

Read 1 Samuel 1:20-22, 27-28 below.

> 20 And in due time Hannah conceived and bore a son, and she called his name Samuel, for she said, "I have asked for him from the LORD." 21 The man Elkanah and all his house went up to offer to the LORD the yearly sacrifice and to pay his vow. 22 But Hannah did not go up, for she said to her husband, "As soon as the child is weaned, I will bring him, so that he may appear in the presence of the LORD and dwell there forever." 27 "For this child I prayed, and the LORD has granted me my petition that I made to him. 28 Therefore I have lent him to the LORD. As long as he lives, he is lent to the LORD."

How did Hannah demonstrate that she loved God more than her son?

If it was me, I'd be thinking online seminary for my young son seemed like a pretty good option now, right? While sacrificing Isaac seems out of the question, leaving your three-year-old to be raised by a priest has its own set of issues. How were Abraham and Hannah able to trust God with such life altering options? Simply put, they walked with God.

Our God is a gracious God. As nail-biting as both of these situations must have been, He rewarded each person's faithfulness a hundred fold (See Genesis 24:1 and 1 Samuel 2:21 for some encouragement!).

Let me be very clear. You will not love God more than other people until you acknowledge that you can't do this life on your own. You won't put Him in first place until you give up your determination to be Miss Perfect. When you come face-to-face with the reality that you missed perfect a long time ago and He still loves you unconditionally, then you begin to see how much He has done for you and putting Him first will no longer be a struggle.

If you want to be a woman who has God as her first love, you must spend time with Him. If you have not implemented what you learned about relational disciplines last week, do not delay any longer. This Bible study is not a substitute for meeting with your Heavenly Father. You must spend time with Him daily to be reminded of His great love for you. The only reason Hannah and Abraham chose God's way when they were faced with the choice is because they had consistently walked with God.

> You will not make a decision of faith when the crisis comes
> if you spend your days barely acquainted with God.

Reread Matthew 10:37 from earlier in the lesson.

Do you think God is being selfish? Yes   No

Why do you think Jesus would make such a strong statement?

We must put God first for a thousand reasons. Above all, He is holy and deserves our undistracted loyalty and faithfulness. There is, however, even another reason we must seek Him above all others. It is only when we seek Him and are aware of His love for us that we are able to successfully be in relationship with other people.

Can you think of a time where you were aware that the love you had for someone was only possible because you knew the Lord had enabled you to love her or him? If so, describe it.

Can you think of a time when you knew that you were trying to love from your own strength and it failed? If so, describe the situation.

When we think about relationships, some might come with the perspective that our families are easy to love while others think it is nearly impossible to love our families. What must happen before we are able to love others with a Christ-like love?

Read 1 John 4:7-8.

> 7 Beloved, let us love one another, for love is from God, and whoever loves has been born of God and knows God. 8 Anyone who does not love does not know God, because God is love.

Where is love from? (v7)

What is required for us to be able to love? (v7)

You may be thinking, "I know people who aren't Christians who love well." Is this verse REALLY true? In reality, we can love out of our own gain. We can return love, but to love as God designed us to love, we MUST be connected to Him.

If you are not convinced, Luke 6:27 tells us to love our enemies. I have never met anyone who can do this without Christ in his or her life! Our day-to-day interactions and relationships may scream the loudest to be cared for, but if we forget our source of love, we will easily fail when we try to love others in our own strength.

We have spent the day seeing how God's word urges us to walk with Him. For many, you know that you need to spend time with God, but somehow the urgent screams louder than the important. If you don't change your patterns now, how many years will pass before you are sensing the Spirit's nudging again? The Lord longs for us to seek Him, but He won't force us!

What was the most meaningful statement or Scripture you read today?

What does God want you to do in response to today's study?

HONORING YOUR PARENTS

KARIN CONLEE

As we saw yesterday, we must grasp the level of intimacy that God desires to have with us. All through my childhood and teenage years, I depended upon my father or my boyfriend to be my security. No person, no matter how great, can fulfill that role. God literally had to physically separate me from both men to get my attention and make me realize I needed Him. God is the only one who can truly meet our needs and never disappoint. We should willingly, joyfully, not begrudgingly, make Him our highest valued relationship. When we do, we can then function out of the peace of our relationship with Him to interact with a chaotic world.

Flip back to Day 1 of this week and reread our value on relationships on the chapter title page. We truly were designed to receive love from Him first so that we can love others. If we try and bypass this first step, it doesn't take long before we've created a train wreck in our relationships and are living with regrets. After all, God chose to put us on earth in the context of human relationships that, from the first moment of our life, were imperfect. Let's spend the remainder of the week exploring and applying God's direction on how we should interact in specific human relationships.

Today, we will look at the relationship of the adult child to her parents. Scripture speaks specifically to the parent/child relationship. Write the following passages:

Exodus 20:12

Genesis 2:24

These are two foundational truths taught in Scripture. Unfortunately, we live most of our adult lives stuck in a tug of war between these two verses. We either honor our parents really well but have struggled with the "leaving and cleaving," or we have had great success at establishing our own family or independence at the expense of our parents being honored. How can we live out both of these truths in a way that brings God glory?

If you are married, which of these two biblical principles do you feel you have been more successful at?

What has been the biggest challenge?

If you are single, how have you seen couples leaving and cleaving in an honorable way? In a dishonorable way? What do you think is the key to making leaving and cleaving honorable?

If we are going to be godly women in this culture, we must be willing to enter into some areas of our hearts and do some work to go against the norms. While navigating our new role as an adult daughter and even a married adult daughter can take some practice, it will be worth it to follow God's way and experience His protection. Today we will focus on the command to honor our parents.

HONORING YOUR FATHER AND MOTHER

Whether single or married, as the adult child in the parent/child relationship, this is the first time we have ever grown up. We have never had a chance to practice how to be an adult in any way, especially as we relate to our parents. Depending upon your personality and the dynamics of your home during your childhood, you might have taken one of these approaches as you entered adulthood:

Run fast:
Perhaps you were the one that decided to get as far away from your parents' authority as possible the moment the high school graduation bell rang. You had decided long ago that you indeed would go FAR away. Maybe it was literal miles or maybe it was a college or job on the other side of town. Either way, independence was not a problem for you. You were ready to spread your own wings and would interact with your parents on a "need-to-know" basis once you left home.

Stay tight:
Perhaps you were not the one to abandon your family at graduation. Maybe your sibling did, but you were loyal and stayed put. Or maybe your education and career took you miles away, but your heart and cell phone were still fully connected. Even now, you enjoy keeping up with your parents frequently and they are mutually grateful for the window you give them into your world.

Do you recognize yourself in either description? Where would you describe yourself between the two options?

While the two scenarios paint extremes, there are often a lifetime of both healthy and unhealthy relational patterns between a child and her parents that lead us to lean one direction or the other. It has only been through my own experience as a parent that I have been able to reflect on my choices made years ago and understand the "why" behind some of my own decisions as I left home. Now as a mom, I have one child who is very similar to me in personality and one who is my opposite. We laugh about the differences...sometimes. How I respond to each child impacts how they move towards me or away from me... and ultimately how I respond impacts how they view themselves.

As we enter adulthood, regardless of the strength or weakness of our relationships with our parents, we are called by God to honor our parents. *Honoring* means *"showing esteem and respect to a person of superior standing."* In Hebrew, it also means *"to weigh"* or *"to make heavy."* In other words, when placing the opinion of your parents on a balancing scale opposite the opinions of your friends, your parents' opinion is going to weigh more because you honor them.[1]

Do you find it easy or difficult to honor your parents?

One thing the Lord has shown me through ministry and parenting is that to some extent, everyone is dysfunctional and everyone has a dysfunctional family. Imperfect families are the result of imperfect parents and imperfect kids! Romans 3:23 says that "all have sinned and fall short of the glory of God." Amazing, if I had just stuck with that, I would have realized this much earlier!

Ironically, there are so many accomplishments, even for the Lord, that are actually birthed from unhealthiness. In my own life, I see where my type A personality was somewhat fueled by my desire to control. My drive was used to accomplish a few good things along the way even though it was really being subconsciously steered by unhealthy motives. Why do I say this? What does this have to do with honoring your parents? Because, some of us need to step back and normalize that our parents have struggles just like we do. Sometimes we even have the same struggle or character flaw they do. The very thing that may drive us crazy about them, may actually be one of our flaws, too... it is called generational sin. If you share the same struggle as one of your parents, it can be a greater barrier in your desire to honor unless you acknowledge the mutual struggle.

If honoring your parents is a challenge, I encourage you to take a step back and try to learn about your parents' lives. What were their challenges? What struggles did they face? What support did they have or lack? How could the issues they experienced possibly influence their relationship with you or the ability to connect with you? You must also keep in mind that unhealthy people unintentionally hurt people. Choose to believe the best about those you are trying to honor. My generation and those who have followed are much more apt to seek help and verbalize our failures. When relating to our parents, it is helpful to realize without the same openness they may not be at a place of articulating their struggles. We are to honor them anyway.

How could learning about your parents' journeys help you empathize with them?

Earlier, we defined what honoring means. Sometimes, the struggle to honor can be clarified by understanding what honoring is NOT. This clarity is also important for those who lean towards "staying tight." You must be sure to continue in the maturing process and not get stuck in the figurative role of a child.

Read Ephesians 6:1-5.

Who is Paul specifically addressing in verse 1?

What are children told to do?

Who is Paul addressing in verse 4?

Who is Paul addressing in verse 5?

In this portion of Paul's letter to the Ephesians, he is giving specific instructions for specific types of people. Children are told to obey. Multiple times through Scripture, including the Ten Commandments, we are told to honor our parents. We should honor our parents at all times, regardless of our age. It is only in the context of being a child, however, that we are told to obey our parents.

Many adult children still function as children. Women can spend a lifetime trying to be Miss Perfect to please their parents. I will always be the daughter of Dave and Lynne Lichtermann, but I am no longer their child.

We must shift our obedience to our Heavenly Father as we move into adulthood.

This shift should occur as we mature into adulthood and should not be delayed until marriage. We are now accountable to the Lord for our actions. Many women feel torn by not following their parents' instructions when they are grown. While honoring means we always show kindness, respect, and humility, we must not get stuck continuing in the role of a child in an adult body.

What difference should it make in your life to acknowledge you are now accountable to God rather than your parents?

Respected author and Biblical psychologist, Henry Cloud, offered this perspective for those still struggling to leave the child role:

(The) inability to get out of the child role and still want parental approval involves
the process of needing something from your parents that you did not get. When there

is something you are still looking for like love, acceptance, approval, validation or other ingredients that parents are supposed to give children to prepare them to be adults; you can be stuck waiting for them to finally grant you what you never had. You never really leave and become an adult because you are still waiting for "something."

The truth is if it hasn't happened by now, they are probably not able to give you what you want anyway. You have to get those things from the people of God He has surrounded you with. They are to be your new spiritual family, and God gave them to you to help you "grow up in all things" (Ephesians 4:15,16). If you are still waiting for your parents to give you something they cannot give, then it is time to grieve that and get on with growing up."[2]

What is the difference between honoring and obeying?

What specific ways can you choose to honor your parents? Bring some ideas to small group to discuss.

There are certainly circumstances that make it challenging to obey the Lord in this area. What if our parents or in-laws may not be believers? What if our parents suffer with mental health issues? What if there has been abuse within our home? What if there has been a divorce? What then? As believers, we are still called to honor our parents. All of these situations will require us to lean more on the Lord and His Spirit to give us wisdom. We must remember that we are not responsible for their actions, but we are responsible for our actions and our responses. Whatever way you express your honor, you should extend grace and recognize their efforts in raising you.

What was the most meaningful statement or Scripture you read today?

What does God want you to do in response to today's study?

Please see our Recommend Reading page for resources to help you if you would like more information on this subject.

LEAVING YOUR HOME
KARIN CONLEE

As I stated yesterday, most of us are pretty successful at honoring our parents or leaving and cleaving, but most of us are not stellar at both. Honoring our parents is a call to all of us. As we leave our teen years, our relationship with our parents must be redefined so we continue maturing as God designed. This transition is critical for us to truly have relationships without regrets. We are no longer called to obey them. Instead, we must be accountable to God.

> The accountability changes, but the need to honor our parents remains the same.

As we turn to the other end of the continuum, we will explore the subject of leaving and cleaving. Obviously, this relational dynamic is encountered as you enter marriage. I have two cautions before we dive in:

1. This study is intended to make you a godlier woman.

- If you are married: Apply the truths to you, not your spouse. God will honor your obedience, not you highlighting "leaving and cleaving" tips for your husband and placing your book by his nightstand! (Remember: There is no Mr. Perfect, either!)
- If you are single: Any married woman would tell you that this topic of leaving and cleaving can wreak havoc early in a marriage, if a couple is not equipped with God's perspective. Explore and absorb as much of God's truth about this subject now so you will be an asset for your future husband.

2. Do not make the mistake of thinking that this does not apply to you if you said "I do" many years ago.

Our relationship with our spouse and our extended families are important enough that an annual (at least) check-up is highly recommended. Speaking as someone who has had her in-laws living very close by for the last five years, (like 25 feet), the dynamics and boundaries change through the various seasons of life. Keeping this as a healthy and open subject between you and your spouse is important to provide clarity and unity in your marriage, especially when you are called to care for an aging parent.

God has designed the process that instructs, "Therefore a man shall leave his father and his mother and hold fast to his wife, and they shall become one flesh." (Genesis 2:24 ESV). The Hebrew word for *leave* comes from a root word that means to "loosen or to relinquish or to forsake." For marriage to work, the spouse needs to loosen her ties with her family of origin and forge new ones with the new family she is creating through marriage.

In Genesis 2:24, who does Scripture say should leave their mother and father?

Why does the woman need to "loosen or to relinquish or forsake" too?

This verse makes sense in the context that the new husband is establishing his own home and inviting his new wife to become one with him. It is the picture of the man being the initiator. He is going and establishing a place to live and then, once able to offer a place to shelter her, he invites his love to marry him and make her home with him. From an emotional standpoint, however, the act of leaving our home of origin and becoming a new family impacts both newlyweds. As the woman responds to her future husband's invitation to join him, she too must loosen, relinquish or forsake various relationships as she weds. Failure to make this transition can explain some of the pressure women feel as they try to live in two worlds.

The need to reorient our priorities and ourselves within this new home usually focuses on two critical areas: decision making and emotional connections. No matter if it has been days or decades since you exchanged vows, you agreed to follow your husband. If you did not trust him to make good decisions, then you should not have married him! As women, we must be sure not to run to our parents to help us make decisions within our marriage. We must trust that as a husband and wife, we can talk through subjects and come to decisions.

If you are married, is there a specific area that you are seeking advice from your family that dishonors your husband?

Certainly, wise counsel is always advisable for a couple when needed, but we must be cautious not to lean too heavily on our parents. Even the most well-meaning parents and in-laws are put in a precarious position when we seek their advice, especially if you are not unified as a couple in your approach. Your husband must know that you trust him implicitly and not sense you distrust him, if you jointly seek counsel.

The second key area is the heart.

> As our marital status changes from single to married,
> we also must change our primary emotional connections.

Our spouse should become our primary confidant. If your husband is not as talkative or engaged, it can be tempting to turn to our family of origin for the level of interaction we desire.

Have you been tempted to have your emotional needs met from your family of origin rather than your spouse? If so, specify how.

I strongly caution you against this pattern. Calling a parent and sharing our deepest needs and dreams with them robs our husband of the level of emotional intimacy reserved for him. It may take some patience and time to develop the level of emotional connection you desire within your marriage, but the investment will be well worth it. It goes without saying that we can maintain healthy relationships with our parents. I would also encourage you to have female friends. Your husband needs to meet your primary emotional needs, but not all of them.

> You want your extended family and friends to have a valuable,
> but secondary role when it comes to your emotional needs.

What are ways you can help develop this dynamic of your marriage? (If this is a strength for you, what is one thing you have done to stay connected emotionally to your spouse?)

If you are single, have you seen your parents engage with your grandparents in a healthy or unhealthy way?

If you are already married, how can you gauge whether you have been able to leave and cleave successfully? Take this simple test below to gauge if you and your husband need to work on leaving and cleaving.

Rank the following statements 1-5 with 1 meaning this statement is very true for you and 5 meaning this statement is very untrue for you.

_____ **My spouse and I tend to get really grumpy when we spend time with our families.**

_____ **My spouse (and/or children) feel like they get my leftover energy.**

_____ **We are consistently receiving financial gifts or aid from our parents with stated or implied strings attached.**

_____ **We are consistently receiving unsolicited advice from our parents.**

_____ **When something good or bad happens to me, I first call a parent instead of my spouse.**

_____ **We often end up arguing about our extended family with both of us defending our families of origin.**

Do you need to work on leaving and cleaving? If you received a lower score, which of these issues do you struggle with the most?

What is one change YOU can make this week?

As with most relationship issues, it is critical for you and your husband to address the core issues each of you are struggling with rather than the symptom. Often jealousy or insecurity surface if a spouse has not made her loyalty clear to her husband over her family of origin.

When we initially prayed through my husband's mom coming to live in a mother-in-law suite attached to us, I had to sort through my emotions. What were my concerns? What was fear and what were legitimate areas that needed to be discussed? Five years later, I can say that I have been able to have a very good relationship with my mother-in-law because there was healthy communication between my husband and me. Obviously, we have a somewhat unique situation, but all couples need to be on the same page regarding both of their parents so they can each be at peace in the various relationships.

If you and your husband have work to do in this area, I highly encourage you to find time when you are rested and in a good frame of mind to gently approach the subject. The majority of leaving and cleaving difficulties can be resolved between you and your husband. Sort out the core issues and then make a unified game plan before involving either set of parents.

It is important to establish healthy boundaries while also honoring each other's parents. As we have said for the last two days, this is not an "either/or" option. As you and your husband develop healthy interactions with your in-laws, you will be a huge asset in the process if you choose to believe the best about your parents and your in-laws. Not enough guidance is given to newlyweds on how to relate to each other's parents. Keep in mind that loving your in-laws is actually loving your husband. Give the relationship time to develop. Just like it takes time for you and your spouse to develop a rhythm and build trust in all areas of marriage, the same is true for our relationships with our in-laws.

Before we conclude for today, I want to address one additional aspect of leaving and, more specifically, cleaving. For some women, leaving is not a problem. We have grown up with multiple generations of independent women. With more women delaying marriage longer than our mothers and grandmothers, it is possible for a woman to have lived independently and made thousands of significant decisions on her own before marriage.

Leaving parents may have come naturally, but the act of coming up under your husband and being grafted as one may still need to be addressed. Earlier in our lesson, I identified that God designed the man as the initiator and the woman as a responder.

Have you considered the fact that your husband is designed as the initiator in your relationship or is this a new concept?

As a single woman, how do you need to begin thinking regarding this area of initiator and responder to prepare yourself for a future spouse?

How can failing to leave your family of origin AND cleave to your husband sabotage your husband's development as the initiator?

How has our culture moved away from embracing a woman's design as a responder?

I have yet to meet a woman who wants to be married to a spineless, opinion-less man. Despite the constant drum beat that we can do it all, at our most honest points we want a strong protector, provider, and warrior. God designed men to be just that. We could remove so much pressure from our own lives if we trusted God with our husbands and stopped trying to do their job for them!

Consider this insightful research and commentary by Mary Kassian:

> When Adam laid his eyes on the woman, he broke into an exuberant and spontaneous poem. "This at last is bone of my bones and flesh of my flesh. She shall be called woman [Ishsha] because she was taken out of man [Ish]" (Genesis 2:23). The first man called himself Ish and the woman Ishsha, and this appears to be a very clever and very profound play on words. Ish comes from the root meaning "strength." So the man said, "I am strength." Ishsha comes from the root meaning "soft." "I am strength; she is soft. She is able to receive; I was meant ...to give."
>
> The implication becomes clear when we observe the biblical meaning of a man's strength. The Hebrew root word is commonly associated with the wisdom and strength and vitality of a successful warrior. It carries the idea of a champion valiantly serving his people by protectively fighting on their behalf... He is strong, directed by inner softness, and she is soft, directed by inner strength...
>
> Man was created to actively and joyfully initiate and give, and the woman was created to actively and joyfully respond and receive and relate. She's the beautiful soft one. Each is a perfect counterpart to the other.[3]

The culture wants us to believe that Christianity teaches that women are to be doormats. How does the thought that "a man is strong, directed by inner softness and a woman is soft, directed by inner strength" help you grasp God's perfect design for both men and women?

For some women, they are desperate to see their husband become the initiator. In the absence of leadership, we can often be like Eve and step in to lead. I beg you, unless you are in physical danger, stop leading. Take your concern to God and ask Him to restore your husband's confidence to initiate. Ask the Lord to show you how you can play a part in answering that prayer. Telling him he needs to initiate will only shut him down further. If you are single, ask God to give you the grace to protect your God-given design to respond as you face a dating culture that screams the opposite.

Ladies, it is when we allow our husbands to initiate that we, in our quieted strength, give them the room to become the valiant warrior God intended. When we choose to remain stubbornly independent or dominating in our marriages, we squelch the greatest God-placed qualities in each of us. Let's be good "cleavers" for our own joy and for God's glory! To choose anything less than God's design is to create unintended pressure for both you and your husband.

What was the most meaningful statement or Scripture you read today?

What does God want you to do in response to today's study?

PASSING IT ON
KARIN CONLEE

Today, we move from our relationships with those a generation ahead of us to the generation after us, our children. No relief, huh? Both generations have sets of dynamics that can strike to the core of our soul with either great joy or anxiety on any given day. Each relationship that the Lord allows is purposeful and powerful; but there is something so dynamic and unfathomable within the privilege of bringing life into this world and then being accountable to set that sweet child on a path of righteousness. If you do not have children, I encourage you to continue with today's lesson. Many of these truths have application outside of parenting. We are all called to make disciples so we can all use these truths. Additionally, if you can learn from the mistakes of others who have gone before you, you will spare your family a difficult learning curve if children are in your future.

My own life provides the segue into this expansive topic. This very morning in my Priority Time, I was in 1 Corinthians 10. Turn and read 1 Corinthians 10:13. As I completed my journaling, I wrote down the question, "Where am I tempted?" I am not exactly sure what I expected to write as my answer, but the Holy Spirit did not delay in bringing my temptation front and center. I am tempted to control. How about you? Do you ever struggle with the desire to control...your children? Immediately, the Lord brought back Mark's comment from the night before. "Mom, lately I feel like all you do is tell me things I need to do and then check to see if I have done them yet." Guilty as charged. Maybe some of you struggle with this too.

Why do we try to control our children?

I know...to protect them, or help them, or teach them. These are all true within reason, but behind all of that, we are often tempted to control out of fear. We fear failure. Sometimes we control because we fear THEY will fail. Other times, we control because we fear WE will fail. Our children may be 2, 12, or 32 and we can still battle this. After all, it is hard to be Miss Perfect if your children don't play along, right? When they are younger, our controlling is very direct. After all, they need substantial leadership. As they grow, our controlling usually becomes subtler.

If you have children, finish this sentence:

I am really afraid my child will_____.

Can you trust your God, who is also your child's Heavenly Father, with this fear?

Is He able to handle your burden?

Is there anyone else more capable for you to trust this burden to?

Our tendency as women can be to try to solve the humanly unsolvable through trying to control circumstances and people. If God has brought something to mind, stop and share your burden with God now. Ask Him for the grace to replace your tendency to control or fear with the discipline of prayer.

I remember one of my child's first "report cards" from Mother's Day Out. My husband and I sat in Chick-fil-A as our children climbed the tunnels and I wiped away tears because I was sure that this less than stellar report signaled doom. I laugh at myself now, but all of us have likely gone down the slippery slope of what-if in our minds. What if they fail a grade? What if they don't make the honor roll? What if they don't go to college? What if they date someone I don't like? What if they never eat vegetables? What if... What if... What if...

As moms, future moms, and even role models, we must correct this issue of fearing the future and controlling by truly entrusting them to the Lord. Is it any wonder that we feel pressure in our lives, if we feel like we have the power and obligation to control the future? Interestingly, if we study Scripture, we see that God wants our families to experience success and has laid out our role in it. As we turn to Deuteronomy 6, we will enter into a scene where Moses is delivering God's instructions to the Israelites.

Read Deuteronomy 6:1-3. What would occur if they followed God's instructions?

Read Deuteronomy 6:4-5. This is an incredibly significant passage. It is known as the Shema that means "to hear." Moses gets their attention and tells them to hear, to take careful notice. What Moses wanted them to hear is the cornerstone of our faith and later, Christ called it the greatest commandment.

What are the Israelites instructed to do?

Read Deuteronomy 6:6-9.

Notice that the Israelites are called to action and THEN called to teach their children to follow, too. Moses' first instruction was to the adults. Moses was addressing the men as the leaders. You cannot live out verse 7, if you do not live out verse 5!

Reread Deuteronomy 6:5 and 6:7. Why is fulfillment of verse 5 necessary before you can be successful at obeying verse 7?

Moses speaks metaphorically here: "Sitting suggests inactivity; and walking, of course, activity. Together they encompass all human effort. Likewise, to retire at night and to rise up in the morning speaks to the totality of time."[4] No matter what time of day or what we are doing, we are communicating something to our children.

If your child were to answer, what would he or she say is communicated most frequently from you to your child?

Convicting, huh? As women following the Lord, I believe our desire is to obey God's Word and to impart a heart for God to our children. So why does it not always happen? Consider one possibility: If you do not love the Lord with all your own heart, soul, and strength, and you try to speak of the Lord from a place of observation not experience, this will seem like a daunting task. I am not just speaking to the question of salvation, though that is to be considered. You may even have a relationship with the Lord, but if it is anemic and does not receive the time and nurture it needs, then it is hard to fulfill God's instructions in Deuteronomy 6:7.

As moms, we constantly need to find ways to streamline and simplify our lives. There is not, however, a shortcut to producing God-honoring, God-protected children. As moms, we always forego things for the sake of our children. How many times do we buy our children something they want instead of something for ourselves? We pass the last strawberries down the table for them to have seconds, knowing we never had "firsts."

> You cannot skip your discipleship process and expect for your children to have a passion for the Lord. If you are not a disciple, you will not produce a disciple.

We must take the time to daily be in His Word and in prayer so that we develop a strong relationship with our Heavenly Father. It is only when we talk to our children and continually impart truth to them birthed from our own love for the Lord that they will desire to follow.

We have had seasons of success and seasons of failure getting our children to complete different devotionals and Priority Times. My hope and trust is that as they continue to grow in their faith, they will begin to have a greater ownership of their own walk. If we just forced them to complete a legalistic routine, I am certain we would do more harm than good. Do you know when I do see their hearts warm towards God? When I come to them in humility sharing something that God taught me about me, not them. They know most of my flaws. When God shows something to me and I share this with them, when appropriate, they rarely look shocked. I have not heard them say, "Wow, Mom I never realized that was a weakness of yours." They usually nod. They have already figured out I am not Miss Perfect! When they see our submission to our Heavenly Father and the results of us humbly seeking Him, our children see a real relationship that makes us a better person... and that is something they will realize they want and need as they mature.

In post-biblical Judaism, the last instruction of Deuteronomy 6:8 was followed literally. Jews would place mini rolled up portions of the Torah in little boxes that were attached to a band and tied around their foreheads. They wanted to constantly be reminded of God's truth.

We might not put portions of the Torah between our eyes, but how should we still accomplish the same objective?

Read Deuteronomy 6:10-18. What does God warn the people about?

The Lord was warning them not to forget Him when they did enter the Promised Land. We may not be headed to a literal Promised Land on this earth with our family, but the truth is still relevant to us.

As a point of application, have you found yourself less dependent upon the Lord when things are going well?

How do you show less dependence on the Lord when things are going smoothly for your family?

What are two to three tangible things that you need to do differently to protect yourself from forgetting the Lord's faithfulness when you are in a season of peace?

Let me contextualize the truths of Deuteronomy 6. God tells us to love Him with all of our being and to teach our children to do the same. The Lord tells us not to forget Him when things are going smoothly and to be prepared to remind our children why we do what we do when they ask. You can make a list and follow this to the letter of the law and still have children far from God. The difference in your children running to God or running from Him will be most influenced by the level of genuine love you have for the Lord. It may be a familiar saying, but it is also very true: your faith will be more caught than taught.

As a parent, we must remember that we too are children of God. Our Heavenly Father needs us to do our part: love God and teach our children about Him. Beyond that, our controlling will not produce the type of relationship in them or in us that is desirable. As moms, we can be so focused on the external behavior of our children that we miss addressing heart issues. As Chris, my husband, would affirm, I can lean towards the area of legalism. At one point, a wise counselor told me that if I always win the external battle, that I may get my children to obey, but I will lose their hearts. As we consider both our relationship with God and our relationship with our children, we must be more focused on the heart than on the behavior. If that makes you worry, have no fear. When our hearts are right, the behavior takes care of itself!

In your own relationship with the Lord, what are you doing that might be considered external, but you are not necessarily obeying from a heart of love? Put another way: where are you just going through the motions?

If you are a mother, what is an example of an outward behavior that you want changed in your child?

What is the issue at a heart level?

Whether we realize it or not, our ultimate goal should be our righteousness and our children becoming righteous. Righteousness is thrown around in the Bible, but what exactly do we mean? A good definition for righteousness is obeying from a heart of love. Ultimately, that is our aim. As we shepherd our children, we must realize that a long list of do's and dont's with hefty consequences may achieve the desired external response, but if your leadership of your child does not move beyond the behavior to the heart, you will likely produce more rebellion than righteousness. Spare your children from the empty pursuit of external perfection and allow them to learn early what God's true purpose is for their lives.

What was the most meaningful statement or Scripture you read today?

What does God want you to do in response to today's study?

BEING AT PEACE

KARIN CONLEE

We have spent the last few days on a journey through a variety of different relationships. While our relationship with God, our parents, our spouse, and our children are some of our most intimate relationships, we have hardly scratched the surface of relational dynamics. Certainly, there are many more that we will not be able to specifically address.

As Gary Smalley says in *The DNA of Relationships*, "Life is relationships. The rest is just details."[5] God wired us for relationships. We usually view our level of joy, success, or regret through the lens of relationships. Everything in life can be going well, but if our relationships are not healthy, all of the other "stuff" does not matter. At the beginning of this week, we set out to show you how women were designed in the context of relationships. Recall the principle that we are DESIGNED to receive unconditional love through our relationship with the Lord and that enables us to share Christ's love in all the relationships God brings to us.

Consider our design as you read Romans 12:18 below.

If possible, so far as it depends upon you, live peaceably with all.

What is most challenging to you about this verse?

To be at peace with all is a tall order. The majority of women would likely feel pretty comfortable if Paul gave us just a little wiggle room. What if the Lord called us to be at peace with just 90% of our relationships? Seems a little more doable, right? There is always that one… or those few. So, how do we obey Romans 12:18?

> We must understand that being at peace with all is not dependent upon the "all."

To be at peace with all men, we must first be at peace with God and at peace with ourselves. Before you can be at peace in your horizontal relationships, you must be at work on your vertical (God) and internal (self) relationships.

As we examine these three spheres of relationships, we must realize that they are interconnected. If we are not at peace with God, then we will not be able to be at peace with others or ourselves. Similarly, when we are not at peace with who we are, we will have a hard time finding peace in our human relationships. All of us can think of a time when we were struggling internally and it caused us to act unbecomingly to someone we cared about. When we are in conflict with someone, we are out of sync with both the Lord and ourselves. We wrestle between the desires of our own flesh to be right and knowing that we should extend the same grace and forgiveness that God extended to us. Do you see how none of the three relationships ever lives in isolation?

Which of the three relationships (God, self, or others) seems to need the most help for you?

To say that we must be at peace means that we must define what that looks like. God is not suggesting that this verse is only possible when all of our life is on the mountaintop. Quite the contrary, peace is not circumstantial. Peace comes through security. The security we need must start from the Lord. We cannot provide our own security (though we try!) and friends cannot provide the security we need (though we sometimes ask this of them). Security comes through unconditional love. If we rewind all the way back to our week on Identity, we will realize that if we do the heart level work on our identity, then we will have the capacity to be at peace with all.

Accepting the fact that God loves us unconditionally is difficult for some. On a scale of 1-10, with 10 being "I completely embrace the fact that God loves me and He will never stop loving me," where would you place yourself?

If you cannot confidently say "10," then I ask you to change your perspective because that is EXACTLY what God does. God does not view us through our fallen nature anymore!

Read Hebrews 10:11-14.

According to verse 11, what did the priests do when they were under the law?

What was the effectiveness of the priests continually making sacrifices? (v11)

How many offerings did Christ make? (v12)

What was the result for those being sanctified? (v14)

"Those being sanctified" are all who have repented of their sins and placed their faith in Christ. If you have a personal relationship with the Lord, then you are being sanctified AND that means you have been perfected for all time!

Read Hebrews 10:15-18.

God gave us the Holy Spirit to remind us of His truth. Then, what does God say about how He views our sin? (v17)

You can be at peace with God because through Christ's death and resurrection, God is already at peace with you. God loves you as His child. He says He will remember our sins and lawless deeds no more! Sometimes we get stuck with this concept because we know we are not living the life God desires. Can He be more pleased with you, YES... but does His love for you change? Absolutely not! Think about it in the context of earthly children. Can I be more pleased with my children, sure! I love it when they obey me and follow my direction, but I don't love them less... even on their most defiant day!

Sometimes we act like the Old Testament priests and forget the incredible sacrifice of Christ. We keep trying to make sacrifices when they are useless and there is no longer a debt to pay. Maybe our pursuit of Miss Perfect would be the female version of Mr. Pharisee? Accept God's love and be at peace.

When you grasp that God loves you, you can begin to be at peace with yourself.

What keeps someone from being at peace with herself?

There is not enough blank space in this book to write out all the reasons women are not at peace with themselves. This lack of peace is usually what drives us to try to be the imaginary Miss Perfect. If we address two primary areas, however, the majority of our battles can be won. First, we must realize that God does not make mistakes. If you can accept this, then you can begin to accept you. God did not make a mistake when He designed you. Remove the pressure to be someone else. You have exactly the strengths, talents, and gifts you need. Decide to become the best you that you can be, but stop being ungrateful for how God made you. Second, stop comparing yourself to others.

What are areas in which you need to commit to stop comparing yourself to others?

What does all this stuff about God and self have to do with friendships? Everything! It is only when we are at peace with God and ourselves that we make a good friend. So often, when we are not at peace internally or vertically, we put unrealistic pressures on friendships. We need unconditional love. We spend time looking for expressions of love and attention as a substitute for what only God can provide. We must have a non-performance-based relationship with God and ourselves before we can have non-performance-based relationships with others.

When we are no longer trying so hard to get something from a friendship, then we are free to give to the relationship. It is at this point that friendships begin to mirror Christ's relationship. Our friendships can begin to be birthed out of our being able to give, not out of our need to receive.

Read Hebrews 10:19-25.

This is written in the context of how the new covenant, through the crucifixion and resurrection of Christ, has made a way for believers to leave behind a system of sacrifice and to now live on mission. Verses 10:19-23 acknowledge that Christ became the ultimate sacrifice and now He faithfully watches over us! We can be at peace because of the new covenant. God looks at us through the lens of the new covenant He created. Centuries later, this truth applies to us!

What should Christ-honoring relationships look like? (v24-25)

What are some specific, practical examples of how you could apply this truth to one of your friendships?

We live in a sinful, fallen world, but we have been given a path through Christ that allows us to be at peace while we are here on Earth. In even the toughest of relational dynamics, there is a way for us to remain at peace with ourselves and avoid the landmines of relational regret. When we are vertically and internally healthy, the opportunity to be at peace with all is within reach. We can love others without expecting or needing them to be perfect while we trust God to be at work on His timetable in them.

What was the most meaningful statement or Scripture you read today?

What does God want you to do in response to today's study?

NOTES FOR THE WEEK

PRAYER WITHOUT PRETENSE

A woman develops her prayer life by simply listening and talking to God.

Day One
PRIORITY OF PRAYER

Day Two
PATTERN OF PRAYER PART 1

Day Three
PATTERN OF PRAYER PART 2

Day Four
PERSISTENCE IN PRAYER

Day Five
PRACTICES, PROMISES, AND PROBLEMS

PRIORITY OF PRAYER

CHRIS KUHLMAN

Two weeks ago, we explored the relational disciplines of spending time in God's Word, meditation, and Scripture memorization. We held off discussing one of my favorite relational disciplines until now... prayer. If I were to ask the average person walking down the street if they pray, the answer I would almost always receive would be "yes." Most people engage in some form of "prayer." But what is prayer? Why is it important? If I were to further probe into the reason behind why people pray, I bet I would discover that it's because they want something they can't get by themselves.

What are the common motivations behind your prayers?

Prayer is so dear to my heart. It draws me into an intimate, loving relationship with my Creator. I have experienced great growth in my life because of prayer. I haven't always had the desire for prayer that I have now. Still today, I constantly fight to give prayer proper priority in my day. It has taken time and practice to get to a place where I have a constant yearning to be in a close relationship with God. I hope through this week that you will develop such a taste for prayer that you will be willing to fight to keep it a priority in your life, too.

Remember when your relationship with your husband or boyfriend was brand new and you couldn't wait to tell him all about your day? If you're like me, you couldn't wait to get him on the phone or see his face over dinner. Maybe you are in that sweet place right now. In this day and age of social media, we can instantly connect with the ones we love. I am constantly amazed at the amount of time that people can spend texting back and forth. They are never without their phone, which is their constant connection. Can you imagine having that same kind of longing for a conversation with God that you do with those you feel especially close to?

A woman develops her prayer life by simply listening and talking to God.

We were designed by God to be in communication with Him. He created us to love Him. Can you have a love relationship with someone without talking to them? Definitely not. You know as well as I do that women were made for conversation! And in God we have someone who loves to listen and asks us to come to Him and share everything. Think about the close relationships you have in your life now.

Would a lack of communication in those relationships create intimacy or distance?

WEEK SIX

Read how the Psalms capture a hunger for God. Circle the word or phrases in these verses that describe this longing for God.

Psalm 63:1,8

> [1] O God, you are my God; earnestly I seek you; my soul thirsts for you; my flesh faints for you, as in a dry and weary land where there is no water. [8] My soul clings to you; your right hand upholds me.

Psalm 119:10

> With my whole heart I seek you; let me not wander from your commandments!

The most magnificent thing on this earth is that God gives each of us the opportunity to know Him. And just like in any healthy, thriving relationship, if we want to know Him we must spend time with Him.

> ## Daily fellowship with God should be the chief goal of our lives.

We must have a deep desire, a passion that will drive us to action.

Many of you are tensing up right now. Some of you may even be realizing that you don't have that deep desire, and there's no way you want to voice that out loud. It's ok. You can get there. You may be thinking of all the pulls you have on your life—work, bills, school, taking care of the house, perhaps children or the desire to be a godly wife. You may think you do not have enough time or peace and quiet to be able to pray. Frankly, some of you don't even think you have the energy. Amazingly, all of these legitimate reasons or excuses will fall away when you see God's activity through your time with Him.

Our biggest obstacle to prayer is ourselves.

Do you have any of the "pulls" listed above in your life? Will you take an honest look at yourself and mark where you are in desiring to have a stronger prayer life?

Place an X where you are now in your desire, and place a cross where you want to be.

No desire   **I am in constant communion**

No matter where you are in your life, He can deepen your relationship with Him through the relational discipline of prayer. Jesus is our example. Today, we will look at a few of Jesus' prayers and tomorrow we will look at His instructions to the disciples when they asked Him how to pray.

Hebrews 5:7 (CEV) says,

> God had the power to save Jesus from death. And while Jesus was on earth, he begged God with loud crying and tears to save him. He truly worshipped God, and God listened to his prayers.

Describe how Jesus prayed in this verse.

It may make you feel a bit uncomfortable to read that Jesus so desperately cried out for God to intervene. Jesus was fully God and fully man, but in His humanity He was feeling the weight of the physical sacrifice ahead and the separation from the Father that He would have to endure to be our Savior. Ponder that. In the very next words we see He worshipped God. He brought every part of His humanity into submission to the will of the Father. He could do that because He had such a strong and loving relationship with the Father. Take a moment to stop and reflect on what feelings and emotions you would have knowing that you were going to endure such suffering.

List some of those feelings and emotions.

God the Son was dealing with those same feelings. Yet because He KNEW the Father, He could rest in the Father's will and know it was best. God knows your feelings, too. He can handle any feeling you bring to Him. God wants us to be honest when we come to Him. He is not looking for clichés, pretense, or pretty poems when you pray. He wants you to come to Him just as you are. GET REAL.

Jesus prayed all the time. He prayed at His baptism, (Luke 3:21) in the desert (Luke 5:16), before choosing His disciples (Luke 6:12,13), at the transfiguration (Luke 9:29), and at Gethsemane (Mark 14:32-39).

When did Jesus pray? Note what each reference says.

Mark 1:35

Luke 6:12

Where did Jesus pray?

Matthew 14:23

Mark 6:46

We discussed this in our week on relational disciplines, but it is worth elaborating on here in the context of prayer. Where you pray determines how you will pray. GET ALONE. Jesus got away so He could be alone with His Father without distractions. We need to be somewhere that we have the freedom to be transparent. From a practical perspective, praying silently is very challenging. I don't recommend it. GET LOUD. Be somewhere that you have the freedom to pray out loud or write out your prayers. Your posture is also important. You may have the desire to kneel. Be somewhere that you have the freedom to move into a position that you desire. Sometimes, we still can get distracted. If that is the case, I recommend keeping a little pad of paper nearby. If a random thought on Miss Perfect's to-do list goes floating through your mind, just quickly jot it down so you don't try to remember it while you are praying.

Prayer was a priority in Jesus' life. He continually sought out a quiet place so He could pray because prayer was His bridge to the Father while dwelling on this earth. It's important to see the relationship Jesus had to the Father through prayer. He always submitted to the authority of the Father.

In the following verses, read and mark the phrase that describes how Jesus related to His Father.

> [19] The Son can do nothing by himself; he can do only what he sees his Father doing, because whatever the Father does the Son also does. [30] By myself I can do nothing; I judge only as I hear and my judgment is just, for I seek not to please myself but him who sent me. (John 5:19,30 NIV)

> For I have come down from heaven not to do my will but to do the will of him who sent me. (John 6:38)

How would developing your prayer life help you to submit more to the Father?

Jesus had a confidence that His Father knew what He needed. We can have that same confidence. Even when we do not understand life's circumstances we can rest assured that God does. How we pray is directly related to what we think about God. If we have a problem with prayer, it is often because we have an inaccurate view of God. If you are uncertain whether God is personal or good, or in control, or concerned about ordinary things, you are bound to conclude that prayer is pointless and you won't do it.

Can God move the impossible? Can He work in my unsaved husband? Can He bring me contentment when I am alone? Can He bring a dead marriage to life? Will He send me a husband? Will He heal my broken family? Can He bring my kids back to Himself? As Christians, we are daughters of the King so we can approach God confidently. The Father delights in our coming to Him. He delights in our joy and brings comfort in our sorrow. He wants to hear about both our greatest needs and our "ordinary" day.

Prayer is powerful and yet uncomplicated. Prayer is simply talking and listening to God. Don't miss the listening! If we do pray, we are notorious for coming to God, unloading our needs, and quickly saying "Amen." Prayer is a two-way relationship, so we must also listen. GET QUIET. Sometimes that seems weird since we don't hear an audible voice respond. So what does listening to God look like? Listening occurs in our prayer time when we stay in an attitude of prayer and let God bring thoughts and answers to our mind. If you take the thoughts and answers and hold them up against Scripture, you can always know if it was God answering or our own idea. If it is in alignment with His Word, it is likely Him. If it is not, then chuck it! So many times we rush through our prayers and then we wonder why we're not hearing God just like when we rush through reading a few verses. A relationship will blossom, if you give it some time!

Because Christ paid the price for our sins on the cross, and because He is our High Priest, we can enter the presence of God boldly, with confidence. In His presence we begin to change. It moves us more than it moves God. I have learned that as I spend time in prayer, my love for Jesus grows into a passion that permeates everything in my life! He is my satisfaction. He wants to be your satisfaction. He can be.

What was the most meaningful statement or Scripture you read today?

What does God want you to do in response to today's study?

PATTERN OF PRAYER PART 1
CHRIS KUHLMAN

Our world has taken a very simple thing and with the aid of the enemy has ended up portraying prayer in such a way that it is common for people to distance themselves from this relational discipline. Maybe you have been to a church or flipped the channels and seen prayer modeled as a very formal, rote part of a ceremony or religious service and wondered, "How can that change my life at all?" Others have seen someone pray out loud in a more relational way, but are convinced that they themselves must not be any good at praying. Even when a group of normal "Chatty Cathys" gather to eat, if it is suggested that someone bless the meal there is usually someone experiencing internal hot sweats hoping it will not be her name that is called.

While formal and public prayers have a place, neither accurately represents God's heartbeat on prayer.

Prayer is most frequently a private discipline.

God desires for us to grow in an intimate relationship with Him by daily communication. If you don't experience that intimacy with God through prayer, you may feel like you are missing out on something in this Christian life. You are, but you don't have to any longer! I want to help you understand how to develop this relational discipline of prayer.

If you are thinking, "I don't really know how to pray," you are in good company. Let's look in Luke 11 and read about how the disciples were thinking the very same thing. The disciples were living everyday life with Jesus and saw firsthand that He spent a lot of time alone with His Heavenly Father. The result was spiritual power and wisdom. Could this happen for them as well? Is this possible for you? Allow this week to be a defining moment in your relationship with God as we see how Jesus wants us to pray.

Read Luke 11:1-4.

How does Jesus address God?

Jesus had an intimate relationship with God. He calls Him Father. This Greek word, "Pater," is used to signify a nourisher, protector. How do these two words color the meaning of Father to you?

Look at some other passages of Scripture that describe our relationship with God.

John 1:12-13

> [12] But to all that did receive him, who believed in his name, he gave the right to become children of God, [13] who were born not of blood nor of the will of the flesh nor of the will of man, but of God.

2 Corinthians 6:18

> And I will be a father to you, and you shall be sons and daughters to me, says the Lord Almighty.

Matthew 6:6

> But when you pray, go into your room and shut the door and pray to your Father who is in secret. And your Father who sees in secret will reward you.

Based on these verses what is our relationship with God?

The fact that we are praying to our Heavenly Father has enormous repercussions. God gave us the parent/child relationship on this earth so we could have some small grasp of how He views us.

One day as I was meditating on Scripture, the Lord showed me two distinct ways to grasp the significance of the fact that a perfect, powerful God is also my Father. We can see God as our "Father who is in heaven" or that "God in heaven is our Father." Do you see the difference? Both are meant to increase our wonder and our joy, so that we can come to Him anytime.

The first way to approach God is to think of His greatness. He is holy, infinite, and eternal. As Solomon in his prayer voiced, "Will God really dwell on earth with man? The heavens, even the highest heavens cannot contain you." God replies in Isaiah 57:15,

> For this is what the high and lofty One says--
> 'I live in a high and holy place,
> But also with him who is *contrite*
> And *lowly in spirit...*'

This God of all power becomes the Father of insignificant sinful people like us, if only we will humble ourselves. This holy, unchanging God stoops down in love and picks us up and lifts us to a place of honor and significance. He gives Himself to us in fellowship and gives us life abundant.

The second way to approach God is to think of Him as our Father and then remind ourselves that He is "in heaven." This means He is free from all the limitations, inadequacies and flaws that are found in earthly fathers. I don't know what kind of father you have had, but even the best earthly father does not compare with our Heavenly Father. If you struggle because your father was absent, or you felt insecure in his love, or you felt betrayed... take heart.

God is a father whose relationship to us is ideal, perfect, and glorious. Dwell on the fact that there is no better father; no parent is more deeply committed to His children's welfare or more wise and generous in promoting it, than God the Creator. You can marvel over the fact that "He is my Father and He's God in heaven; He's God in heaven and He's my Father!"

Before we move to the next aspect of prayer, also consider the fact that we pray to our Heavenly Father defines who we are NOT praying to. Remember that we do not pray to a genie in a bottle, an impersonal tyrant, or an equal partner. Our relationship with Him matters.

When a child comes to her parents, why do the parents listen to her? Because she is their child. It doesn't matter how old she is. When children come to their parents and want to spend time with them it brings joy to the parents' hearts. For the same reason we listen to our children, God listens to us. We don't give our children everything they want just because they come and crawl up in our lap, but we do love it that they want to be so close to us. When they come and don't talk in full sentences or with a great vocabulary it makes no difference to us. We just enjoy the time together and especially enjoy the desire they have to be with us.

How should seeing God as your Heavenly Father shape how you pray?

Flip back to Luke 11:2.

Father,_____ _____ _____ _____.

He is not just our Father, He is our holy Father. We must wrap our minds around the knowledge of His holiness and His uniqueness; there is no one like Him. If we truly call Him Father and acknowledge His holiness, we cannot come to Him in any other way but humbly. As we develop the relational discipline of prayer, we will move closer to God. The closer we get to God the more we will see His holiness and our sinfulness. For this reason, prayer should never create pride but only cause humility. Realizing that He still wants us to come to Him should give us the desire to give Him glory. What comes out of our mouths then is from a heart that is being sanctified by His Holy Spirit. It is when we believe God can do all things, that He moves the heart of man, that He provides for all of our needs, and that He rewards those who diligently seek Him.

Father, hallowed be your name,

_____ _____ _____.

It is God who rules. He is sovereign. That means everything He does, He does for a reason, for His purpose. His purpose for each one of us is to conform us to the likeness of His Son.

> Prayer is not a way to get your way.
> Prayer is a way to get God's will accomplished in us and among us!

We come to Him. We lift up His name. We come in humility emptying our earthly desires to make room in our hearts for His will, His desires, and His rule in our lives. This is why we can't just have a monologue when we pray, we must be still and listen. We must ask God to show us when we are praying our will instead of His.

God's kingdom is so much more than a place. It begins with a relationship that is happening even now on this earth. It exists wherever people allow Jesus to reign in their lives. So, the kingdom of God is a place of grace. It is where the damage done to us by sin is repaired; grace proves to be what the kingdom is all about. Any request for a new display of God's grace by (1) overcoming the enemy and his reign in me and those around me; (2) limiting the effects of evil in this world; or (3) allowing the goodness of God to reach out to others through my life, is all a part of "Your kingdom come."

Bible scholar David Guzik says,"To pray, our Father, requires faith, because he who comes to God must believe that He is. To pray, Your kingdom come, requires hope, because we trust it is to come in fullness. To pray, Your will be done, requires love, because love is the incentive to obey all of God's will."[1]

In praying "Your kingdom come" we are inviting the Father to do something in us. This requires us to be ready to say, "Start with me, use me to be an answer to my prayer."

What are you praying right now that God may want to use you to answer?

Sometimes we pray hoping that God will work in spite of us, certainly not using us! What if it requires me to deny myself or deny something I am holding on to? We pray for God to clean up others' lives but we are not ready to clean up our own lives, making excuses for what we selfishly want to hang on to. Can you pray "Your kingdom come" and really mean it? We are asking for God to strengthen our relationship with Him and to extend that relationship to others so that His will can be accomplished. The purpose of prayer is not that our selfish will be done but to bring our will in line with His will.

Is this a new thought for you? How will you allow it to change your prayer life?

Start with me, Lord. Am I willing to deny myself? Do I want His will to be done even if it's different than what I am asking? I realize that I don't know what's best. I don't always know the direction to go. Wanting God's will to be done may involve quite a personal struggle.

When Jesus was in Gethsemane, He struggled intensely because He did not want to endure the suffering and the rejection that was coming. But through great struggle and turmoil He humbled Himself and became obedient to death (Philippians 2) and said, "Not My will, but Yours be done" (Matthew 26:39,42). What it cost Him to pray this we will never know. What it may cost us to accept God's will we cannot say either. But we are asking God to teach us all that we should do and to make us both willing and able.

> Whether you turn to the right or to the left, your ears will hear a voice behind you, saying, "This is the way; walk in it." Isaiah 30:21 (NIV)

What was the most meaningful statement or Scripture you read today?

What does God want you to do in response to today's study?

PATTERN OF PRAYER PART 2
CHRIS KUHLMAN

Yesterday we began looking at prayer through the relationship we have with God. We pray as a child to a perfect, all-knowing Father. If we didn't have Him as our Father, we would never be able to exchange our selfishness and begin to desire His will. God puts the question to us - What am I to you? I think of relationships today. I work closely with young people, and so many are dealing with relationships with the opposite sex. They often come to me with questions and problems early on in their dating relationship. The first thing I always ask them is if they have defined the relationship. Define your relationship with God. The defining helps us to move in a direction that will complement the relationship. He says, "I am your Father and you are My daughters if you have come to Me through My Son." We want our relationship with the Father to be a growing and thriving one.

Now let's return to the passage in Luke 11:2-3.

Father,
Hallowed be your name,
Your kingdom come.

_____.

The phrases we have looked at in Scripture so far are based on our secure relationship with God and His will. Jesus was demonstrating to the disciples that we should begin our conversation with God acknowledging our relationship and how He is set apart from us. This is not meant to be a prayer formula. It is simply good to remember His love and His superior ways to shape the rest of our conversation.

We commit ourselves to live wholly for God and then naturally we go to our requests. We ask Him to provide our needs for today. We can come to Him for the most mundane of our needs. And He wants us to! Our prayer life enables us to deny our self sufficiency and humbles us so we acknowledge our dependence on God.

> God is concerned about every need we have, physical and spiritual.
> He wants to supply them all.

Most of us can easily see God's blessings in our lives. Whether it is good health, a warm house to live in, good friends, or a healthy marriage, we know that all of these gifts are from the Lord. We acknowledge them as good gifts when we enjoy and delight in them. But if we don't acknowledge God as the giver of those good gifts, we are simply being ungrateful. There is a book by Ann Voskamp called *One Thousand Gifts*. In it she invites her readers to embrace the everyday blessings that God gives as gifts to each of us. If you are struggling to see God's gifts in your life then I would encourage you to get the book and have your eyes opened to the amazing goodness and grace that God gives each of us every day. Take joy in the little things and see them as gifts from the goodness of God's heart to you.

We ask for our "daily bread" just as the Israelites were told to gather their manna - enough for each day. When the Israelites gathered more than they needed, it rotted. God wants His children to realize their daily dependence on Him for their everyday needs. He gives us what we need for the day.

Describe the difference between want and need.

Jesus was not telling the disciples nor us to ask for what we need based on our greed or what we think we need. If what we ask for is not met, maybe it's not really a need, or maybe it's just not His timing. What God gives us is all we need. He will provide our every need every time, in His time. Will you be content with what He provides and then be grateful for it? This is the real test of faith.

How many times have you heard children ask for something and end their plea with "but I neeeeeeed it?" Sometimes they add the statement, "but everybody else has it!" As you well know, sometimes children get their wants and needs mixed up. So many times I come to the Father just like my children have come to me. I decide there is something I need and then I start to beg. God is not stingy with any of His giving. If He has not provided, ask Him to give you His perspective. Sometimes God offers us the greatest protection when He chooses not to give us what we are begging for Him to provide.

Let's continue in Luke 11:2-4.

> **Father,**
> **Hallowed be your name,**
> **Your kingdom come.**
> **Give us each day our daily bread.**

_____

_____.

In this prayer, we move from the physical to the spiritual. Just as we need physical nourishment for our bodies, we need spiritual cleansing and forgiveness because we're sinners. Scripture presents sin as "missing the mark"–that is missing the mark of perfection. Sin is lawbreaking, rebellion, and pollution according to God's standards. We cannot pay God back for our sin. We owe Him, with no way to pay. It is only Christ's work on the cross that can pay that debt.

Early in my walk with Christ, I wondered about confession. If Christ's death paid for *all* my sins, past, present, future, then why do I need to mention my daily sins to God at all? I learned that confession is necessary for me to continue in a healthy relationship with Him. As one of God's adopted daughters, my daily failures never cancel my position in the family, but they do affect my fellowship with my Father. I need to say "I'm sorry" for the ways I disappoint Him or let Him down. Those of you who are parents can relate. You certainly would not disown your child every time he or she were disobedient to you, but there is a break in closeness when a child disobeys. However, when that child asks for forgiveness, there is a sweet restoration that takes place.

Have you had confession as a regular part of your prayer life before now?

It is essential that confession be a consistent part of your prayer life. It is also essential that confession be specific.

> **If we keep our confession generic, we are quick to minimize our own sin and therefore, more likely to commit it again.**

When we move from "forgive me of my sins" to "Lord, I am so sorry I gossiped about Jane today. I know that it hurts You when I speak against one of Your children," we are truly acknowledging where we need His help. We will also be much more attuned to the Holy Spirit's nudge the next time the specific opportunity to sin returns.

It is because we are forgiven that we can forgive others. Paul tells us in Ephesians 5:1 to be imitators of God. The unforgiving Christian brands herself a hypocrite, but when we forgive others it brings glory to God because it is an imitation of what He does for us. We will learn to forgive only when we begin practicing forgiveness towards those who have hurt us. This is not easy, but God never said it would be, He simply requires that we do it.

There have been times when I have obeyed in this area, and then there have been plenty of times I have held onto my pride and been disobedient. When someone hurt me, I wanted him or her to pay, and I wanted God to okay my actions and my hurt. When I looked at Scripture I only found that I was to forgive. Never am I permitted to continue on in unforgiveness towards another person, regardless of the wrong committed against me. God receives much glory when we deny ourselves and depend on Him to help us love others and forgive their offenses toward us. We can relinquish the wrong done to us knowing that He has forgiven us of our unpardonable debt, but we cannot do this in our own strength. It is only possible when we are abiding in Christ.

Take a few minutes to think about specific areas in your life where you need to seek God's forgiveness. Is there an offense you need to forgive of another? Ask God to give you the strength and the desire to forgive those who have offended you. Whether on the topic of relationships, identity, or prayer, God will not leave the issue of forgiveness alone. As women seeking to leave behind our goal of perfection, we must be willing to forgive others for their shortcomings, too.

What is the last element we are taught to pray about?

Luke 11:4b_____.

This is a cry to the Lord for protection. The word *temptation* here means trial or test. It's a situation that God allows to reveal where you are in your faith. It is out of His love that He tests us, to prove what is in us and to show how far we've come. His purpose is to strengthen us and help us move forward. He knows our weak spots. He knows the places that we have messed up in the past. He knows how easily we get "sucked" into our familiar sins. We each have a tendency to fall to our own fleshly desires.

Life is a spiritual minefield, and left on our own we will be blindsided and fatally fall to each blast. But in asking the Lord to "lead us not into temptation" we are asking God to keep us from walking headlong into that familiar sin. We are asking the Lord to prevent us from getting sucked into the place where we are so easily able to fall.

Whenever we are tested, Satan is lingering right around the corner waiting to exploit the situation and make us question God. We need to lean into our relationship with the Father and pray for the strength to do what is right, when inwardly we are pulled toward the temptation that would seek to steer us off course.

As we have said with almost every element of relational disciplines, we must be specific in our prayer life. When we come to pray regarding protection, we should be specific. Does God need us to be specific? No. Yet, think about how our faith is impacted if we are generic or specific. For example, if you are praying over a child you can pray, "Lord, protect Susie from temptation." Or you can pray, "Lord, Susie will face temptations at school today to lie and to believe lies about herself when she is among her friends. I pray that when she is with her friends she will believe what is true about her. Protect her from falling into the temptation to project herself as someone other than who she truly is. I ask You to protect her from conversations that could cause her to fall into temptation again. Guide her to friends that will build her up. I pray that when she hears something negative and is tempted to believe the lie that she is not good enough, that You would remind her she is fearfully and wonderfully made." Think how your faith will grow when you begin to see Susie talk about her progress in handling conversations and picking friends!

Think of a specific victory you've had over a temptation in your life. How did you overcome it?

When you have experienced defeat in temptation, what led you there?

Here is the bottom line. We need temptation and trials in our lives; they are what grow us. But when we are tempted God always provides a way out. Jesus tells us to come to the Father for help before we walk into the path of the blast so He can lead us in another direction. We are not going to be taken out of this minefield called life, but having a loving Father to direct our steps can keep us from getting crippled and rendered ineffective while we're here.

Take a minute right now to ask God *specifically* to "Lead you not into temptation."

What was the most meaningful statement or Scripture you read today?

What does God want you to do in response to today's study?

PERSISTENCE IN PRAYER

CHRIS KUHLMAN

We have spent the last two days looking at the Lord's prayer as a model to show us how to pray. Jesus did not desire for us to merely recite this prayer from memory. He wanted His disciples (including us) to see how we can relate to God. As way of review, let these key thoughts help you as you pray:

1. Father - We are praying to a loving Father
2. Holy - We can trust Him because He is perfect and unlike any other
3. His Kingdom - We must ask Him to help us align ourselves with His will
4. Provision - He cares about our daily needs, ask Him
5. Forgiveness - We seek specific forgiveness from God and ask for the grace to extend it to others
6. Temptation - We can come to Him to ask for protection (be specific)

Look back to Day One of this week and fill in the Key Reminder words to avoid some common pitfalls in prayer:

1. Get_____ - skip the clichés and be honest with God

2. Get_____ - pray somewhere you won't be distracted

3. Get_____ - pray out loud or write your prayers out in a journal

4. Get_____ - don't forget the listening part when you pray

As we study the significance of the Lord's prayer, God can open up our hearts and minds and lead us into the next level of intimacy. My prayer is that you will become impassioned with a desire to come to our Father and lay before Him your heart and to experience the deep, deep love He has for us. While we completed the portion of Jesus teaching on the Lord's prayer yesterday, Jesus still had a precious truth about prayer that He wanted to teach us.

Read Luke 11:5-8.

I don't want you to get the idea that God is like this grouchy neighbor. Anyone who knows what it's like getting all the kids to bed and finally getting there yourself knows what an imposition a late night knock can be. But Jesus is using extremes to get His point across. If this selfish neighbor will get up and get you what you need because of your persistence, how much more would your loving Father give you what you need? He is the opposite of this so-called "friend"... He never sleeps, and He desires that you come to Him no matter the time of day. He wants to supply you with good things and He never gets impatient.

How does it help you to know that Jesus tells us to be persistent?

Jesus is using this illustration to show the virtue of persistence. If persistence finally paid off for a needy neighbor knocking on the door of his grouchy neighbor, we can be confident that our persistence in prayer to our omniscient, loving, Heavenly Father will bring blessing. It isn't that God is reluctant to provide so we have to keep coming back to get Him to change His mind, but He wants persistence from us because it benefits us. It keeps us in a constant place of recognition of the Giver of all gifts. Go back to the first page of today's lesson and write in "Get Persistent" as the fifth reminder to avoid pitfalls in prayer.

Persistence in prayer prepares us for the answer He gives. But what do you do while you are waiting to protect yourself from doubting God or giving up? One incredibly practical tool is your journal. In our week on disciplines we introduced the value of having a journal to write out what God teaches you when you are in His Word. It is equally beneficial to use this journal in your prayer time. If you pray out loud, go back afterwards and jot down the specific things God led you to pray about. As God answers, note that in your journal, too. When you are trusting God to respond to your prayer, the enemy loves for you to forget all the other prayers God has answered. Your journal becomes an amazing tool to help you recount God's faithfulness. Let's look at one last account to help us persevere in prayer.

Read Luke 18:1-8.

In order to help you understand the context of this parable, you should know that the "courtroom" Jesus spoke of was a tent that was moved from place to place as the judge covered his circuit. The judge set the agenda. Anybody could watch from the outside but in order for you to be accepted and have your case tried usually meant bribing one of the assistants so that he would call the judge's attention to the case. The widow had 3 obstacles to overcome:

1. She was a woman and had little or no standing before the law. Women did not go to court.
2. Since she was a widow she had no husband to stand with her in court.
3. She was poor so she could not offer a bribe to have her case heard.

According to verse 1 why did Jesus tell His disciples this parable?

Don't miss this!!!! Jesus knew we were going to struggle with growing weary in prayer so He left us this love letter that tells us exactly what to do and how to think, so we don't lose heart.

When was the last time you felt like giving up praying for something? What was it?

I have been at this point a few times, especially lately. I am praying for something very dear to me, and I have no control over the outcome. In other words, I can't make what I am praying for happen. I have realized I am a control freak! But I am totally dependent on God for the answer. This causes me to ask the question, "Can I trust you, God?" When I allow the enemy to turn my thoughts from being focused on God and the truth of WHO He is to being focused on myself and my inadequacy and limitations, I find myself doubting God and believing the lies of the enemy. The enemy feeds me lies like, "God doesn't care about that part of your life." "God can't really answer that prayer, it involves another person." It is a slippery slope, and it is dangerous when we find ourselves there. But when I take these thoughts captive and cling to His promises, I am able to persevere.

Prayer is more than the words of our lips. It is the desires of our hearts. And when our hearts are continually desiring Him and His will for our lives, we "pray without ceasing." Again, Jesus is arguing the lesser to the greater by saying, "If a poor widow got what she deserved from a selfish judge, how much more will God's children receive what is right from their Heavenly Father!" Unless you see that God is pointing out contrasts, you might get the impression that God has to be "bribed" or "argued" into answering prayer. God is not like this judge, for God is a loving Father, who is attentive to our every need and wants us to come to Him.

We must remember that what is most important to God is our relationship with Him. Everything in life is to be viewed in light of that relationship.

God's delays are not inactivity, but preparation.

The moment we send Him our request, God is at work! The answer is coming! Don't give up. We stop praying because after some time of pouring out our hearts to God we can't see anything happening from our perspective. We live with the pain. We are allowing the circumstances and our own expectations to get between us and God instead of surrendering our ideas and expectations to Him.

Steadfast prayer requires faith and knowledge of what God wants to accomplish - knowing God and His plan. It's a time of searching and discovery. God always knows what's best for us, He wants what's best for us, and will only give us what's best.

Are you praying for something or someone now and you can't see the answer? God is faithful. He hears and is working. There is such joy in answered prayer, especially when it has been bathed in months or years of tears and yearning. If you are in a period of waiting, take comfort in these truths:

Psalm 9:10 (NIV)

> Those who know your name trust in you, for you, Lord, have never forsaken those who seek you.

Psalm 10:17 (NIV)

You hear, O Lord, the desire of the afflicted; you encourage them, and you listen to their cry.

Psalm 145:18 (NIV)

The Lord is near to all who call on him, to all who call on him in truth.

My aunt Pat prayed for my uncle David's salvation for 30 years. He knew my aunt had a relationship with God but he had no desire for the same. In the fall of 2002, David was alone in the field preparing to harvest corn. He was oiling the chain of the corn picker while it was running and he slipped. The chain grabbed his pant leg and instinctively he reached out his hand to brace himself. Not only his leg but both arms were pulled into the running machinery. His arms and leg were trapped and were being pulled further and further into the picker. His first impulse was to cry out to God for help, and at this point the tractor stalled, shutting down the picker. There was no way for him to free himself. It was only David and God for 3 hours. He didn't think he was going to make it. With each passing moment his prayer became more fervent and sincere.

After 3 hours, his brother thought he heard something and ran to the field to find David in this state. It was another 2 hours before the rescue workers were able to free him. God was answering a 30 year long prayer. Was this the way Pat wanted God to answer? No, not really, but she knew that His ways are far beyond our ways. Not only was God answering Pat's prayer for her husband, but God was actively pursuing their son Todd through this ordeal. Pat could tell that God was working and He gave her a sense of encouragement she had never felt before. God gave her the strength, peace, and grace in the midst of the difficulty because He was doing an even greater work.

One week after the accident, God broke Todd and he humbly accepted Christ. One month after the accident, David walked into church and wept as he too accepted Jesus Christ as his Savior. Thirty years of persistent praying and God answered abundantly, with the salvation of David and Todd.

David, Pat, Todd and the whole family will tell you to keep on praying. God is working!

What was the most meaningful statement or Scripture you read today?

What does God want you to do in response to today's study?

PRACTICES, PROMISES, AND PROBLEMS
CHRIS KUHLMAN

I want to be your biggest cheerleader when it comes to prayer. I am so moved and encouraged by stories of answered prayers. They reveal that God is still working and is in the business of transformation. He uses prayer to change us, to grow us, and to draw us intimately to Himself. Are you putting into practice the truths you are learning this week concerning prayer? I hope so!

Today, we will finish by looking at three dynamics surrounding prayer. We are going to look at how to pray Scripture, what God promises us regarding prayer, and some common hindrances in prayer. While time and space will necessitate that we address each briefly, they are each too important to omit, so let's get going!

PRAYING SCRIPTURE

All week long, I hope you have observed that prayer is simple yet profound. Are you grasping that prayer is a relational discipline that is very real and personal? Prayer is simply talking and listening to God. One way that I have grown tremendously in my prayer life is through praying Scripture back to God. This is a powerful way to see how God's Word is always personal and applicable. In case you have not done this before, let me show you how. Open your Bible to Psalm 119 and let's start with verses 129-136.

Begin by writing down everything you see about God...who He is, what He does, etc..
I will help you with the first ones.

> **v129 Your testimonies are wonderful**
>
> **v130 Your Word gives light**
>
> **v132**
>
> **v133**
>
> **v135**

Now, when we pray these truths back to God, we are telling Him who He is. Do you know first hand that His testimonies are wonderful? His testimony is His Word. Circle the verses above that meant the most to you.

What can you pray from these verses that will increase your desire for Him? Here are two examples, then you give it a try.

v129 Because Your Word is wonderful I want to obey You. Help me when I struggle to be obedient.

v130 You have promised to give me understanding. When I don't know.... You are my light.

v131 (an open mouth suggests wanting it to be filled)

v132

v133

v134

v135

v136

What you are asking for is more of Him! Do you see? When our eyes are focused on Him, He is the only one who can satisfy us.

What do I need for today, according to these verses?
v133

v134

"Redeem me from man's oppression..." Where are you feeling "squeezed" right now? What may be giving you anxious thoughts? Redemption was extended to us when we surrendered our lives to the Lord. We are now daughters of the King!

v136

Who do you know that is not keeping God's law? Is it someone in your family? A friend or a coworker? Are you carrying that burden? Let God know how deeply it affects you and how much you want their relationship with Him to be redeemed. Are there areas that you are not being obedient and you need to come in humility and confession before Him?

If praying Scripture is new to you, I hope that you have experienced the presence of God in a personal way that will draw you back to this place again and again. As we discussed in our week on disciplines, these relational disciplines are intertwined. As you are in your Priority Time, you can pray Scripture back to Him to get your heart set as you prepare to spend time in His Word. You can stop and pray Scripture back to Him as He reveals truth about Himself while you are in His Word, or throughout your day. He is always ready to hear from you.

PROMISES AND PROBLEMS

While the subject of prayer can be extremely fulfilling, it can also be extremely frustrating. God's Word has so many promises, yet many well-meaning Christians still find prayer somewhat confusing or disappointing. Consider two of the amazing promises given in God's Word:

John 14:13-14

> [13] Whatever you ask in my name, this I will do, that the Father may be glorified in the Son. [14] If you ask me anything in my name, I will do it.

What is our promise from Jesus?

John 16:23-24

> [23] ...Truly, truly I say to you, whatever you ask of the Father in my name, he will give it to you. [24] Until now you have asked nothing in my name. Ask, and you will receive, that your joy may be full.

According to this verse, how are we told to pray?

Jesus is so passionate about this promise for His disciples and for us. Six times, Jesus commands us to ask whatever we will. We want His answer to our asking, our knocking, our seeking, yet our experience and His promises don't seem to match up sometimes. How many of us are getting our prayers answered? What holds us back from seeing these promises fulfilled?

I want you to know that you can have complete confidence in God's promises! Every word of Scripture is true. The reasons we seem to have a disconnect between our asking in His name and His answering usually fall into two categories. First, we don't grasp the fullness of God's truth in this area, and second, there may be something in our lives that is a hindrance to our prayers. Let's look at both so we can experience the joy of answered prayer.

As Jesus continually mentions that we should pray "in My name," we must grasp what that means. It is not just a phrase that we attach to the end of a prayer that causes it to be supernaturally FedEx'd to God. "In My name" means that we are asking according to His desires not ours. It means Christ is "Lord" (master) of our prayer lives. 1 Corinthians 12:3 tells us that we will only say Jesus is Lord by the Holy Spirit. So our prayers must be "approved" by the Holy Spirit. In other words, He endorses them for payment by God. We are praying as He would pray if He was in our place. Whoa! Does that change your thinking about what you pray for? "In My name" is according to all He is and all He has accomplished. Prayer that is truly offered for Christ's sake cannot fail.

This concept of praying according to the Lord's will is best illustrated in Psalm 37:4 which says, "Delight yourself in the Lord, and He will give you the desires of your heart." We like the idea that God will give us the desires of our heart, but the key to that occurring is in the first phrase. If we delight in the Lord, then our desires will change. If we are spending time learning who God is and growing in our love for Him, then our desires will move into alignment with His desires. If our desires are the same as His, He will joyfully answer "yes!" because He alone knows what is best. Again, it is not magic. Praying His will requires us to cultivate a relationship with God.

God is not looking for Miss Perfect before He answers our prayers, so don't stress if you are still learning how to approach prayer from God's perspective instead of yours. Come to Him honestly. You can bring a desire to Him and then tell Him without pretense, "Help me to know how to pray about this as You see it." Then be still. Listen. Let God put His perspective in your mind and begin to pray what He shows you. For example, maybe you come to the Lord praying, "Please sell our house." As you are still, God may remind you that His timing is perfect or that the underlying issue is about much more than a physical house. As those thoughts come to mind, pray in accordance with God.

If you have been actively pursuing the Lord but still feel like your prayers hit the ceiling, then examine your own life and make sure that you are not limiting God's activity. We need to get on our knees and allow His Spirit to search us and see if we have hindered our prayers by:

- Sin - Are we hanging on to something in our lives that God says needs to go?
- Idols in the Heart - An idol is anything that we put before God. Ezekiel 14:1-3
- An Unforgiving Spirit - God answers our prayers based on being forgiven sinners through Christ's sacrificial death, but God cannot deal with us as forgiven sinners if we are not forgiving those who have wronged us. Mark 11:25
- An Unwillingness to Give - The Christian who is stingy in her giving cannot be mighty in prayer. Proverbs 21:13, Luke 6:38
- Wrong Treatment of a Spouse - Look into our home life. 1 Peter 3:1-7

Do you sense the Holy Spirit showing you an area that you need to address? If so, what is your first step of action?

The beautiful thing about God is that He is not a God of hide and seek. If you sense conviction, then deal with it. I highly encourage you to deal with it NOW. Do not let another day go by. God does not hide conviction. If there is an area that He is wanting you to address, He will show you. He cannot contradict His character and answer your prayers if you are knowingly living in disobedience, so you must take action. On the other hand, if you do not sense conviction, then don't beat yourself up. Again, God does not hide conviction. You can trust that God is at work behind the scenes and the promises of God are being accomplished. Persevere as Jesus told us we should.

God created prayer. He wants us to come to Him and He wants to answer our prayers. He receives glory when His children see Him answer. Our faith is increased when we see Him respond to our smallest and biggest need. Take time today to deal with anything that may be hindering you from experiencing the joy of seeing God respond. Then embrace the journey of seeking Him and anticipating His response.

What was the most meaningful statement or Scripture you read today?

What does God want you to do in response to today's study?

NOTES FOR THE WEEK

PURITY WITHOUT PRESSURE

A woman discovers the power of purity by pursuing pure pleasures instead of impure pleasures.

Day One
PURE BEAUTY PART 1

Day Two
PURE BEAUTY PART 2

Day Three
PURE DECISIONS

Day Four
PURE PROTECTION

Day Five
PURE INTIMACY

Day One

PURE BEAUTY PART 1

KARIN CONLEE

Just the words *purity* and *beauty*, independent of each other, conjure up a thousand different thoughts and images.

What are your first thoughts when you hear the word "beauty"?

What do you think when you hear the word "purity"?

From white snow-capped mountains, to runway models, to *Little House on the Prairie*, to failed diets and desperate regret, the threads of beauty and purity are powerfully woven into a woman's life. In our culture, we seldom put the two words together. In the 21st century, there is beauty and all of its nuances and then there is purity, an altogether separate strand. Over the next two days, we will consider them in isolation. At the end of the week, we will see how the two are linked.

BEAUTY

If you were to ask a room full of women, "Are you beautiful?" there would be a moment of pause. Could you answer the question in a group setting? To say "yes," seems somewhat prideful and yet to say "no" seems to admit defeat as a woman. There is pressure either way. Would you not wonder what every other woman was thinking as one looked at you while you made your answer audible? Well-known authors and speakers, John and Staci Eldredge describe the battle with beauty like this...

> Beauty is, without question, the most essential and most misunderstood of all of God's qualities—of all feminine qualities, too. We know it has caused untold pain in the lives of women. But even through the pain, something is speaking. Why so much heartache over beauty? We don't ache over being geniuses or fabulous hockey players. Women ache over the issue of beauty—they ache to be beautiful, to believe they are beautiful, and they worry over keeping it if they can ever find it.[1]

How would you describe how you orient yourself to beauty?

Earlier in Week 1 of our study, we noted that beauty was one place that we might mistakenly try to place our identity. By the sheer amount of money we spend on haircuts, color, product, manis and pedis, not to mention the more aggressive approaches to acquire a certain look, the argument is compelling. So is it all vanity? Do we just pick a cover model to be our goal as we strive to be Miss Perfect? Are we all just suckers for marketing?

To answer the question, we must go back to grasp God's purpose in creating woman. Back in the Garden of Eden, before the fall and before sin, there was an amazing creation being brought forth. There was a faultless man in relation to a perfect God. There were increasingly complex living creatures coming forward to be named by Adam. Everything was good, but not right. What God added when He added Eve was not only a companion for Adam, but beauty. All of God's qualities of beauty, creativity, and relationship were at the pinnacle in the creation of Eve. Ironically, for a short period of time there actually was a Miss Perfect. Yes, the earth had beauty in her landscape before Eve, but God-breathed beauty was a beauty that revealed more of Him than any other creation.

Women were created to embody beauty. Now before you go down the slippery slope of questioning whether you live up to that billing, STOP! Women are beautiful, EVERY SINGLE ONE OF US. It is one of the glorious ways that we bear the image of God.

Try to put the magazine covers out of your mind, and ask the question: What beauty is esteemed in Scripture? If we want to please God in every other way, why not ask what He esteems as beautiful? There is no doubt God made us pleasing for a man to look at, but we miss so much if we think in secular terms alone.

Read Proverbs 31.

What physical description are we given of this worthy woman?

Who thinks well of her?

What is she affirmed for?

Is her specific appearance mentioned?

What does verse 30 say?

There are several other notable women in Scripture. Think of Mary, the mother of Jesus, Martha and Mary, and Elizabeth. Of just these four women, have you ever considered what information is given regarding their physical attributes? None!

Look up the following passages and write what God did find important to affirm.

Read Luke 1:30. What do we learn about God's views towards Mary?

Read Luke 1:34-45. Why do you think God found favor with Mary?

Read Luke 10:38-42. What did the Lord affirm was good?

Now, I know what some of you are thinking. "What about....?" There definitely are beautiful women mentioned in Scripture. Sarai, Rebekah, Queen Vashti, and Esther's physical beauty were noted, as were a few more. I think, however, all of us would agree that these women are more significant because of their role in God's story than because of their physique.

We must remember that God does make us beautiful, both internally and externally. It is a gift given to us, not a goal we are pressured to reach.

> After all, the beauty and discovery of a woman has amazing parallels
> to God's longing for us to discover Him.

Our beauty is a picture of His beauty. Our beauty is a mystery to be explored and discovered just as He longs for us to discover His mysterious beauty as we grow to know Him intimately.

The dilemma is not "is beauty important?" It is. God created beauty. It was so important that He made you beautiful. "Beauty is an essence that dwells in EVERY woman."[2] The struggle comes because we have redefined beauty to be purely external. Now, we spend little time cultivating true inner beauty and so much time searching for the secrets of external beauty.

Read 1 Peter 3:3-4 below.

> [3] Do not let your adorning be external–the braiding of hair and the putting on of gold jewelry, or the clothing you wear– [4] but let your adorning be the hidden person of the heart with the imperishable beauty of a gentle and quiet spirit, which in God's sight is very precious.

How does Scripture direct us to deal with this dueling issue?

What is precious in God's sight?

Honestly, how much time do you spend each day making yourself look good?

How much time do you spend each day cultivating your internal beauty through relational disciplines?

If these times are out of balance, what is one step you will commit to make to begin correcting this imbalance?

The issue of beauty is not either/or. Nowhere in Scripture is physical beauty condemned. What is condemned is taking pride in God-given beauty and giving excess attention to physical beauty while ignoring matters of the heart.[3]

As women, we must embrace that we are beautiful by design. Then with appropriate understanding of what makes us beautiful, we dig deep into our relationship with God. We allow our own unique, internal beauty to be developed, and as we bathe in the affirmation of our identity in Him, we can, with balance, enjoy sharing our external beauty appropriately. "The only things standing in the way of our beauty are our doubts and fears, and the hiding and striving we fall to as a result."[4] As we conclude, let's breathe in the reality that we are His beautiful daughters. Tomorrow we will explore how our beauty should work in sync with God's purity.

What was the most meaningful statement or Scripture you read today?

What does God want you to do in response to today's study?

PURE BEAUTY PART 2
KARIN CONLEE

We pick up today where we left off yesterday. We attempted to paint the picture of what beauty truly is. Our physical beauty should not be dismissed as nonspiritual and it should not overshadow the internal beauty that, when nurtured, brings forth our best. Our understanding of beauty as a believer, however, will remain murky if we do not also comprehend how purity is involved.

As Elizabeth George describes in *A Woman's Calling*, there are multiple definitions of purity.[5] Generally, we all relate to the concept of pure being without stain or guilt. When something is pure, it is clean and free from pollution.

Read Titus 2:3-5.

> [3] Older women likewise are to be reverent in behavior, not slanderers or slaves to much wine. They are to teach what is good, [4] and so train the young women to love their husbands and children, [5] to be self-controlled, pure, working at home, kind, and submissive to their own husbands, that the word of God may not be reviled.

This cornerstone verse on the conduct of women speaks to purity being a value we strive for as a woman. What do you think when you read this verse?

Our responses vary greatly based on our experiences and understanding of Scripture. For now, I want to isolate our focus to purity. The Greek word for pure here is *hagnos*. It is derived from *hagios* which is used in the New Testament for holy, Holy of Holies, and Holy One.

When you think of pure with the understanding of where this word came from, how does your definition of pure change?

Originally, the idea of purity had its practical application in the ritualistic cleansings under Mosaic law. As time progressed, Jesus came to show that it was not simply about our external cleanliness, but it was about the internal removing of guilt and stain. We were called to be holy, separate, and pure. Interestingly, humanity took the concept of purity and beauty, tried to minimize them to a list of do's and don'ts, and missed the greater picture.

As women seeking to discover God's purpose for our lives, we must reconnect purity and beauty. When purity and beauty are reunited, we can gain an accurate picture of how to be what God desires. It is not ignoring our beauty and de-feminizing ourselves, but it is also not flaunting our beauty in a way that distracts or tempts others. This understanding is sadly missing from the modern church.

Have you ever been aware of someone at church that did not consider her call to holiness when she thought of how to display her beauty on a Sunday?

Have you ever struggled yourself with knowing what was appropriate as you try to wed the fashion magazines' latest styles with your desire to be pure?

If you have observed an immodestly dressed woman at church or even struggled yourself, it does not take much imagination to know the problem is exponentially greater in other environments. We have heard forever that WE, the people, are the church. While the level of formality may differ from event to event, women who follow the Lord are called to demonstrate pure beauty in EVERY environment, not just on Sunday mornings.

As women, we tend to forget how God created man. Christ follower or not, men are very visual. While we may think it is innocent attention we are asking for, it is much more dangerous. When we wear low cut tops, low-waisted pants, and short skirts, we have not only ignored our call to pure beauty, but we have caused our sons, friends, and husband's friends to stumble. May I be so blunt to say that no one, outside of your husband, should be privileged to see your breasts! They are beauty to be enjoyed by him and him alone. Big or small, no one else even needs a hint of your beauty. If you are single, do not share the mystery of your beauty with a man who has not taken your hand in marriage.

Though I doubt most Christian women, single or married, set out to sabotage a marriage or to cause men to stumble, I can think of men who have shared with my husband that they had to switch Sunday classes because a woman's clothing was repetitively too revealing. I can only imagine how embarrassed and heartbroken the woman would be if she knew that her poor choice caused such action to be necessary. I have also had to gently tell women that their attire was distracting when they were on stage for a friend's baptism.

Why are we tempted to reveal too much of our bodies to those other than our spouse?

So often, women do not even realize the motive of their actions. The woman who has not found her identity in Christ will look to others to affirm her. Where we seek affirmation is different for each of us, depending on our strengths and past experiences. For some of us, the last place we will go to fill this void is our body. We might choose to get attention in other ways. Some, however, believe, "If I can get a man to notice my body, then I must be beautiful. I must be worth loving."

> The woman who is confident in who she is in Christ and in her inner beauty will have no need to flaunt her beauty because she is secure in who she is.

Sometimes, the woman who flaunts herself seems the most confident. In reality, it is usually an internal cry for love and affirmation sadly misdirected. If you relate to this pattern of behavior, I highly encourage you to confide in a trusted friend or your small group leader. Your clothing choices are merely a symptom. Addressing the heart need will bring you a freedom and security you are longing to experience. No amount of head turning will fill the void you need to fill.

We have mentioned how men are negatively impacted by our inappropriate clothing choices, but let us not overlook the way that the enemy can use the same indiscretion to cause other women to struggle.

When an immodestly dressed woman is in your presence, how does it make you feel?

In the most innocent of cases, it can be awkward. For women who have been abandoned by their husbands for another woman or have navigated marriage through an affair, a woman flaunting her beauty is more than just indiscretion, it is painful. For God's glory and our protection, we must take our call to pure beauty seriously.

While the Bible does not speak to specific legalistic measurements of our clothing, the heart and intention is definitely clear.

How does 1 Timothy 2:9-10 describe what our approach to clothing should be?

What does verse 10 show is more important than the external?

Before we move forward, look at the end of verse 10 again. Who should heed these truths?

The NASB translation says this "is proper for a woman making a claim to godliness." Are you a woman claiming to follow God? We must not forget who we represent as we dress ourselves.

Is this passage saying that gold, pearls, and costly brands are forbidden? No. (Now, you might check out Dave Ramsey, but we'll leave stewardship for another study.) Paul is expressing that we should dress with PURE beauty. It is not the outside alone that makes us beautiful. Our beauty and our purity must permeate from the inside out.

Over the last two days, we have dealt with some very personal and very practical areas where we can possibly be misusing the beauty God gave us. Take a few moments to pray and reflect on what God has revealed to you.

How does God want you to respond?

If you have been convicted about your immodesty, confess that specifically to the Lord. Do you need to take some practical steps and modify your wardrobe or how you carry yourself?

List any specific action steps you need to make.

Many of us have chased the desire to achieve some type of external beauty. In the world of airbrushing and editing, what we are comparing ourselves to and what we are striving for is not even real. Miss Perfect became unattainable with one bite of fruit. What IS real is the opportunity to acknowledge our God-given beauty and to enjoy our femininity in the context of purity. We must refuse to compromise ourselves and our dignity to get the world's affirmation. Embrace your pure beauty and rest in the affirmation of the King.

What was the most meaningful statement or Scripture you read today?

What does God want you to do in response to today's study?

PURE DECISIONS

KARIN CONLEE

―――――――――

The subject of pure beauty is an important concept to grasp. I hope in the last two days you have been able to drink in the fact that you already possess beauty. God gave us our beauty. There is no pressure to go find it! Instead, we are told to set our beauty apart from the world's warped ideas and keep our beauty pure. Understanding accurate definitions and having some reasonable boundaries in your clothing choices, however, will be of little use if you have not determined that you truly embrace God's view of purity as your own. Even the most modestly dressed woman can easily choose to seduce a man if she has not genuinely aligned her desires with God's desires.

It is analogous to the doctor who knows all the implications of smoking to the human body and yet chooses to smoke anyway.

Knowledge means nothing if we do not act upon it.

If we examine our lives for any length of time, we can see areas where we know the truth but don't live by it. Don't we all know we should floss daily? Don't we all know we should eat less fat and more vegetables? We have the information to do what it right, but sometimes we lack the next step of making application. In the area of purity, we cannot afford to stop with the information. We MUST apply God's truth.

Have you decided to embrace the power of purity? Let's look at what God makes available to those who choose His way. Read 2 Peter 1:3-11.

What did God's power grant us? (v3)

How can we have these things? (v3)

Why did God grant us His promises? (v4)

What do we escape if we choose His way? (v4)

What qualities need to be in us and increasing? (v5-7)

What happens if you practice these qualities? (v10)

> A woman discovers the power of purity by pursuing pure pleasures
> instead of impure pleasures.

As we discussed in day 2, purity is synonymous with holiness. Purity is so much broader than keeping the physical act of sex within marriage. Purity is deciding to be set apart and completely different than the world. Purity brings blessing and protection. If we choose God's way, we will be pure, not just sexually, but in every aspect of our lives. If we have virtue, knowledge, self-control, steadfastness, godliness, brotherly affection, and love in us and increasing, we will never fail! This is a promise from THE Promise Keeper.

What description is given of the person that chooses to go against God's instructions? (v9)

God has laid it out very plainly. We can follow His way and never fail, or we can go the world's way and be like a blind man. What is your decision?

Read 1 Thessalonians 4:3-5 below.

> ³ For this is the will of God, your sanctification: that you abstain from sexual immorality; ⁴ that each one of you know how to control his own body in holiness and honor, ⁵ not in the passion of lust like the Gentiles who do not know God.

What is the will of God? (v3)

How are we to control our bodies? (v4)

How do those who do not know God control their bodies? (v5)

In our culture, the statistics for divorce run scarily similar between Christians and those who do not proclaim Christ. The Gentiles were the unbelievers in Paul's time period. Are you a Christ follower or a Gentile? What would your actions communicate? Do you conduct yourself with holiness and honor or do you allow your lust to control you?

> If we are offered the path of holiness as a way to never fail, and we choose to embrace this path, then we have some decisions to make.

We cannot intellectually assent to this path and then continue walking the same path as everyone else. There are two specific ways that I want us to apply these truths. Both applications apply for every stage of womanhood.

1. MEDIA

Some of the greatest deterrents from walking a path of holiness are the distractions of the world. One of the most effective distractions is the media.

Whether married or single, how does the media cause you to stumble in the area of purity?

If we continue to fill our minds with images of impurity, we will eventually give up the battle of holiness. You can't continually take garbage in and not be tainted.

What SPECIFIC AND PRACTICAL changes do you need to make in your intake of media to guard your mind?

Read 1 John 2:15-17.

> [15] Do not love the world or the things in the world. If anyone loves the world, the love of the Father is not in him. [16] For all that is in the world–the desires of the flesh and the desires of the eyes and pride in possessions–is not from the Father but is from the world. [17] And the world is passing away along with its desires, but whoever does the will of God abides forever.

While the Bible may not name names, like *Desperate Housewives*, it makes it very clear what we should not love.

What two things are we told not to love in verse 15?

Circle the three specific descriptions of what Paul tells us are in the world.

Where do these 3 things come from?

What is passing away? (v17)

Who abides forever? (v17)

What does it mean that the one who does the will of the Father will abide forever?

Look up Titus 2:11-14.

What are we told to renounce? (v12)

How should we live? (v12)

What does God want us to wait for? (v13)

Aside from the media, what other things encourage you to live outside of God's plan in the area of purity?

What changes do you need to make to decide to live a life protected by purity?

2. RELATING TO MEN

Not only must we guard what we expose our eyes to, as believers we must also be responsible with how we interact with men. As we discussed earlier, there is an element of purity that would call us to never cause another man, single or married, to stumble by tempting them.

This call extends beyond our wardrobe. Flirtatious and even just extremely friendly behavior can cause both parties to stumble.

SINGLE WOMEN

As a single woman, while you would certainly interact with other single men, you would still want to do so in such a way that keeps the relationship pure. Please prayerfully consider applying these principles to guard your purity:

With single men:
- Do not pursue a man. If a man will not lead in dating, then you risk the high probability that he will not lead you in marriage.
- Spend time together in public places where you will both be protected from greater temptations.

> **What are some ways that single women casually interact with single men that may cause both to stumble?**

Frequently, we skip through the natural progression of building a relationship and move to intimacy too quickly. Once physical intimacy is ignited, the relationship has just short-circuited healthy growth. Often conflict in the relationship is "resolved" through physical intimacy. Problems are swept under the rug as passion may soothe the offense. The couple no longer works through issues, setting them up for struggles if the relationship continues.

With married men:
- Do not Facebook, text, or email a married man without copying his wife.
- Do not drive in a car alone with a married man, including on business.
- Do not eat a meal alone with a married man, including on business.

MARRIED WOMEN

While any woman can certainly be physically attracted to a man, it is usually a married woman's emotions that stir her attraction toward a man outside of her marriage. She can begin to believe subtle lies that someone else can bring her what her husband has not.

Married ladies, guard your marriage by making decisions to limit interaction and social media contact with men outside your family. Invest your precious time in cultivating the marriage God gave you. For your friendships with other couples, you should have primary connection with the wife.

May I recommend for you to also apply these protective measures for men outside your family:
- Do not Facebook, text, or email a man without copying his wife.
- Do not drive in a car alone with another man, including business.
- Do not eat a meal alone with a man, including business.
- Do not give face-to-face hugs with other men…stick with a handshake or side hug.

If you read the section prior to this for single women, you will notice the precautions are almost identical. Getting married gives us permission to be more relaxed with how we interact with our husband, but it is not a license to be irresponsible in the way we relate to other men.

Some of you may be thinking, "Really? Is that realistic?" Several years ago, my husband shared this approach of not driving or eating alone with a woman to a friend who frequently traveled for his company. Under conviction, the next time his friend took a business trip he decided to honor this principle. Did he take some heat from his colleagues? Yes, for a few days. Is there evidence that God honored his willingness to care more about his purity and protecting someone else's purity than his popularity? Absolutely.

Why must we make God's call to purity more important than our popularity or comfort?

It is easy to read truth and agree, but never take the steps to change established patterns of behavior. Taking action immediately upon feeling conviction is important for replacing old habits. As we conclude, pray over the truth you read today and any adjustments that you need to make. Once you have prayed, get busy making changes. There is no time like the present. Maybe you need to remove some programs from your DVR schedule or de-friend some men that you do not need to be communicating with through Facebook. If you are doing your Bible study at a time that you do not have the necessary tools handy to make changes, then set an appointment or alert in your calendar to remind you to make those changes when you are home. Make decisions to protect you and your family from having to deal with the pain of broken trust.

What was the most meaningful statement or Scripture you read today?

What does God want you to do in response to today's study?

PURE PROTECTION
KARIN CONLEE

As we have said, God made us each a beauty with a mystery for our spouse to enjoy and discover. It is the most beautiful and mysterious part of all of creation. Genesis 2:22-25 should leave you little doubt of the enormous creativity, sensitivity, and tenderness of our God.

Read Genesis 2:22-25.

What do you think when you read this portion of the creation account?

Our world has it all wrong. Our culture sends contradicting, but all tragically wrong, messages. We are encouraged that sex with anyone at any time will bring pleasure. We are also told we can have physical intimacy and move on. We are told purity is old fashioned and passé. The reality is that there is incredible power in purity. As a woman who keeps herself for her husband, she has held a treasure for him to delight in. In saving herself, she has guarded her mind from painful flashbacks and guilt. She allows herself the opportunity to be completely vulnerable to one who has committed to care for her. She has also kept herself a mystery to be enjoyed as it was intended.

So how do we protect ourselves from the enemy's lies in this most vulnerable area? Regardless of your marital status, the enemy will desire to attack. Let us look at how we can be protected both outside of marriage and inside of marriage.

As we have referenced several times through this study, our desire to be loved is a driving force within us. That is not an error that God made. He created us with a longing to be loved so that we would seek Him and find satisfaction in Him first, then in our human relationships.

> Unfortunately, we frequently fall into the same trap as Eve in the area of our sexuality: We doubt God's plan and timing and think we know better.

As a single adult, when you desire intimacy, it is tempting to believe that this bite of the fruit... just one time, or with just one person, can be of no harm. Just like Eve, however, many a woman has awoken to realize that in that one "bite" she has just had her eyes opened to a world full of disappointment and pain. What looked like ecstasy has become excruciating. What looked like a garden has become a forest of darkness. The physical act is long over when the emotional wounds are still gaping.

Read 1 Corinthians 6:15-20.

Why is protection from these lies so important? (v15)

Do you view your body as your own?

How do your actions confirm this answer?

Who does your body belong to? (v19)

Why? (v20)

As beautiful as the Genesis 2:24-25 passage is that we read earlier in the lesson, what image does Paul paint of the Corinthian believer becoming one with? (v16)

What is different about being physically intimate outside of marriage than EVERY other sin? (v18)

Do you see the need for protection? The sin of sex outside of marriage is immensely more damaging because we are sinning against ourselves as well as God.

As I write this today, I am recovering from a dislocated kneecap. It was a silly, freak accident. No one intended any harm, but somehow the 10 seconds of rough housing that dislocated my kneecap led to over $1000 worth of doctor visits, physical therapy, and MRI's…and that is with insurance! The accident occurred eight weeks ago, and today was the first day I have been able to jog (shuffle)…for three minutes, mind you! The doctor said I should have a full recovery, but I may never be able to kneel on it again.

As I thought about this minor incident, I have been thankful that it was not worse. I did not have to have surgery. I was not exposed to infection in an operating room nor will I have visible scars from surgery. In a few more weeks, hopefully, no one will ever be able to tell that I had this injury.

I began thinking how analogous this situation was to the dangers of sex outside of marriage (Stick with me, I promise!). When you allow your emotions to get involved with someone outside of the marriage covenant, you may break up and you may have some healing to do from a broken relationship. In a few months' time, with the love of the Lord, friends, and family, you can be back to yourself and most people who will meet you will not know of your trial. But if you have had sex with that person, it is like you have had surgery. You will forever have a scar and be at risk for great infection of the soul. You see, the two become one flesh whether you want them to or not... whether you intended for them to or not. I have heard it described as trying to tear apart two pieces of paper that have been glued together.

This sin is different than any other. My friend, if you have not embraced that God's way of intimacy is for your good and protection, I challenge you to stop your justifying. The cost of disobedience in this area will far outweigh any cost of obedience (I speak from experience of having failed in this area and then having to take a costly stand and risk losing a significant relationship to be right with God). It does not matter whom you please, including yourself, if you displease God. And it does not matter whom you displease, if you please God.

Before we move on, I must address the concept of secondary virginity. While God's heart breaks over our sin against our bodies, it broke enough that His Son's death covered forgiveness for these sins as well. You can choose to ask for forgiveness, and through Godly sorrow and repentance, you can become a woman who once again walks in purity.

It is never too late and never too early to leave behind a choice that will destroy you.

If you are sexually active now in ANY context other than your own marriage, I urge you to begin the healing process now.

In an age where divorce is so common, some who have divorced will begin other sexual relationships after their divorce by justifying, "I have already lost my virginity, why does it matter?" God's word addresses sexuality after marriage.

Read 1 Corinthians 7:8-9.

> 8 To the unmarried and the widows I say that it is good for them to remain single as I am. 9 But if they cannot exercise self-control, they should marry. For it is better to marry than to burn with passion.

Who is Paul addressing? (v8)

What does he recommend? (v8)

What should they do if they do not have self-control? (v9)

Paul, a single man, is saying, "stay sexually pure as I am." If you cannot, then you should marry. Without getting into all of the nuances of divorce and remarriage, the point that must be made is that even the widow is warned not to have sexual relations outside of marriage. Why? Every sexual encounter forms a bond. A bond that is painful to break. You must remain pure in your singleness, no matter the reason, to guard yourself from becoming bonded to someone who has not committed to caring for your heart within marriage.

Even if you don't want to share this in a group setting, write what it is that keeps you from receiving God's warning, if you struggle in this area.

What are the possible consequences from continued disobedience in this area?

Some of you are in the midst of circumstances that make this subject very raw. May I encourage you to seek the Lord and obey the truth of Scripture, regardless of the cost. I say this not with a finger pointing at you, but with a broken heart. The scars of obedience will heal, but the scars that result from continued disobedience are far more painful. For others, you have people that you care for that are ensnared in this tragically common sin. Can you commit to pray for God to show them the protection of His way? Can you commit to being available to lovingly speak truth to them, if God chooses to use you to help them see the protection He offers?

What was the most meaningful statement or Scripture you read today?

What does God want you to do in response to today's study?

PURE INTIMACY

KARIN CONLEE

With slight hesitation and a huge prayer, we dive into a subject today that will likely make each of us, including me, uncomfortable. Yet this frequently omitted subject is in dire need of being addressed. Even if you are not currently married, I encourage you to engage in today's work so you can learn now how to see God's design in sexual intimacy. For the reasons we studied yesterday in Genesis 2:24 and 1 Corinthians 6:18, sex can be an incredibly painful and shameful subject. God designed a husband and wife to experience the celebration of their union, yet for many the marriage bed becomes a source of anxiety, not celebration.

The strong emotions may stem from previous sexual partners or from being the victim of a sexual crime. If this is true for you, I ask that if you have not had healing in this area that you do not put off dealing with your hurt any longer. While this resource is not designed to meet this need, it is a very legitimate need. Please ask your small group leader or pastor for assistance in locating a qualified counselor to help you. Our tendency is to minimize the impact that wounds in this area can have on the rest of our marriage. While addressing such a sensitive topic is difficult, there is only hope for healing if the subject is honestly addressed.

Outside of the traumatic situations, there remains a large percentage of women who silently struggle. He wants it too much. I want it more than he. I feel used. We are always too tired. I think he is disappointed in me. I am not interested. Every time we go on a date, he expects some. Why doesn't he seem interested in me? You get the point!

Basically, the enemy uses any angle he can to try to take this most intimate celebration of unity and make us avoid it.

Read 1 Corinthians 7:1-5.

In this portion of Paul's letter to the church of Corinth, he is responding to questions that they had regarding sexual practices. Remember, Corinth was a place where there was much perverse sexual activity (sound familiar?).

Why should each man have his own wife and each wife her own husband? (v2)

What should a husband give his wife and a wife give her husband? (v3)

The ESV (English Standard Version Bible) says, "The husband should give to his wife her conjugal rights, and likewise the wife to her husband." In the NASB (New American Standard Bible), it says we should fulfill our duty.

When your husband married you, he in essence said, "I will deny all other women and entrust you alone to meet my sexual needs." Wow! How we lose sight of that basic fact in the fog of what we think we want, feel, and deserve. Scripture affirms in verse 2 that the temptation of sexual immorality is real. That is one reason we are encouraged to marry.

> As a single, if you do not love a man enough to be willing to meet his sexual needs for the rest of your life, then do not marry him and do not sleep with him.

Who has authority over the wife's body? (v4)

Who has authority over the husband's body? (v4)

Now this study is specifically designed for women. You will have a tendency to want to deflect to the "what about him?" conversation. A marriage is a two-way relationship, but it is not 50-50. It is 100% - 100%. Therefore, I encourage you to learn and apply God's Word to you and do not get distracted by how your husband could improve. We all can use vast improvements!

When is the one time that you might deprive one another? (v5)

Who decides if there will be a period of abstaining? (v5)

Why should you come back together again? (v5)

Does the passage suggest this is an open ended amount of time or a specific, limited about of time?

If it were no big deal to have a mediocre sexual life, I think the Bible would make that clear. Instead, Paul speaks to the opposite and warns that there is danger in abstaining too long. Again, I do not say these things oblivious to the fact that some women's stomachs are literally turning. I beg you to talk to someone with a Biblical perspective about your specific situation, if that is you. In cases of abuse and where there has already been unfaithfulness, there is much more work to be done outside of the bedroom. You need someone trained to gently guide you on a path of recovery.

To those of us in fairly healthy marriages where there is not abuse, I urge you to heed the warning AND grasp what the marriage bed is supposed to celebrate. Consider that your intimacy with your husband is to celebrate that God has given you each other so you are not alone in this fallen world. Your marriage is not perfect because two imperfect people married each other, but by God's grace you can learn to see the best in your husband and celebrate that. We cannot wait until we think our husband has loved us well enough to be intimate.

We will sabotage the most sacred relationship God gives us on earth if we try to stand in the place of judge.

Another danger of our culture is how sexuality is portrayed. We get such skewed images from media that we have all but forgotten that sex is to be a celebration. It is the most intimate picture that as husband and wife; we are one. It is not about how good or lousy we feel that we look when we are undressed. Sometimes we make it so much about our fears that we forget that we are celebrating the relationship.

In the beginning of my marriage, I made a commitment to never say no to my husband. While that is a step in the right direction, my view fell far short of what intimacy could be. Your husband is not looking for someone to simply meet his physical urges, though we must understand he has them and trusts us to help him meet them in a God-honoring way. He is also not looking for Miss Perfect in the bedroom. We must remove this self and world-imposed pressure and see what truly matters. Your husband simply wants you to celebrate pure intimacy with him. A man may have a release by going through the motions with a willing wife, but the desire of his soul is to know that he can cause his wife to experience sexual fulfillment.

What first step can you take to make your physical life better in your marriage?

For some, this may start with asking God to change your attitude. For others, you may need to have a vulnerable conversation with your husband.

Would you be willing to lovingly engage in an honest conversation with your husband about how he views your sexual life as a couple?

It may start with a question like, "I want our physical life to be satisfying to you. What is one way that I could encourage you in the area of our intimacy?" You would be amazed how asking the question alone can begin to bring unity and oneness back to the forefront of your marriage.

Even the best of marriages can struggle in this area from time to time. Transitions are especially important times to guard against de-emphasizing this area of our marriage. Whether the transition comes in the form of the addition of a baby, illness, injury, starting a new job, your children staying up later, or caring for an elderly parent, do not allow the enemy to convince you that it is okay to continue neglecting this area of your marriage.

We'll stop here for today. If you are married, you know the rest of your homework assignment!

What was the most meaningful statement or Scripture you read today?

What does God want you to do in response to today's study?

NOTES FOR THE WEEK

WEEK EIGHT

CONTENTMENT WITHOUT CONDITIONS

A woman discovers contentment by abiding and depending upon Christ for rest in the midst of labor.

Day One
MORE THAN A NAP

Day Two
LEARNING TO REST

Day Three
EASY AND LIGHT

Day Four
I AM NOTHING

Day Five
PUNY LITTLE BRANCH

MORE THAN A NAP

CHRIS KUHLMAN

For many years, I felt as if contentment was just one step away. My performance-driven mindset made me think if my life looked good from the outside I would feel good on the inside. Even now after being a Christian for many years, there are times when I have to stop and remind myself of who I am in *Christ*. As we discussed in week one, our value comes from Christ and Christ alone. We should never move too far from the truth that our identity comes from the Lord or we will get off track.

A woman discovers contentment by abiding and depending upon Christ for rest in the midst of labor.

If you've been around Christians a little while, you've probably heard words like peace, rest, and joy thrown around like little charms we suddenly get to wear when we start a relationship with Christ. But what happens when your son gets kicked out of school, or your fiancé breaks off the engagement, or your boss tells you you've been downsized? We are left disappointed because our walk with Christ hasn't measured up to what we thought it would be. We run this rat race trying to be better and comparing ourselves with every other woman to see where we rank. We are left feeling frustrated, unworthy, and alone. What would it take for us to get off the treadmill and rest?

List some areas you feel anxious about right now.

When you hear the word "rest," what images come to mind?

Maybe you're dreaming of a comfy lounge chair stretched out on a beautiful beach with the crash of waves in the distance. While our first thoughts of rest may go to the few stolen moments when we aren't rushing from one meeting to another or cleaning up after someone else, Paul tells us in Philippians 4:7 "The peace of God, which surpasses all understanding, will guard your hearts and your minds in Christ Jesus."

The kind of rest we are talking about this week is much deeper than the need for a nap or a good night's sleep. We need relief from a heaviness that goes from day to day and that has nothing to do with our physical sleep, but everything to do with the heaviness of our hearts. The rest we are discussing is best defined as being able to take ease or be content.

What percent of the time would you say that you are "at ease?"

When you sense that you are not at rest or at ease, how do you try to find contentment?

Does your approach have long lasting results?

The world might suggest a weekend getaway, taking the day off from work, or a massage. While all three sound appealing, these approaches rarely bring lasting contentment at the heart level. We are merely addressing the symptom not the core source of our unrest. We need the weight on our shoulders lifted, not just massaged! Don't you agree?

The type of rest or contentment we need is found through Christ, but it doesn't just happen on its own. In order to find rest, there are certain things we must do. Let me illustrate what I mean. One night my daughter, Kendal, was baking cookies for an event. She did everything correctly, but she added the wrong amount of flour. Needless to say, she did not get the result she was hoping for! Finding rest is the same way.

> We have to follow the directions God gave us to find rest
> in order to get the result we desire.

One of the first things we must recognize is what robs us of the ability to be content. God's word warns us that we must stay away from some unhealthy behaviors. We can all get trapped in our thoughts from time to time. We can all overextend ourselves and be committed to too many things for a season, but if these patterns are reoccurring in your life then they are likely just symptoms. To have a state of mind that is at peace regardless of circumstances, we must see the "why" behind our choices. We must understand the underlying enemies that push us to repeat unhealthy choices that keep us in a state of unrest. Read the following verses and on the line below each, write down the primary enemy of rest mentioned.

Psalm 73:2-3

> [2] But as for me, my feet had almost stumbled, my steps had nearly slipped. [3] For I was envious of the arrogant when I saw the prosperity of the wicked.

Psalm 73:21-22

[21] When my soul was embittered, when I was pricked in heart, [22] I was brutish and ignorant; I was like a beast toward you.

Hebrews 3:18

And to whom did he swear that they would not enter his rest, but to those who were disobedient?

Hebrews 3:19

So we see that they were unable to enter because of unbelief.

We learn from these verses that the enemies of rest are envy, bitterness, disobedience, and unbelief.

Which of these do you struggle with the most?

List one or two recent experiences where, in retrospect, you see that one of these enemies robbed you of rest.

Today we have taken the first step and defined what keeps us from experiencing the rest or contentment that God desires for us. Tomorrow, we will learn the antidotes to these qualities, so we know how to withstand the temptation to fall prey to these enemies. For now, we need to look back to our initial question, I asked, "What are you anxious about right now?"

Now that you know some of the major enemies of rest, write down which enemy(ies) of rest corresponds with your anxiety(ies).

In Matthew 11:28 (NASB), Jesus says, "Come to Me, all who are weary and heavy-laden, and I will give you rest." Jesus tells those who are weary to come to Him. The Greek word for weary means "those tired from hard toil" and the Greek word for burdened or heavy-laden means "those loaded down."

Do those characteristics describe you more than being "at ease?"

Are you exhausted from trying to work things out in your own way? Have the choices you've made created a heavy burden in your life? Have the choices of others made you feel you have inherited a burden? We have just begun our study on contentment, but I want you to know from the very beginning that rest is possible. Contentment is possible. Peace is possible. We truly can become women who live out God's purpose for our lives with peace instead of pressure. God has given us His Word and His Holy Spirit as our guide. I beg you to stop trying to control your way to peace. It will never happen. Believe me, I have tried. Instead, let us prepare our hearts to be open to following God's path to peace this week.

What was the most meaningful statement or Scripture you read today?

What does God want you to do in response to today's study?

LEARNING TO REST

CHRIS KUHLMAN

Yesterday, we learned the four enemies of rest. Do you remember what they were?

Write the enemies of rest below. Look back on yesterday's lesson if you need to.

Today, we will learn the antidotes for those enemies of rest. It might sound contradictory to pair learning and rest together. Memories of all-night cram sessions in college might come crashing back, but I learned this lesson during my years of playing piano. When I was eight, I began taking lessons and continued through college. It took years of practice and playing to be able to sit down and confidently play for people. Because of the work I put in years ago, I am able to enjoy playing now.

Write down an example of something challenging you have learned how to do after much practice?

How long did it take you to learn?

In our key passage this week on contentment, Matthew 11:28-29, Jesus says,

28 Come to Me, all who are weary and heavy-laden, and I will give you rest. 29 Take My yoke upon you and learn from Me, for I am gentle and humble in heart, and YOU WILL FIND REST FOR YOUR SOULS. (NASB)

What does Jesus say we will find, if we learn from Him?

We have to learn that rest and learning don't happen overnight. In the verses above, Jesus describes two qualities of Himself that lead to rest for our souls. Write these two qualities below.

We are told to be gentle and humble in heart. In other translations of the Bible, the word *gentle* is interchanged with *meek*. In our minds, both of these words leave us thinking wimpy or weak, but meekness is actually far from weak!

Meekness is strength or power that is under control.

It is when we could be assertive, but choose not to be. Meekness is neither putting ourselves down nor having a prideful spirit. The meek person is not occupied with self at all. Meekness stems from trust in God's goodness and control over the situation. When we are meek, we don't feel compelled to exercise our power because we can trust that God will exercise His authority and His way is best.

What is one situation in your life currently where you have the ability to be assertive, but you need to choose to exercise gentleness or meekness instead?

Are you willing to make a commitment to try following the Lord's example and willingly choose to exercise meekness in this situation?

The second quality Jesus describes about Himself is that He is humble in heart. Read Philippians 2:5-8 and circle the word "humbled."

5 Have this mind among yourselves, which is yours in Christ Jesus, 6 who, though he was in the form of God, did not count equality with God a thing to be grasped, 7 but made himself nothing, taking the form of a servant, being born in the likeness of men. 8 And being found in human form, he humbled himself by becoming obedient to the point of death, even death on a cross.

How did Christ exemplify humility for us?

If you are familiar with the Easter story, write down some of the circumstances going on around Christ in the few days leading up to His death?

Christ perfectly exemplified humility for us, and this humility created rest even in the middle of all the chaos around Him as He went to the cross for us. Think back to when Christ was in the Garden of Gethsemane. He acknowledged His own humanity in the garden when he said, "Father, if you are willing, remove this cup from me. Nevertheless, not my will, but yours be done." At the same time that He revealed how He felt, He also simultaneously exercised humility and acknowledged God's will would be done. He humbled Himself and followed God's way.

This should encourage us greatly. When we discuss contentment and rest, God does not expect us to be indifferent robots. We can see a circumstance and lift up our cries to Him.

What we do after we lift up that cry determines if we will have contentment or not.

Do we acknowledge God's sovereignty and humbly trust Him as we walk through the trial like Christ? Or do we abandon contentment and allow our pride to step in, attempting to control our circumstances?

Let's review. What is another word that means "gentle"?

On a scale of 1 to 10 with 1 being I am NEVER meek/gentle, and 10 being I am almost always meek/gentle, how would you rate yourself with being meek?

On a scale of 1 to 10, how would you rate yourself on being genuinely humble? (1= never humble and 10=almost always humble)

How would those closest to you rate your meekness and humility? meekness: humility:

No matter where you are on the scale, are you motivated to change your behavior to become more meek and humble like Christ, knowing that it will give you rest for your soul?

Yesterday, we learned what robs us of rest: envy, bitterness, disobedience and unbelief. It is crucial for us to learn how to be meek and humble because these qualities strike a direct blow at those enemies that steal our rest. Our generation has been taught to take care of ourselves first. And while we love that idea that God wants us to rest in Him, we balk at the idea that rest comes from being meek and humble. Many times humility comes through a fall or humiliation. When we lose something we have clung tightly to, we are humbled, and that humility creates rest, *if* we seek to learn from Christ. We can be humbled when we have set all our hopes on a dream that is shattered. We can be humbled when we blow it in a relationship. We can be humbled when God makes our sin known to other people.

Describe a time where you learned humility through failure.

Whether through personal failure or unexpected crisis, when we are stripped of everything else, Christ becomes more to us than we could ever have hoped or imagined. This is why times of tragedy and crisis can be our biggest seasons of growth IF we lean into Christ. We can trust God because we know only God knows what's best, wants what's best, and gives what's best.

When our middle son, Taylor, was 22 months old, we found out that he needed to have open heart surgery. Tim and I were young parents and were shaken to the core with this news. It brought us to a place where we were facing God with our greatest fear. What if He decided to take Taylor from us? Could we trust God's perfect love for us even if we lost our son? Could we rest in our complete dependence on Him and trust Him to bring us through this circumstance? Or were we dependent on the outcome? This crisis drove us to our knees, and we had to decide if we would believe God no matter the outcome. God chose to bring Taylor through the surgery without any complications. But, He taught us a very important life lesson that we have had to rest in again and again.

While times of crisis or disobedience tend to get our attention and moves us towards humility, God desires to teach us humility through obedience. After all, one reason He had His Son come and dwell among us is so that we would have a tangible example of how to live out this life in humility.

So we don't always have to learn lessons the hard way, what are some ways in your life that you can proactively practice humility?

I once heard a story of two painters who each painted a picture illustrating his idea of rest. The first painted a still quiet lake among far off mountains. The second painted a thunderous waterfall with a fragile birch tree bending over the foam. At the fork of a branch, the rapid churning of water sprayed in the direction of a robin sitting on its nest. The first picture was only stagnation; the latter was rest. For in rest there are always contrasting elements - tranquility and energy, quiet and turbulence, construction and ruin, fearlessness and fearfulness. If you feel like you're hanging on to the thinnest branch of that birch tree today, take comfort in knowing that only in our complete dependence on God can we be meek and humble and truly find rest.

What was the most meaningful statement or Scripture you read today?

What does God want you to do in response to today's study?

Day Three

EASY AND LIGHT
CHRIS KUHLMAN

Yesterday, we discovered that when we learn to be meek and humble we find rest. In order to be meek and humble, we have to relinquish those areas we are still trying to control. Today, we'll learn how to relinquish those trouble areas.

When I was in 5th grade, I learned how to sew. When we started sewing dresses, we had to pay special attention to the "yoke." The yoke was the part of the dress that fits over the neck and shoulders and holds the front and back pieces together. If the yoke isn't sewn just right, the dress won't hang correctly when it's worn. Jesus used the word *yoke* in Scripture too. Let's review yesterday's key passage along with one additional verse.

Read Matthew 11:28-30 below.

> [28] Come to Me, all who are weary and heavy-laden, and I will give you rest. [29] Take My yoke upon you and learn from Me, for I am gentle and humble in heart, and YOU WILL FIND REST FOR YOUR SOULS. [30] For My yoke is easy and My burden is light. (NASB)

Did you see the word *yoke*? A yoke serves to "couple two things together."[1] Go ahead and circle the word *yoke* both times it appears in these verses.

How does Jesus describe His yoke?

Hebrews 4:3a says, "For we who have believed enter that rest..."

What quality is necessary to enter rest?

This verse from Hebrews 4 is a picture of the requirement of the Israelites to exercise belief in order to find rest. In this context, this use of the word *rest* actually refers to a physical place. The Israelites had to believe God and step across the Jordan river to claim the promised land. Without this faith, they would have continued wandering in the wilderness. Just like the Israelites, we must exercise belief in God in order to experience rest.

> True rest is impossible without belief in God.

If we believe in Him, we will come to Him. If we come to Him, we can take on His yoke and find rest.

Because of what Christ did for us on the cross, our old nature has been defeated, and we act on that truth by joining Christ, by taking His yoke upon us. It begins with faith. The alternative to believing leads down a different path. If we don't believe in God, then we rely on ourselves and become self-dependent. We go on carrying our own burden and receive no rest.

Imagine someone came to you one day and asked you to hold her box for just a minute. You agree and begin holding it. A few minutes go by and the box that originally seemed so light now feels a little heavier. Several hours go by and she still hasn't returned. Your arms are starting to feel sore and the box feels like a giant boulder. This is how it is when we carry our own burden. We think we've got it under control at first. It seems manageable, but slowly we start to realize we're sinking and our arms are quivering. Our burden is heavy, but Christ's burden is light.

The burden Christ asks us to carry is humility.

Fulfilling His desires and His mission becomes the purpose of our lives.

What do you think about trading in your burden in exchange for the burden of humility?

Which burden is lighter?

A few years ago we took a vacation to Colorado to go skiing. My son Taylor is a snow boarder so Tim and I decided to try snowboarding! We borrowed the snowboarding boots from a friend who had the sizes we needed. The first day, I put those boots on, and I stayed out on the slopes learning how to snowboard. But the boots did not fit me just right. They were slowly rubbing an area on my shin. The more I stayed out on the slopes, the more it caused friction until my shin was raw. I couldn't wait to get those boots off! But when you have boots that fit perfectly, there is nothing like the exhilaration of zooming down the side of a snow-covered mountain. You get to the bottom and you feel alive and ready to do it all over again!

When we do things our own way and wear a yoke we weren't designed to wear, we experience irritation and pain. But when we take on Jesus' yoke, one that fits perfectly, we are able to go through life with humility and our hearts will find rest. Christ knew that our lives would not be an easy one. He knew we would be burdened. Jesus is saying to us, "Carry it as I do. Take this life as I take it. Make your viewpoint My viewpoint. Interpret it the way I interpret it.

Change your perspective to My perspective. For My yoke is easy, works easily, sits right upon your shoulders and makes the burden light."

Have you ever carried a burden in your own power? If so, describe what that was like.

Have you ever been carrying a burden in your own power, but then finally realized you couldn't do it anymore and surrendered that burden to God? How did it feel when you finally surrendered?

Our souls are made for activity. When we are set free from our own burden, we have the strength to do something else. As Christians, rest does not mean laziness. A yoke is used for work.

> The difference is that the work of Christ energizes us, whereas the work of being in control ourselves leaves us feeling broken and inadequate.

Remember, a yoke is used for work. Actively seek out where you see the Lord working and join Him there. This will look different for every woman, but God has a special purpose for you. Jesus' yoke makes hard work light. Just like the yoke on my sewing dress had to be created just right so that it would fit correctly, Jesus also has designed a yoke that fits us like a glove.

Have you had an experience where hard work was light because you were doing it to bring the Lord honor? If so describe it below.

Have you ever had an experience where your work for the Lord felt especially burdensome? If so, take heart. Sometimes it takes some trial and error to find the place that God wired us to serve. Look to see where the body of Christ affirms your gifting and trust God with the journey as He leads you to your place of greatest impact for the kingdom. If you are under His yoke, He will lead you where you need to be used.

Look up these verses and write down what instructions are given to find rest.

Jeremiah 6:16 -

Matthew 11:29 -

While all of our burdens will not disappear, the weight of them depends upon our choices. When we learn to be humble like Christ, we are able to see our circumstances differently. We are able to gain perspective. Have you taken Christ's yoke upon you? If not, are you ready to? The only way we will be able to be a woman of rest in our crazy, busy lives is if we join with Christ and become humble just as Christ did for us.

What was the most meaningful statement or Scripture you read today?

What does God want you to do in response to today's study?

Day Four

I AM NOTHING
CHRIS KUHLMAN

Over the last three days, we have talked about both the enemies of rest and the qualities that create rest. We must keep these on the forefront of our minds so that as situations arise, we can evaluate our thinking and respond in a way that will allow us to rest instead of falling prey to the enemies that rob us of the peace again.

Write down the four enemies of rest:

Write down the two qualities that create rest:

Today, I want to explore another aspect of rest because rest isn't just the absence of anxiety.

> ### Rest is a contentment regardless of our circumstances.

When we have come to a place of contentment, we will have joy.

Jesus came to this earth to bind up the brokenhearted, to proclaim freedom for those who are held captive, to open the doors of the prison we have put ourselves in.

Read Isaiah 61:3. This is what He wants to do for those found mourning in Jerusalem and for all of His children.

> to grant to those who mourn in Zion—
> to give them a beautiful headdress instead of ashes,
> the oil of gladness instead of mourning,
> the garment of praise instead of a faint spirit;
> that they may be called oaks of righteousness,
> the planting of the LORD, that he may be glorified.

What does He want to give us instead of ashes?

What does He want us to experience instead of mourning?

What does He want us to have instead of a faint spirit?

What does He want us to be called?

Why does the Lord want to do all this?

Did you notice earlier when I said Jesus came to bind up the brokenhearted? Most of us did not have to get much past adolescence to get a taste of being brokenhearted. Sometimes our hearts get matted down, hard and dry, until there is no way that joy is going to spring from them until they are broken up, softened, and able to accept truth. There are many things that can cause our hearts to become hard. Sometimes it is our own stubbornness. Sometimes it is pain.

Are there any areas of your heart that you feel are hard and dry right now? Describe those below.

If you listed any areas, right now take time to ask God to soften it with His Word, and confess any sin that may be keeping you from agreeing with Him by the truth of His Word. When you are done, read John 15:1-11.

Why did Jesus tell the disciples this parable according to verse 11?

Write a couple of areas in which you could use a dose of joy!

From our text we know the following:

Jesus is the_____. (v1)

God the Father is the_____. (v1)

And we are the_____. (v5)

The branch grows out of the vine and there it lives and grows, and in time, bears fruit. It has no responsibility except to receive sap and nourishment from the root and stem. It is a life of total dependence. The branch has nothing; it depends upon the vine for everything. Jesus must be everything to us. We need to learn to depend totally on Him—moment by moment. The vine does the work and the branches enjoy bearing the fruit! Christ is the source of joy just as He is the source of rest. As we take His yoke upon us, we learn from Him. We, as His people, share His life, and therefore, we share the benefit of joy and rest.

What does the vine do? It sends its roots out into the soil, under the ground—sometimes a long way out—for nourishment and to drink in the moisture. It then takes that moisture, minerals, and good stuff from the soil and turns it into sap, which it uses to make the fruit. The vine does the work. The branch just receives the sap and the result is grapes. All the responsibility of the work is on Christ. How does He fulfill it? By the Holy Spirit who dwells in us. The relationship between the vine and the branches is the living connection that is constant. Just as the sap flows continuously, the Holy Spirit flows through us continuously. Morning by morning, day by day, hour by hour, and step by step. No matter what work we have to do we go to Him in utter helplessness. Yes... we come as one who knows nothing, is nothing, and can do nothing. TOTAL DEPENDENCE!

> If I am something, God is not everything.

But when I become nothing, it allows God to become all - that is what is meant by "abide in Me" in verse 4.

Using Jesus' analogy, do you spend more time acting like the vine dresser, the vine, or the branch?

How does your answer above help explain your level of contentment?

Which role should experience the most rest - the vine or the branch?

Look back at John 11:5. Fill in the blank.

Apart from me you can do_____.

The branch has nothing except what it gets from the vine. It sounds ludicrous to think of a vine trying on its own to produce fruit. Yet, that is exactly what we try to do. You and I have nothing but what we get from Jesus. The life of the branch is one of deep restfulness. When I am resting in Christ, I have left everything with Him. I can't help but be full of joy.

What are you trying to do on your own?

When the heat wants to dry up the branch, the branch trusts in the vine to bring moisture to keep it fresh. What a truth for us! The branches get rained on; they sometimes have to endure immense heat with seemingly no relief. But it's not up to that branch to find relief. It rests totally upon the vine for its nourishment and for its needs to be met. We, too, have to endure the rain and the heat that life brings us. There are circumstances that sometimes overwhelm us to that point where we feel we might drown. Or circumstances can leave us dry and weary. Sit back and rest in God. Know that you are not meant to work it all out but to be a branch abiding in the vine, depending on Him. It is a relief to me when I give up my way of trying to work everything out. It is exhausting and I end up restless! But I can rest knowing that Jesus is my everything, and He is going to work out what He has already purposed for me.

Read these encouraging words from 2 Corinthians 4:7-9.

> 7 But we have this treasure in jars of clay, to show that the surpassing power belongs to God and not to us. 8 We are afflicted in every way, but not crushed; perplexed, but not driven to despair; 9 persecuted, but not forsaken; struck down, but not destroyed.

Who does the power belong to? (v7)

Who does not have power? (v7)

Even when we might be afflicted in every way, perplexed, or struck down, write down what we are NOT:

we are NOT_____(v8)

we are NOT driven to_____(v8)

we are NOT_____(v9)

we are NOT_____(v9)

Are you grasping that we were not created to be in control? From the analogy of the vine to Paul's description to Corinth, there is no confusion that God is in control. This is such a sharp contrast to how we live and view our lives. Are you willing to try life as God designed?

What areas are you committing to surrender control of to God today? Please share these with a friend or small group leader so she can help hold you accountable.

Everything in this world will scream that we should take control. Yet, the tighter we grip the neck of our every circumstance, the less peace we have. The more we try to play God in our lives, the less content we become.

God offers us a path of rest, but does not force us down His road.

How much longer will you continue wondering what rest is like? I dare you to try His way one decision at a time.

What was the most meaningful statement or Scripture you read today?

What does God want you to do in response to today's study?

PUNY LITTLE BRANCH

CHRIS KUHLMAN

We have learned this week how to find rest and even joy in the midst of trying circumstances, but you may be wondering if it's really possible. When I'm facing a crisis in my life, can I really find rest and joy?

In a letter from Hudson Taylor, a missionary to China, to his mom, Taylor wrote, "..I have continually to mourn that I follow at such a distance and learn so slowly to 'imitate my precious master.'" His regret was that it took him so long to release everything to His Master. His friend, Mr. Judd, wrote about his change. "He had been a toiling, burdened one before, with latterly not much rest of soul. It was resting in Jesus now and letting Him do the work - which makes all the difference....in the practical things of life a new peace possessed him. Troubles did not worry him as before. He cast everything on God in a new way, and gave more time to prayer.

Instead of bondage, liberty; instead of failure, quiet victories within; instead of fear and weakness, a restful sense of sufficiency in Another."[2]

Mr. Judd saw a transformation in his friend, Hudson Taylor. What do you desire for those closest to you to see as you learn to find contentment in Christ?

At this same time, Mr. Taylor wrote in a letter to his sister,

> "I know that if I could abide in Christ all would be well, but I could not. I would begin the day with prayer, determined not to take my eye off Him for a moment, but pressure of duties, sometimes very trying, and constant interruptions apt to be so wearing, caused me to forget Him. Then one's nerves get so fretted in this climate that the temptations to irritability, hard thoughts and sometimes unkind words are all the more difficult to control. Each day brought its register of sin and failure, of lack of power. To will was indeed 'present with me', but how to perform I found not...Is there no rescue? Must it be thus to the end - constant conflict, and too often defeat?"[3]

How can you relate to Hudson's frustration?

Let's keep reading the words of Hudson Taylor...

There was nothing I so much desired as holiness, nothing I so much needed; but far from in any measure attaining it the more I strove after it, the more it eluded my grasp, until hope almost died out, and I began to think that - perhaps to make heaven the sweeter - God would not give it down here.

I knew full well that there was in the root, the stem, abundant fatness but how to get it into my puny little branch was the question...I saw that faith was the only requisite - was the hand to lay hold on His fullness and make it mine. But I had not this faith.

But how to get faith strengthened? Not by striving after faith but by resting on the faithful one. I saw it! 'If we believe not, he abideth faithful.' I looked to Jesus and saw that he had said, 'I will never leave you'. Ah there is rest! I thought. I have striven in vain to rest in Him. I'll strive no more. For has he not promised to abide with me - never to leave me, never to fail me? He never will.

As I thought of the vine and the branches, what light the blessed Spirit poured direct into my soul! How great seemed my mistake in wishing to get the sap, the fullness *out* of Him! I saw not only that Jesus will never leave me but that I am a member of His body, of His flesh and of His bones. The vine is not the root merely, but *all* - root, stems, branches, twigs, leaves, flowers, fruit. And Jesus is not that alone - He is soil and sunshine, air and showers, and ten thousand times more than we have ever dreamed, wished for or needed. Oh, the joy of seeing this truth!

The sweetest part, if one may speak of one part being sweeter than another, is the rest which full identification with Christ brings. I am no longer anxious about anything, as I realize this; for He, I know, is able to carry out His will and His will is mine. It makes no matter where he places me or how. [We should not] look upon this experience, these truths, as for the few. They are the birthright of every child of God...And it was all so simple and practical![4]

Ladies, I want you to know that I am a woman who desires to apply the deep treasures of truth of Scripture to my life. My desire is to live a life that is always desiring more of Jesus. In the past few years I can say I have experienced a resting in Jesus that I have not experienced before. This rest is available to you, too.

God desires you to experience the fullness of His rest.

For me, it is enveloped in remembering Christ's redemptive work on the cross. It is an acknowledgement of His GREAT love for me and a recognition that I deserve nothing good, but that out of His love He chose to bring me into relationship with Him. That relationship is like any other and it grows with experiences, with trials, and with great delights. I am able to rest in Christ today because I KNOW Him in a way that I can depend and rely on Him. It doesn't mean that I never have times of worry, but that when I feel that restlessness I know I need to get back to that place of total surrender on Him. He is my Savior, my Rock, my Provider. It is more important to me today to live in His presence than for my circumstances to change. I pray for you that you too will enjoy His most rapturous love. It is there I have found abundant peace and joy and rest.

As we close out our week, take some time and answer the following questions:

Am I resting or restless? What is causing me to feel restless?

What percent of my energy do I spend trying to control different aspects of my life?

Is there something I want—that I think will make me happy—that I don't have? What is it?

Am I caught in a sin and I know I'm not at a right place with God?

What specifically am I struggling to believe that God can handle in my life?

What pressure or pull in my life am I allowing to overwhelm me instead of trusting God's hand?

As we close this week, pray and ask God to teach you meekness and humility. For only when we learn these qualities and realize that our ultimate contentment is in Christ alone can we find rest and joy. It is available if we are willing to learn.

What was the most meaningful statement or Scripture you read today?

What does God want you to do in response to today's study?

NOTES FOR THE WEEK

MISSION WITH MEANING

A woman discovers her mission by seeing her life from God's perspective and engaging those around her.

Day One
RUNNING THE RIGHT RACE

Day Two
RUNNING WITH GRATITUDE

Day Three
RUNNING HIS WAY

Day Four
WHY WE RUN

Day Five
RUNNING FORWARD

RUNNING THE RIGHT RACE
KARIN CONLEE

We have made it to the last week of our study of *Miss Perfect*! I hope that you will finish strong this last week. You have been a trooper to persevere through some areas that are sometimes easier left undisturbed. I urge you to consider that the week that seemed the hardest to swallow may be where you need to revisit and allow the Holy Spirit to continue to teach you. God does not stop His work when we finish a study if we remain open to His promptings!

As we have looked at God's holiness, our identity, our relationships, our relational disciplines, our attitude, our purity, and our contentment found in Him, we come full circle. Each week has been intended to be a building block that, when constructed, puts us smack dab in the middle of living out God's mission. We are going to spend this week seeing what this looks like. As it relates to mission,

> ## A woman discovers her mission by seeing her life from God's perspective and engaging those around her.

Our intent in creating this study was to identify the most critical components of a woman's life that, if lived in agreement with God's Word, could enable her to fulfill her God-given mission. What peace we would have if we were living in a place of being exactly who God desires us to be as a woman, a friend, a wife, or a mother! With a high level of confidence, I can say that if you proactively work towards health in these nine areas, your life will be ripe to reap a huge harvest from what you are sowing. Yes, we will fail in these areas at different times, but God will honor our perseverance if we continue seeking His way and participating in His mission. Doesn't each of us long for a life that matters and a life free from self-inflicted landmines? While being a follower of Christ does not protect us from pain and trials, following God's design is the only way to live a life of purpose without pressure.

Through this study, we have closely examined different subjects. We spend much of our personal life at this vantage point, too. We frequently see our lives through a microscope, solely looking at the details of our own little world. I confess that much of my time revolves around the needs and feelings of the Conlee household. As we move forward, let's explore how our little world should fit into God's big mission.

If we can step back and get a broader view, we would realize that we have been created as women to play a beautiful, fulfilling role in this thing called life. There is so much more to our story than just getting up and being busy all day long. Even the joys of specific seasons of life are just that...seasons! We are not the mother of toddlers forever. We aren't in the workplace forever. We are not running the carpool forever. We must not get so locked in on a season that we miss God's activity and larger calling as a woman on His mission. The problem is that sometimes the path to the starting blocks of God's mission for our lives is cluttered with distractions. It is as if we stop at McDonald's, forgetting that we actually had reservations around the corner at Ruth's Chris Steakhouse. We must leave this week wrapping our minds around the mission that God has for us so we don't miss the spectacular journey we were designed to take.

We will learn about our mission through Paul in 1 Corinthians this week. We enter into Paul's letter to the church in Corinth. Among other subjects, he addresses how they should engage a culture of both religious and irreligious people. Since Paul first saw his need for Christ, he has made his life about pointing both groups of people to his Savior. As believers in the 21st century, our goal must be the same: to point everyone, religious or irreligious, to our Savior. Paul returns to one of his common analogies and paints the picture that we are in a race.

Please read 1 Corinthians 9:24-25 below.

> [24] Do you not know that in a race all the runners run, but only one receives the prize? So run that you may obtain it. [25] Every athlete exercises self-control in all things. They do it to receive a perishable wreath, but we an imperishable.

How many of the runners run in a race? (v24)

What two types of wreaths can people run for? (v25)

What do you think the two wreaths represent in Paul's analogy?

Paul knew that the analogy of a race would resonate with all the Corinthians who were very familiar with the Isthmian games. Even today, we can all relate to the analogy of a race, right? Don't you feel like you live life in a race? Whether a Jew, a Greek, a believer, or an unbeliever, I think everyone runs a race. Everyone has suited up and moved out of the starting blocks. The question is, "Are you going after the perishable wreath or the imperishable wreath?"

As we talk about our mission as a woman following the Lord, which wreath would those closest to you say you are seeking? Why would they say that?

Paul echoes God's message of excellence. All of us should run and run in such a way that we should win. Unfortunately, just because you have exercise clothes on and work up a sweat does not mean you are on God's mission. Truth be told, most of us probably fluctuate back and forth in our hearts and actions as to which prize we want. No wonder we always feel so much pressure!

> We don't have time to run two races. One will limit the other.

What would it look like for you in your current stage of life to focus purely on pursuing the imperishable wreath? Be specific. What is one thing you would need to start doing or stop doing to make sure you are running for the right prize?

Read 1 Corinthians 9:26-27.

> 26 So I do not run aimlessly; I do not box as one beating the air. 27 But I discipline my body and keep it under control, lest after preaching to others I myself should be disqualified.

Paul now turns and uses himself as an example in his metaphor. Why does Paul say he trains with discipline? (v27)

Paul runs with aim and boxes with focus. He disciplines his body and keeps it under control. Paul is not describing P90X or his success at a circuit class. His point is that he lives in such a way that his life is in alignment with what he says. Paul cares so much about God's mission that he wants to make sure there is nothing in his life that others would see as a contradiction to what he proclaims.

In light of this being our last week, as you think back over our 9 topics this semester, is there anything in your life that contradicts the message of Christ?

If so, what step do you need to take so that your life is not a contradiction to God's mission? Who do you need to tell so you have some accountability to follow through?

As if he could hear our own internal battle, Paul continues his letter with a reminder of the past and a warning that we cannot miss as we consider the temptations of choosing our own race over God's.

Read 1 Corinthians 10:1-5.

What experiences does Paul remind them that their fathers had? (v1-4)

The Israelites had a pretty good list of spiritual accomplishments. It might be equal to someone's modern day "Christian resume" that included baptism, attending Sunday School, going to church camp, and feeding the poor.

What was God's perspective of these men? (v5)

What action did God take against them? (v5)

When we think of God's strong commentary on the Israelites in light of Paul's analogy of running races, I think it is fair to say that these men were running the race for the right reason, but they were not running it well. God was not pleased with the Israelites and chose to exercise His judgment by having an entire generation die in the wilderness (1 Corinthians 10:5). We should be vividly reminded that it is not our external actions alone that determine how well we are running. Our attitude really does matter to God. God's people did follow God's direction part of the way, but then they grumbled and forgot about God's mission.

Read 1 Corinthians 10:6.

Why should we care about the Israelites' disobedience?

Paul is telling the church at Corinth to learn from the mistakes of those who went before them.

Read 1 Corinthians 10:7-11 and list some of the specific ways that the Israelites sinned and got distracted from accomplishing God's mission.

How are their sins like our sins today?

Paul hits some pretty major categories of sin. Paul mentions sexual immorality, testing Christ, and grumbling as different ways that the Israelites abandoned God's mission and made their own idols. Then Paul concludes with a warning to the Corinthians.

Read 1 Corinthians 10:12.

Paraphrase 1 Corinthians 10:12 into your own words or draw a picture to represent his warning.

Paul is telling us to not get too confident. If you think that you are not in danger of falling into temptation, you should think again!

What amazing hope does Paul give us in 1 Cor 10:13?

Rest assured, temptation is a real thing and is a common experience for the entire human race. By God's grace, however, He will protect us by always providing a way of escape!

The Israelites did not set out to sabotage themselves. Don't you think that the first steps to their idolatry were just harmless reflections that things were not going as they hoped? A little dissatisfaction with God's way of doing things quickly led them down a slippery slope. If we are not staying connected to the Lord, we too can ever so subtly move away from God's mission and be tempted to just pursue our own goals.

In your spiritual journey, have you ever sensed you were living with God's mission consistently on your mind? If so, describe that time.

In your journey with the Lord, have you ever looked back and noticed that you had unintentionally moved from God's mission to your own? In retrospect, what caused you to lose focus on His mission?

In what ways do you try to force God's mission to fit into your plan?

As we conclude today, let me just normalize that all of us will come to these truths from a different path. Some of us may have never even truly considered God's mission before now. Others may have walked closely with the Lord at one point, but now sense distance. It sounds so harsh, but...

> When we are focused on anything other than God's plan,
> we are committing idolatry just like the Israelites did.

Let us not continue to repeat their path of trying to live out our own mission. None of us want to spend our whole life pursuing something perishable. We must realize that we can leave behind this frustrating life of trying to get all the external things right. There is no need to go another day under the self-inflicted and world-inflicted pressure. Tomorrow, we will see how we can choose a much greater journey.

What was the most meaningful statement or Scripture you read today?

What does God want you to do in response to today's study?

RUNNING WITH GRATITUDE
KARIN CONLEE

Yesterday, I asked you to take a step back from your own circumstances and to consider God's big picture mission for your life. I am hoping that you come today with conviction that you want to run the race with excellence for the right prize.

> In our busyness, it is so easy to be lulled back into just accomplishing tasks and to forget that when we took on the name Christian we also took on a new mission.

In my interactions with women, I find that there are generally two points where we get derailed in our journey as believers on mission. We'll address both struggles over the next few days. When we overcome these two obstacles, we are primed to live as God intended so don't check out now! We'll tackle the first one today and tomorrow we will learn about the second one. The first struggle that women (and men) can face is that we aren't genuinely excited about God's mission. GASP! Doesn't that sound horrible? But isn't it true? You might consider God's mission and mistakenly lump it into the other areas of Christian duty. As humans, we try to boil God's plan down to a list we can accomplish. It would be the same thing as asking someone to either eat a warm cinnamon crunch bagel or to eat a picture of a cinnamon crunch bagel. Two radically different experiences!

Honestly, how excited are you by the thought of making your life about God's mission? (Be honest either way!)

If you are excited, what do you think inspired that excitement initially? What continues to fuel your excitement?

What do you think moves someone from their agenda to God's agenda?

Before we go any further, I think it is important for us to continue to reflect on Paul's journey. Yesterday, we saw how determined he was to give his best to being on God's mission. Why did he see the importance in being on God's mission? After all, before Paul became a believer he had plenty of power and he was not exactly in need of a mission. There are two elements that

I believe were the keys to Paul's wholehearted devotion. I pray that through studying Paul, we will allow these perspectives to propel us on our mission for the Lord.

Many will remember that Paul was originally named Saul. He encountered God through a blinding light on the Damascus road. Read Acts 9:1-9, 17-22.
When Saul took on a new identity as a Christian, he also took on a new mission! His entire life became devoted to a purpose greater than himself. From the verses you just read in Acts, do you sense that Saul, who was soon renamed Paul, felt forced to proclaim what had happened to him?

Paul did not put on a load of guilt with his new name. He didn't grovel and pout and then get out a list of things to do that would keep God off his back. Paul was not forced by the disciples to tell his story. Even when his life became endangered in the next few verses, he was determined to carry out God's mission.

Think of it this way: when a woman marries she takes on the name of her husband. Why? Because they become one and share an identity. When you take on your husband's last name, you become an integral part of carrying out the mission God has for you as a couple. As politically incorrect as it is, you actually become his helper to accomplish God's mission through your husband. My job is to help Chris Conlee be the best Chris Conlee he can be. I joyfully and willingly accepted that role by marrying him.

> **If you were to get married and then tell your husband that you don't want anything to do with his life or purpose, what type of marriage would you have?**

> **If you give your life to the Lord and then tell God you don't want anything to do with His purpose or mission, what type of relationship would you have?**

> **How have you done this?**

When we take on the name of Christian, we take on His identity and His mission. Being on mission is not just about raising money and going out of the country, though Paul did the later. It is also about who we are right where we are. We have the privilege of becoming an integral part of His plan to love people and lead them to hope through a relationship with Christ. Out of gratitude for what God did and belief in who He was, Paul chose to begin a new race and to run it well.

> **As a reminder for yourself, list out what your relationship with the Lord has saved you from and how you have been blessed as a result of your salvation.**

Gratitude was the first reason Paul made himself available to God's mission. Are you still grateful for God's work in you? Most women can usually feel their feelings when they contemplate those they love. Contemplating God's goodness to you should move your soul in your love for the Lord, not just be an intellectual exercise! May our gratitude compel us as we run His race!

The verses leading up to Paul's race analogy shed an important light on the second reason Paul lived a lifetime committed to God's mission.

Read 1 Corinthians 9:1-5, 19.

Do you see a theme repeated in verses 1 and 19? What do you think it is?

If you were to read Chapter 9 in its entirety (which I highly recommend), you will realize that Paul comes from a perspective of freedom. Whether applying it to his right to eat, to drink, to receive provision from his ministry, or to take a wife, Paul clearly understands that he is free to do so. He is not bound by all the rigors of the law. He freely chooses to give up some of his freedoms for a greater mission and is trying to show the believers in Corinth how they should use their freedom.

> When you surrendered your life to the Lord, He changed your identity and gave you the freedom to choose to be on mission.

We are free—without pressure—to take on His purpose. We can rewind all the way back to the Garden of Eden where we started and realize that as we are free to choose to love God, we are also free to choose to be on mission with God. Being on mission offers us the greatest opportunity for protection and to experience the joy of being a part of God's story, but it is still a choice we have to make.

Does remembering that you have the freedom to choose to be on mission with God change your perspective?

Read 1 Corinthians 9:19 again and continue through verse 23.

What does Paul choose to do with his freedom in Christ? (v19)

Why does Paul make this choice? (v19)

Paul takes his freedom and willingly decides to serve others in such a way that more will come to know His Lord. Wow!

What are you actively doing with your freedom in Christ?

Do not dismiss the previous questions as condemning. Think where Paul started! He was killing Christians. We are all on a journey of seeing the magnitude of God's mission and joining it. Please prayerfully consider the following:

What is one choice you could make to use your freedom to engage in God's mission exactly where you are in life right now?

If you continue reading 1 Cor 9:20-23, you would see that Paul wanted to be used in the lives of Jews, those under the law, those outside the law, and the weak. If Paul were alive today, he might say that he wanted to reach the Jews, those tied up in legalism, the criminals, and the destitute. Paul laid it all on the line for the Lord.

What types of people might God desire to use you to reach?

Circle any occurrence of the word "all" in 1 Corinthians 19:22b-23 below.

22b I have become all things to all people, that by all means I might save some. 23 I do it all for the sake of the gospel, that I may share with them in its blessings.

What did Paul hold back from being available for God's mission?

Is there any part of your life that you are holding back for your own mission? (Consider your time, your reputation, your resources, your comfort, your pride.)

What is one specific step you can take to release what you have previously withheld from use on God's mission?

As we conclude today, I hope that you will grasp that Paul's devotion to God's mission was not forced religious duty. Paul made a choice to serve the Lord out of gratitude to the One who did not leave him in his sin. We started today acknowledging that one of the biggest obstacles we can face in our spiritual journey is that we are not excited about God's mission. If you continue denying what God has done for you and take credit for creating your own path, you will remain ungrateful and unmotivated to actively be on God's mission. You will keep the daily pressure of trying to maintain whatever dysfunctional pursuit of perfection you have created. Why are you holding out? How much fun are you having trying to be Miss Perfect on your mission? May we choose to be like Paul and allow our gratitude to lead us to exchange our control for the freedom of joining our Lord on His mission.

What was the most meaningful statement or Scripture you read today?

What does God want you to do in response to today's study?

RUNNING HIS WAY

KARIN CONLEE

So far this week, our study on mission has made us deal with several pretty significant questions. We looked at them initially through Paul's analogy of running a race. Let me rephrase the same questions in the context of our design as women:

- Am I living my daily life on God's mission or my mission?
- Have I made an intentional choice to be on God's mission?
- Am I committed to being completely devoted to God's mission?

I mentioned in Day 1 that there were two areas where women get derailed in our journey as believers on mission. The first area we addressed was our excitement. The second area is much more subtle. In some ways, the American church itself condones and perpetuates this second mindset. I want you to know before we dive in that there is balance to this subject. At the same time, Christian women in particular have swung the pendulum so far to one side that I feel a need to encourage us to examine the context of Scripture for a picture of what our lives should look like as women.

If we, as women who love the Lord, can navigate through the landmines of feminism and come to adulthood with a biblical view of our role as a woman of God, there is still another hurdle to cross. We cannot become the casual Christian that the enemy will settle for us to be. The hurdle: defining our lives by our role as a mother. This hurdle exists for both those who are currently moms and those who long to be moms. Breathe. I have likely offended some of you already. Let me reassure you that the women writing this and even the women editing this who have children love their children and their role of mother to the core of their being. We would desire no less for you. What we must consider, however, is if this notion that our family is our only ministry is actually biblical or just convenient.

Again, I knowingly walk on eggshells. There is certainly context and stages of life, but if we are truly on God's mission then we must grasp that while we are, for a season, highly engaged in discipling our own children, that this discipleship should not happen in isolation from the rest of God's work. In reality, our ministry is to our family...

> We must realize we have an earthly family and a spiritual family.
> God's mission will have us engaged in both.

Today, I want to allow the consistent patterns of Scripture to help us have clarity on our roles and what God values. I want us to consider what women are in Scripture and why God has them there. Let's cast a wide net to start. I'll save your fingers from flipping for the first few.

As I assess Old Testament passages that involve women, we have Eve, Sarai, Haggar, Rebekah, and Rachel that have primary roles. Each of these women was the mother of a primary Biblical figure. God gives us the back-story to the beginning of creation through Adam and Eve, then proceeds to give us the context of how Isaac, Ishmael, Esau and Jacob, and Jacob's twelve descendants were born. Interestingly, Sarai, Rebekah and Rachel were all barren for a period of time. After we move from the mothers of these spiritual giants, however, most of the interaction around women changes.

Humor me in a little exercise. Look at the names of the women below and write what you believe was the main reason the Lord included mention of her in Scripture. If you are familiar with these women in Scripture, you are welcome to do this from memory, but I have included key verses to assist you.

Esther - Esther 7:3-4 (below; and see also Esther 2:4-8, 15-17; 8:1-8 for context)

[3] Then Queen Esther answered, "If I have found favor in your sight, O king, and if it please the king, let my life be granted me for my wish, and my people for my request. [4] For we have been sold, I and my people, to be destroyed, to be killed, and to be annihilated. If we had been sold merely as slaves, men and women, I would have been silent, for our affliction is not to be compared with the loss to the king."

Mary, mother of Jesus - Matthew 1:21, Luke 1:26-31, 38; 2:7; Acts 1:14

Mary Magdelene - Luke 8:1-3 (below; and see also Mark 15:40-41, 47; 16:9-11)

[1] Soon afterward he went on through cities and villages, proclaiming and bringing the good news of the kingdom of God. And the twelve were with him, [2] and also some women who had been healed of evil spirits and infirmities: Mary, called Magdalene, from whom seven demons had gone out, [3] and Joanna, the wife of Chuza, Herod's household manager, and Susanna, and many others, who provided for them out of their means.

Martha and Mary - John 11:19-22 (below; and see also Luke 10:38-42; John 11:1-3, 38-44)

[19] and many of the Jews had come to Martha and Mary to console them concerning their brother. [20] So when Martha heard that Jesus was coming, she went and met him, but Mary remained seated in the house. [21] Martha said to Jesus, "Lord, if you had been here, my brother would not have died. [22] But even now I know that whatever you ask from God, God will give you."

Lydia - Acts 16:14-15 (below; and see also Acts 16:35-40)

[14] One who heard us was a woman named Lydia, from the city of Thyatira, a seller of purple goods, who was a worshiper of God. The Lord opened her heart to pay attention to what was said by Paul. [15] And after she was baptized, and her household as well, she urged us, saying, "If you have judged me to be faithful to the Lord, come to my house and stay." And she prevailed upon us.

Priscilla – Acts 18:26 (below; and see also 18:2, 18)

[26] He (Paul) began to speak boldly in the synagogue, but when Priscilla and Aquila heard him, they took him and explained to him the way of God more accurately.

Whether it is Esther being used to save the Jewish people, or Lydia opening her home, or Priscilla explaining that Christ has come as the fulfillment of John the Baptist, all of these women were referenced because they were contributing to God's mission. Scripture does not even bother to mention whether many of these women were wives or mothers. Even Mary, the mother of Jesus, had purpose outside of birthing the Son of God! We see her in Acts as a part of the early church. They were all playing their role in accomplishing God's purpose.

If we go back to the mothers of the Patriarchs, even their stories are so much bigger than raising children. Think of the life Sarah lived accompanying Abraham as he followed the Lord's direction. I am sure she had to have grit and conviction to willingly put herself in many of the positions they experienced.

During our week on Purity, we looked at Mary's prayer of praise in the book of Luke to get a glimpse into her deeply rooted trust and love for God. In our week on Relationships, we referenced the faith of Hannah as she longed for, received, and then gave up Samuel. Do you see the same pattern emerging? Their stories are not just about babies and motherhood; they are about faith. May that be said of our lives, too.

If God blesses you with children, let your story and my story be about a faith so contagious that the children God entrusts us with are drawn into a lifestyle of worship, adoration, and joyful service to the Lord. If we get everything else in motherhood right (good luck with that!), but get living out our faith wrong, then it is all wrong. Living a vibrant faith is the greatest responsibility of motherhood. In the same breath, if God's mission for you does not include biological children, you are called to no lower a level of faith. All women, with or without biological children, shape this world and have the opportunity to engage in spiritual motherhood. Our faith or lack of faith will shape those He puts into our path to influence.

Let's look up one more to drive the proverbial nail in the coffin.

Read Luke 1:5-7, 39-45.

What do we learn about Elizabeth's faith through an extended period of barrenness? (Luke 1:5-7)

What does Elizabeth's response to seeing Mary indicate about her faith?

I would argue that God entrusted some specific women with children who were front and center Biblical characters BECAUSE they were women on mission. Think of Mary and Elizabeth. They did not just end up with men used of the Lord...and in Mary's case, the Savior. God strategically placed those children in the wombs where they would be a part of an earthly family that lived out God's mission. Joseph and Mary were not skipping synagogue...nor were they just going through the Judaic motions. Elizabeth did not just get lucky with a good kid! No, there is evidence that these women sought the face of God. She and Zechariah were called righteous! I believe as God says, that He seeks to and fro for a heart that is completely His; that He chose these women because He knew they would not allow their children to become their gods, but instead would usher them into a family of faith that actively lived out truth.

Whether or not you are on mission should not be a function of your age, your stage of life, the number of children God blesses you with, whether you work outside your home, whether you are poor or rich. We should all be on God's mission. We must not wait to start contributing to God's mission until we are out of college, or until we are secure in our careers, or until our children are out of diapers, or they have made it to kindergarten. As seasons pass and we are retired or empty-nesters, we should not think that our time on God's mission has faded either! Lord help each of us if we think that American retirement somehow equates to spiritually coasting in our final decades of life.

> From our spiritual birth until our physical death, we should be on God's mission.

God's mission is why we were created! Anything less will ring hollow and void over time.

We started out the day wrestling with the fact that defining our life solely by our role as a mother can be a hurdle in being on God's mission. While the American culture at large may no longer hold motherhood in esteem as much as it once did, within the Christian culture you can safely rest with this philosophy. This hurdle is equally true for someone who has young children, has grown children, or has no children. We can make motherhood our idol whether we are in the midst of raising children or wishing we were, especially if we think that raising biological children is our only mission. We have seen that the totality of Scripture embraces the precious role of women in raising children, but it is the faith of women and their obedience in a much broader scope that caused the Holy Spirit to inspire men to write of the great women of our Biblical heritage. Make your life something worthy of writing about!

You have worked hard today! Thank you for persevering. Tomorrow, we will see how we can make living God's mission possible right where we are.

What was the most meaningful statement or Scripture you read today?

What does God want you to do in response to today's study?

WHY WE RUN

KARIN CONLEE

Yesterday, we were reminded that our purpose in life is much greater than our roles or our season of life. In some ways,

> **Our relationships serve as agents to encourage us and refine us so that we are better equipped to be on God's mission.**

In our culture, however, we can subtly allow these relationships to become our substitute mission. The question that begs to be asked is, "How are we supposed to do it all?"

Early in my dating relationship with Chris, he gave a set of golf clubs to me. The plan was for me to learn to play so we could enjoy the game that consumed so much of his time and energy as a collegiate golfer. I was a senior in high school when I received the clubs. I was genuinely interested, but I told him that I would need to wait until life slowed down in college before I had time to learn. After all, your senior year of high school is a busy time! As I attended Wake Forest and later Rhodes, I found the semesters quickly passed and I promised that when I had a regular 9-5 job that we would have all our weekends and evenings for me to learn and play. Graduation and marriage came and went while the clubs collected dust. We had four years before God gave us a child. Every waking moment seemed filled, now with work and assisting Chris in ministry. I was naively convinced that only a stay-at-home mom might have the luxury of learning such a hobby. Then, I became a stay-at-home mom and realized life was just as busy as before. I have now passed those clubs on to my daughter. Not surprisingly, she does not have much time to use them either.

It is a spooky analogy, right? In some ways, we treat God's mission and our walk with God just like that set of clubs. We have good intentions and have nothing against God. It even sounds like a good idea and use of time. As women, however, it can seem like *Mission Impossible* to take care of all our earthly responsibilities and be the woman of God that He designed us to be.

How do you relate to the struggle of finding time to make God's mission a priority?

When you hear the term "God's mission," what do you think?

I want to acknowledge that the battle is real. The truth is, the Lord is perfectly aware of the battle and has warned us.

Read Ephesians 6:10-12.

Satan is so hard at work trying to undermine God's activity and deceive generations that we as a society do not even believe in God. But what does he do with those who already have the Holy Spirit within them? He gets us distracted with good things. Good is the enemy of great! There is likely not a woman alive today that feels like she can live up to all of the spoken and unspoken expectations on her life. Isn't this where most of the pressure comes from? What are we to do? We subconsciously know that being Miss Perfect is impossible, right? So we quietly put what is most important to us in first place and hope that the nudge to live for more than our little world does not reoccur too often. We spend each day of our lives doing good things that, apart from God's mission, will have little eternal impact.

Over the last nine weeks, we have covered a lot of ground. We have urged you to pursue the Lord in each area so that your life could be the beautiful contribution to God's mission that you were designed to make. The reality is that if you have a relationship with the Lord, then the Holy Spirit is within you. God gave us the Holy Spirit to teach us, convict the world concerning sin, judgment, and righteousness, and to glorify God (see John 16:7-15). We are actually restraining the Holy Spirit by choosing our own mission instead of God's.

Do you ever sense that battle within you of knowing you were created for some greater purpose? If so, please describe the battle.

What prevents you from being on mission?

What do you think are your practical and logistical obstacles to being on God's mission?

I told you earlier this week that we would explore how to bring our world into alignment with God's mission. Regardless of our stage of life, we have both the realities of our world and how God designed us. May I propose to you that the simplest way to grasp how to choose God's mission comes back to our first two weeks of study: God's holiness and our identity.

Being on mission is not adding Christian activities to your busy schedule.

When we grasp how amazing God is and why He created us, then everything we do and think will be accomplishing God's mission. Let's return to 1 Corinthians for the last time to see what this looks like.

Read 1 Corinthians 10:31-11:1 below.

In 10:31, what does Paul tell us to do to the glory of God?

Now before you get too excited that God's mission is just about eating, consider the context from which Paul writes. In previous verses, he has told the believers in Corinth that they are free from the law. They no longer have to follow all of the Jewish laws because Jesus fulfilled the law. Now, their focus is greater than following rules. Everything they do should be done in such a way that God receives the glory.

What are some things in your life that you do on a daily basis that you would do differently if you were doing them with the purpose of glorifying God?

Identify two specific tasks or areas that you are going to ask the Lord to remind you to do in such a way that He receives glory. Write those 2 areas below.

Reread 1 Corinthians 10:32.

What three groups of people does Paul say not to offend?

Paul is reminding them that how they conduct themselves has an impact on others' receptivity to the Gospel. In parallel with Paul's audience, we too must make a decision not to offend the religious, the irreligious, or the church. Paul was taking the news of the Messiah to the Jews and Gentiles. We too are on mission to take the Gospel to those who resist God and those who do not grasp what a relationship with God truly means. Paul was not telling them to agree with the Jews and Gentiles. To share the news of Christ required that truth be spoken, but it should be the truth of the Gospel that offends, not the people of God. Through God's grace and wisdom, we are to be actively engaged with people around us in such a way that we honor what the church represents while not needlessly offending those we are trying to reach.

Reread 1 Corinthians 10:33.

Whose advantage does Paul seek?

Why does Paul seek the profit of many?

Paul understood God's magnificence and his own identity. Paul realized his life was for the purpose of sharing with others all the grace and forgiveness that he had received. Paul lived his life looking at the big picture.

How often do you seek the profit of many instead of your own?

If we go back a few verses in Paul's letter, we can see this same theme reiterated in 1 Corinthians 10:24:

Let no one seek his own good, but the good of his neighbor.

What is one situation where you could choose the advantage of many or the good of others right now... rather than your own way?

We will conclude with 1 Corinthians 11:1. Read it again.

I hope that you see that being on God's mission has nothing to do with your age or stage of life. Being on mission is about who you are and what you do right where you are! If God wants to move you, He can do that, but where He has you today is your mission field. Paul could not have spent his entire Christian life doing religious things without an internal conviction. Remember, he understood his freedom. He grasped that he was a new creation because of God's saving grace and then because of his new identity, every encounter he had changed. He never looked at life the same again.

My prayer for you is that you will follow Christ the way Paul did. Whether you are single, the mother of five, or a grandmother, when you live on mission everyone around you will be impacted. Your friends, children, co-workers, or grandchildren, will see a life with purpose. Will some of your activities change? Yes! You will be like Paul and be compelled to put yourself in the flow of God's activity. You will choose to prioritize worshipping and connecting with other believers. You will see the opportunity to serve and give as a way to carryout your God-given purpose.

If you are in the process of discipling your children, scoop them up and let them be a part of your journey. Some of our best memories as a family occurred when we were serving others together as a family. Will some of your activities remain just the same? NO! You will now understand that God needs you to be His light at the gas station, in the drive-thru line, and at the dry cleaners. You may be going the same places, but by God's grace you go as a new woman ready to bring hope to all who encounter you.

Who can you specifically love "as you are going"?

We are guilty of categorizing missions into a box of fund raising letters, strange foods, and different languages. The reality is that God gives us the privilege of being on mission in our very stage of life and in our current location. No money is even required, if you have been using that excuse.

God's mission is our purpose.

The pressure we feel to be Miss Perfect does not come from God. The opportunities to be used by Him are gifts, not burdens. We put the pressure on our backs when we decide to try to be what the world desires us to be instead of who we were created to be. Release yourself from the endless pursuit of worldly expectations, and enjoy living out God's purpose right where He has you.

What was the most meaningful statement or Scripture you read today?

What does God want you to do in response to today's study?

Day Five

RUNNING FORWARD

KARIN CONLEE

We have made it! Congratulations! As we wrap up the study, there are two things we want to accomplish before we turn the last page. First, I want to send you off with a plan of action that is memorable, understandable, and doable. Second, with your help, we are going to leave you with a resource to help these truths stay on your heart as you move past your daily homework of *Miss Perfect*. Forgotten truth is useless truth.

As Chris Kuhlman and I approached our first writing deadline, I had this light bulb moment as I was studying. After months of research and writing, it dawned on me that there were three underlying qualities that would allow women to have success in all nine of the areas we discussed. Since you made it to the last day of this last week, just consider this your bonus cheat sheet gift for being faithful to finish what you started. Remember how we started the study? Here was our premise:

> ### A woman discovers God's purpose by embracing the humility, identity, and perspective of Christ so that she can be known by love.

In every week we wrote, these three qualities kept resurfacing: humility, identity, and perspective. There are no shortcuts to spiritual maturity or biblical womanhood, BUT, if we can understand that having our identity in Christ, exercising genuine humility, and gaining God's perspective on our daily lives is key to our victory, then we will be three-quarters of the way there!

Think of it this way: If you have your *identity* in Christ and exercise *humility*, then you will come to relationships at peace with who you are and without a desire to prove yourself. When it comes to purity, if you are looking at it from God's *perspective* and find your *identity* in who Christ made you to me... not in some man's approval, then purity becomes very possible. Do you see the pattern emerging? One last example... When it comes to relational disciplines, many women have good intentions but don't actually develop the disciplines. If you come to relational disciplines with genuine *humility*, then you see that you can't possibly live this life in your own strength and you see your need to spend time with God.

So... if you need something to remember as you give up being Miss Perfect and continue pursuing God's purposes, then you should...

> ### Just remember to work on becoming Miss H.I.P.

Corny? Yes. Cheesy? Absolutely! Memorable? Yep! So as both a reminder and an encouragement as you continue to bring your life into alignment with the Lord in the areas we have discussed this semester- If nothing else, work on developing the *humility, identity,* and *perspective* of Christ and you will be going the right direction.

Now, it is your turn. At the end of each day of homework, you should have been answering two questions. These questions were designed to help recognize where the Holy Spirit was revealing truth to you and how you needed to respond and apply this truth to your own life.

I want you to spend a few minutes going back through each chapter of homework. Review your answers to these two questions at the end of each day. (If you did not answer these questions, notice what you have highlighted, what verses spoke to you, and your answers to personal questions.) On the following page, list the one or two most critical truths for you to remember for each week. Also list any action point or steps of obedience that the Lord prompted you to make.

If you have not acted upon the commitment yet, don't believe the lie that it is too late to obey. It is never the wrong time to do the right thing.

It has been a joy to be on this journey with you! Chris and I are co-laborers with you. Our prayer is that somehow, beyond our human limitations and flaws, that God has chosen to speak into each of your hearts through the pages of His Word and our time together. We encourage you to stay connected to other women seeking to follow the Lord. Only the Lord has all the answers, but we need other women in our lives to continually encourage us towards Him and to remind us of what truly matters as we are constantly inundated with lesser things. Will you join us in leaving behind the impossible goal of trying to be Miss Perfect? Let's exchange the pressure of this world for the privilege of carrying out our God designed purpose. There is no greater satisfaction.

Week 1

>**I need to remember:**
>**Action Point:**

Week 2

>**I need to remember:**
>**Action Point:**

Week 3

>**I need to remember:**
>**Action Point:**

Week 4

>**I need to remember:**
>**Action Point:**

Week 5

>**I need to remember:**
>**Action Point:**

Week 6

>**I need to remember:**
>**Action Point:**

Week 7

>**I need to remember:**
>**Action Point:**

Week 8

>**I need to remember:**
>**Action Point:**

Week 9

>**I need to remember:**
>**Action Point:**

One last request: Tear this sheet out of your workbook. All of my completed Bible studies are on a bookshelf. *Miss Perfect* will join the ranks soon. Keep this sheet somewhere visible and accessible to remind you how God spoke and what steps you need to continue to take as you pursue His likeness.

NOTES FOR THE WEEK

MENTORING QUESTIONS

WEEK ONE: IDENTITY
KARIN CONLEE

As you approach this week's topic of Identity, the mentor needs to be willing to be vulnerable and share where you have been convicted. The mentee will be encouraged when your personal struggles are discussed in light of how God has renewed your mind in this area. Always leave your discussion with the focus on how God and His Word will transform these areas.

Which area of mistaken identity were you the most convicted by:

· POSITION?
· WIFE?
· MOTHERHOOD?
· BEAUTY?

1. POSITION

· After reading that section of the lesson, did you recall a time where a position or job gave you an added sense of importance or purpose?
· If so, did you ask God to show you why you felt that way...what the root cause was? For example, was it pride?
· If so, are you facing current areas where pride is a problem?

2. WIFE

· If you are not yet a wife, what expectations are you expecting your future husband to fulfill that only God is able to?
· If you are a wife, what expectations have you put on your husband that only God can fulfill?
· If you are no longer a wife, what unmet expectations in your former spouse are you harboring that truly only God can fill?

3. MOTHERHOOD

· How have you elevated motherhood to replace God in your life?
· Have you made your children an idol?
· Are you angry with God because your expectations for motherhood have not been fulfilled?

4. BEAUTY

- How do you apply the truth of 1 Peter 3:3-4 to combat the world's definition of beauty?
- What practical measures do you need to take? For example, do you need to eliminate fashion magazines or blogs?

We've talked about your struggling in one or more of the above areas, but on Day 3 you looked at how God transforms your identity. Describe specific ways God has made you a new creation in light of 2 Corinthians 5:17-21. This passage refers to old things passing away, new things have come. Discuss specifically... "My old self was....but He made me new by..."

- What types of agreements do you need to break in order to free yourself from a false identity? (Refer to workbook page 18.)

Mentor be sure to address this question, being vulnerable to share your own personal experience with this.

- How is your heart aching because you have been deceived and have gone against the grain of God's definition of womanhood?
- How are you embracing the role of nurturer & encourager God has created you for?
- If you are not embracing this role, what is holding you back?

Can you honestly say "I love God and He loves me, therefore I am okay"? (Refer to workbook page 26.) If not, help her begin to see how removing the layer of circumstances and/or criticisms and getting back to the very basics of her being God's daughter can help her change her thinking. Lies we believe and false agreements are what need to be addressed.

WEEK TWO: HOLINESS
CHRIS KUHLMAN

As you approach this week's study, the mentor needs to be willing to be vulnerable and share specific ways in which she has compromised the holiness of God in her own life and be willing to share how God redeemed her from it. Your overarching goal of this week is to help your mentee grasp the vastness of our God.

- How has your view of God been inaccurate? What areas do you "control" in order to maintain a false sense of security? How is an accurate view of God able to help you relinquish control in that situation?
- In what areas do you sense God is showing you a hardening of your heart because you did not receive from Him what you desired?
- On page 32 holiness means to be set apart and totally different, unique. Are there areas of your life you have compromised God's expectations of holiness? In what practical ways does your life reflect the holiness of God?

- In the lesson you learned that you will yield to that which you fear the most. In what areas have you elevated a fear of some thing over your fear of God? Find a Scripture that places your focus on the One who can conquer this fear.
- Do you truly believe that only God knows what's best, wants what's best, and gives what's best? If so, how is this changing your life?

WEEK THREE: ATTITUDE
KARIN CONLEE

Be careful in the area of attitude to strike an appropriate balance between being real with your own struggle, but not allowing your own inconsistencies to become justification for your mentee to excuse her choices. Use your role as mentor to provide encouragement and accountability for you to grow in this area, too.

- How have you allowed other people to be your standard instead of the Lord when it comes to attitude?
- What prevents you from applying the principles of Luke 6:27-28:
  - Love your enemies?
  - Do good to them?
  - Bless them?
  - Pray for them?
- In what ways has God shown you mercy? Because you have received mercy, who do you need to extend mercy to?
- How does the mercy you've received change the way you interact with all people... neighbors? Strangers at the grocery store? The guy who cuts you off in traffic? Your child's teacher? A critical spouse?
- How do you manage the tension between offering unconditional love in an environment where you can't offer unconditional approval?
- Do you give permission for someone to point out your blind spots?
- Have you shifted your thinking from "How am I being affected by this situation?" to "How can I use this situation to point someone to my King?" How could that shift change the outcome?

WEEK FOUR: DISCIPLINES
CHRIS KUHLMAN

There are many types of mentoring, but the greatest gift you can impart to your mentee is the gift of being able to hear from the Lord for herself. In this week on disciplines, I urge you to challenge your mentee to begin a Priority Time. This will allow her to be self-feeding when your mentoring concludes. Most believers know they should, but don't. Encourage your mentee to start small. Fifteen minutes everyday is more beneficial than an hour three times a week. If she starts small, God will increase her appetite! You as the mentor must model what you are teaching. If this is new to you, start with her. If you continue mentoring beyond the *Miss Perfect* curriculum, your Priority Time can become your curriculum as you help your mentee process applying the truth God is revealing.

- Day 1 is intended to help women move from "I should" to "I want to have a Priority Time." Pride is often the core reason why we don't commit. We would never say that, but our actions shout, "Lord, I don't need You today" when we don't spend time with Him. Your mentee must see that she can't live out the Christian life as God intended without being connected to Him.

- Explore this subject with the following types of questions:

  - What do you want your relationship with the Lord to be like in 5 years?
  - Will you have that, if you keep doing what you are doing now?
  - What are you doing with the time that should be spent with Him?
  - What practical steps can you make to protect time to be with the Lord daily?

If they have begun a Priority Time or have an established one, spend your time helping them apply the truth of the passage to their current life. For example:

- What is one truth God showed you in your Priority Time this week? Engage them in conversation so you can help them know if they are interpreting the truth correctly. There is one truth but MANY applications. Make sure they understand God's Word correctly first, then move to application.
- How does that truth apply to you right now?
- What is the first step you need to take to obey?

On the subjects of meditation and memorization:

- Talk to them about what they observed in the John 3:16 exercise.
- If possible, develop some accountability in the area of meditation and/or memorization through your mentoring relationship to help them establish this fruitful discipline. Ask them what topics they think would be helpful to meditate on and/or memorize.

WEEK FIVE: RELATIONSHIPS
KARIN CONLEE

After Day One, the age and stage of life of your mentee will play a large part in where you spend your time in discussion this week. Relationships are very complex. Allow God to use what you have learned through Him to help your mentee. Make sure you continually keep God's Word as the plumb line. Cloudtownsend.com is an excellent website for resources on establishing healthy relationships, if you need a biblical resource to help your mentee navigate and process through past or current struggles. If your mentee needs help with significant relational wounds, walk along side her as she seeks and gets professional help. Do not feel the pressure to be a counselor, but be willing to help her research a solid Christian counselor and then be an ear as she processes truth, where appropriate.

- Who is your first love? If it's not God, why?
- When it comes to honoring your parents, which of the two categories do you struggle with:
  - honoring your parents?
  - leaving & cleaving?
- If honoring your parents is your greater struggle, what practical steps can you take to better understand them?
- If leaving & cleaving is your greater struggle, what practical steps do you need to take to make your spouse your primary confidant?
- Are you imparting a heart for God into your children? If not, do you see yourself as being merely an observer of the things of God or one who experiences the movement of God in your own life? How do you move from observing to experiencing?
- Where is your current greatest struggle:
  - in your relationship with God?
  - in your relationship with yourself?
  - in your relationship with others?
- If your struggle is being at peace with God, review Hebrews 10:15-18 and consider what God says about how He views our sin.
- If your struggle is being at peace with yourself, in what areas will you no longer compare yourself to others?
- If your struggle is being at peace with others, review Hebrews 10:19-25 and consider how you can become an encourager in those relationships.

WEEK SIX: PRAYER
CHRIS KUHLMAN

Prayer is a precious and private discipline, but many times someone will give up or minimize prayer, if she does not have any guidance through a challenging season. The conversation on prayer can be very healthy, freeing, and motivating. If you are not where you want to be in your own prayer life, then seek out the help of a woman that you know has developed a healthy prayer life. There is nothing worse than someone trying to mentor someone in a discipline that she does not herself own. Go together and learn from another godly woman and begin to implement what you learn from her as your mentee does, too.

- What has been your orientation to prayer before this week?
- What has been your biggest struggle with prayer?
- Was there a new truth or idea about prayer that encouraged you or challenged you this week?
- How does grasping that God is our Father help you make prayer more relational? (If she has had a negative orientation to her earthly father, help her see the peace a perfect Father wants to provide. God is broken over her experience, too.)
- Reviewing the beginning of Prayer Day 4, how can the reminders to Get Real, Get Alone, Get Loud, and Get Quiet help you make strides in your prayer life?

- Are there specific prayers that you need encouragement to persevere in prayer with? (As a mentor, this is a great opportunity to allow God to use you to support your mentee. Perhaps she has a specific burden she has been carrying for years. Join her in praying about it. Talk through how to pray through this request from God's perspective as she waits for His answer.)
- If your mentee is struggling in prayer, ask her if the Lord convicted her of a specific area that she needed to address to prevent her prayers from being hindered. If so, help her to take steps of obedience to be forgiven.

WEEK SEVEN: PURITY
KARIN CONLEE

As a mentor, you have been given permission to speak truth into your mentee's life. Do not avoid tough subjects, but always address them with tenderness and mercy. For someone who has maintained purity, help them to keep a high view of this value. Help them to see the power that is available through maintaining purity. For the mentee who has had failure in this area, you must point them to God's mercy. The picture of Jesus telling the adulteress that she is forgiven and she should "Go and sin no more" is an excellent example of showing them compassion without compromise. She must see that she has a new beginning when she repents, but then must take great cautions to sin no more.

Review 1 Cor. 6:12-20:

- This week you learned that your body is not your own but a temple of the Holy Spirit, bought with a price, so that it might glorify God. How does this truth affect your future decisions on purity?
- What are some patterns in your life that have opened the window for you to have impure thoughts or be physically impure?

For example:
- Were you overly flirtatious with someone?
- Did you end up alone somewhere, unsupervised?
- Were you inappropriately dressed?
- Did you share personal/emotional concerns with a man who is not your husband?
- What are some boundaries you need to set up to prevent future opportunities from becoming impure either in thought or deeds?
    For example:
    - I will get rid of inappropriate clothing.
    - I will not be alone under ANY circumstances with a person of the opposite sex who is not my spouse.
    - I will remove movies, music, and reading material that cause temptation.
    - Have you failed to live up to Christ's standard of purity in any area that continues to cause you to stumble?

If so, memorize Romans 8:1 "There is therefore now no condemnation to them which are in Christ Jesus." Ask for forgiveness, receive God's forgiveness and reevaluate boundaries in your life. Invite accountability for the new boundaries you are establishing today.

WEEK EIGHT: CONTENTMENT
CHRIS KUHLMAN

As American Christians, we look for contentment in all the wrong places. Help your mentee to see that the peace she longs for cannot come from any source other than God. As we are moving towards the end of the *Miss Perfect* curriculum, help her to see that she must prioritize what will provide contentment by saying "no" to what the world tells her will satisfy, and saying "yes" to the Lord's call to come to Him.

- What robs you of the ability to be content and why? (The enemies of rest)
- Where do you continually feel compelled to exercise your power because you are not trusting God to exercise His authority?
- How are you exchanging your burden(s) for Christ's burden of humility? How have Christ's desires and His mission become the purpose of your life?
- What work are you doing in your own power that is draining you? What work of Christ are you doing that is energizing you?
- What are past ways God has been faithful that you need to remember today? Will you choose to rest in Him because of His faithfulness?

WEEK NINE: MISSION
KARIN CONLEE

This is a great week to practically live out with your mentee! Help your mentee see how she can use the gifting she has to be on mission in the everyday path of her current life. Model this by doing something in your life with her that shows mission in action right where you are.

- Which prize do you want...a perishable or imperishable one? Does the race you are on reflect the prize you desire?
- In what ways do you lack gratitude towards God for having placed you in your current circles of influence? How can you become excited to invest in the people you currently do life with?
- In what ways has God redeemed your history and given you a ministry that brings encouragement to people you are uniquely equipped to speak to?
- As a woman, God calls you to nurture life in others. This does not hinge on traditional motherhood, but we are all called to leave a spiritual legacy of Christ followers. How are you investing in others to accomplish this mission?

As you wrap up the last chapter of *Miss Perfect*, this is the time to help make sure that she is not living her life just going through the motions, but that she is intentionally making choices that honor God's priorities. From a discussion standpoint, help her to really evaluate her life from a "big picture" perspective.

- What changes does she need to make?
- What has God revealed to her through the study that she still needs to act upon?
- Where is she still letting the world's expectations dictate her life?

MENTORING NOTES

ENDNOTES

BIBLES USED

- American Standard Version (1901), Public Domain.
- Amplified Bible (Grand Rapids, MI: The Zondervan Corporation and the Lockman Foundation, 1987).
- Contemporary English Version (New York, NY: American Bible Society, 1995).
- New American Standard Bible (Anaheim, CA: Foundations Publications, Inc. ,1998).
- New English Translation (NET) (Biblical Studies Press, L.L.C, 2006).
- New International Version (Colorado Springs, CO: Biblica, Inc., 1973).
- New Living Translation (Carol Stream, IL: Tyndale House Publishers, Inc., 1996).

WEEK 1

1. Robert Lewis and Jeremy Howard, *The New Eve: Choosing God's Best for Your Life* (Nashville, TN: B&H Publishing Group, 2008), 5.
2. Ibid, 6.
3. John Rosemond, *The New Parent Power* (Kansas City, MO: Andrews McMeel Publishing, 2001).
4. Neil Anderson, *Who I am in Christ* (Ventura, CA: Regal from Gospel Light, 2001).
5. Blue Letter Bible. "Dictionary and Word Search for katallassō (Strong's 2644)." Blue Letter Bible (cited 19 April 2012). Available online: http://www.blueletterbible.org/lang/lexicon/lexicon.cfm?strongs=G2644
6. Henry Cloud, "Relational Freedom, One Step at a Time, 4: Please Release Me!" CCN Weekly Solution Series (New Life Ministries, 2007).

7. Robert Lewis and Jeremy Howard, *The New Eve: Choosing God's Best for Your Life* (Nashville, TN: B&H Publishing Group, 2008), 43-44.
8. Ibid, 44.
9. Ibid, 45.
10. Ibid, 47.
11. John DeFoore and Marion Sue Jones, personal communication with Karin Conlee (Boerne, TX: Consultant Services, May 2010).

WEEK 2

1. W.E. Vine, *Vines Expository Dictionary of Old and New Words* (Nashville, TN: Thomas Nelson, inc. 1997), 414.
2. ThinkExist.com Quotations. "Frederick W. Cropp quotes," ThinkExist.com Quotations, 1 March 2012 (Cited 18 April 2012). Available from the Internet: http://en.thinkexist.com/quotes/frederick_w._cropp/
3. J.I. Packer, *Knowing God* (Downers Grove, Illinois. InterVarsity Press, 1973), 101.
4. Ibid, 107.
5. Louie Giglio, "7:22 by Passion Ministries." (Northpoint Church. Atlanta, GA. 1999) Keynote Speaker.
6. W.E. Vine, *Vines Expository Dictionary of Old and New Words* (Nashville, TN: Thomas Nelson, inc. 1997).
7. Jonathan Edwards, *Lover of God: The Essential Edwards Collection* (Chicago, IL: Moody Publishers, 2010).

WEEK 3

1. "Attitude." Dictionary.com (cited 20 April 2012). Available from the Internet: http://dictionary.reference.com/browse/attitude
2. Guzik, David, "Study Guide for Luke 6." Blue Letter Bible, 7 July

2006. 2012 (cited 20 April 2012). Available from the Internet: http:// www.blueletterbible.org/commentaries/comm_view.cfm?AuthorID=2&contentID=7914&commInfo=31&topic=Luke
3. Ravi Zacharias, "The Harvard Veritas Forum." (Norcross, Georgia: Ravi Zacharias International Ministries, 1992).
4. Guzik, David, "Study Guide for Luke 6." Blue Letter Bible. 7 July 2006 (cited 20 April 2012). Available from the Internet: http://www.blueletterbible.org/commentaries/comm_view.cfm?AuthorID=2&contentID=7914&commInfo=31&topic=Luke
5. Ibid.
6. Matthew Henry, "Commentary on Luke 6." Blue Letter Bible, 1 March 1996 (Cited 20 April 20 2012). Available from the Internet: http://www.blueletterbible.org/commentaries/comm_view.cfm?AuthorID=4&contentID=1647&commInfo=5&topic=Luke

WEEK 4

1. Adrian Rodgers, *ADRIANISMS: The Wit and Wisdom of Adrian Rogers* (Memphis, TN: Love Worth Finding Ministries, 2006).
2. Brother Lawrence, *Practice of the Presence of God* (Grand Rapids, MI: Spire Books, 1958), 21.
3. Sir Ken Robinson, "Divergent Thinking." YouTube.com (Cited 1 May 2012). Available from the internet: http://www.youtube.com/watch?v=tnOnaKHZ3_k
4. Ravi Zacharius, *The Grand Weaver: How God Shapes Us Through the Events of Our Lives* (Grand Rapids, MI: Zondervan Books, 2007).

WEEK 5

1. Sarah Bubar, "Honor and Obey: The Dividing Line for Adult Children." Girls Gone Wise. 14 March 2011 (cited 20 April 2012). Available from the Internet: www.girlsgonewise.com/honor-obey-the-dividing-line-for-adult-children
2. Cloud-Townsend Resources, "Questions and Answers." (Cited 18 April 2012). Available from the internet: http://www.cloudtownsend.com/resources/question-answers
3. Mary Kassian, "The Genesis of Gender." True Woman, Mary Kassian's True Woman '10 (Cited 19 April 2012). Available from the Internet: www.truewoman.com.
4. Eugene Merrill, *The New American Commentary Volume 4 on Deuteronomy* (Nashville, TN: Broadman and Holdman publishers, 1994), 167.
5. Dr. Gary Smalley, *The DNA of Relationships* (Carol Stream, IL: Tyndale Publishers, 2007).

WEEK 6

1. Guzik, David. "Study Guide for Luke 11." Blue Letter Bible. 7 Jul 2006 (cited 2 May 2012). Available from the internet: http:// www.blueletterbible.org/commentaries/comm_view.cfm?AuthorID=2&contentID=7919&commInfo=31&topic=Luke

WEEK 7

1. John and Staci Eldredge, *Captivating: Unveiling the Mystery of a Woman's Soul* (Nashville, TN: Thomas Nelson, 2005), 77.
2. Ibid, 222.
3. Sarah Bragg, *Body. Beauty. Boys* (Birmingham, AL: New Hope Publishers, 2011), 43.
4. John and Staci Eldredge, *Captivating: Unveiling the Mystery of a Woman's Soul* (Nashville, TN: Thomas Nelson, 2005), 224.
5. Elizabeth George, *A Woman's High Calling: 10 Ways to Live out God's Plan for Your Life* (Eugene, OR: Harvest House Publishers, 2011).

WEEK 8

1. W.E. Vine, *Vines Expository Dictionary of Old and New Words* (Nashville, TN: Thomas Nelson, Inc, 1997).
2. Dr. and Mrs. Howard Taylor, *Hudson Taylor's Spiritual Secret* (Chicago, IL: The Moody Bible Institute of Chicago, 1989), 156-164.
3. Ibid, 156-164.
4. Ibid, 156-164.

RECOMMENDED READING

Identity

Grace for the Good Girl, written by Emily Freeman
The New Eve, written by Robert Lewis
The Me I Want to Be, written by John Ortberg

Holiness

Holy Discontent, written by Bill Hybels
Knowing God, written by J.I. Packer
The Knowledge of the Holy, written by A.W. Tozier

Attitude

How People Grow, written by Dr. Henry Cloud and Dr. John Townsend
Lord Change My Attitude, written by James MacDonald
One Thousand Gifts: A Dare to Live Fully Right Where You Are, written by Ann Voskamp

Spiritual Disciplines

The Way of the Heart, written by Henri J. Nouwen
The Life You Have Always Wanted, written by John Ortberg
Desiring God, written by John Piper

Relationships

Intimate Allies, written by Dan B. Allender
Boundaries, written by Dr. Henry Cloud and Dr. John Townsend
Everybody is Normal Until You Get to Know Them, written by John Ortberg

Prayer

The Circle Maker, written by Mark Batterson
The Kneeling Christian, written by unknown Christian
Praying the Names of God, written by Ann Spangler

Purity

Teaching True Love to a Sex at 13 Generation, written by Eric Ludy and Leslie Ludy
When God Writes Your Love Story, written by Eric Ludy and Leslie Ludy

Contentment

Humility, written by Andrew Murray
Absolute Surrender, written by Andrew Murray
Jesus + Nothing = Everything, written by Tullian Tchividjian

Mission

Right Here Right Now, written by Alan Hirsch and Lance Ford
The Next Christians, written by Gabe Lyons

All

The Cost of Discipleship, written by Dietrich Bonhoeffer
Purpose Driven Life, written by Rick Warren
Where is God When It Hurts?, written by Philip Yancey